HOW TO FIND OUT IN
PSYCHOLOGY
A guide to the literature and methods of research

Other titles of interest

BISHOP
Canadian Official Publications

BORCHARDT
How to Find Out about Australian Bibliography

BORCHARDT
How to Find Out in Philosophy and Psychology

BURMAN
How to Find Out in Chemistry

BURRINGTON
How to Find Out in the Social Sciences

CHANDLER
How to Find Out, 5th edition

CHANDLER
International and National Library and Information Services

CARROLL
Recent Advances in School Librarianship

CHERNS
Official Publishing: An Overview

GREENBERG
How to Find Out in Psychiatry

PEMBERTON
Bibliographic Control of Official Publications

PEMBERTON
How to Find Out in Mathematics, 2nd edition

WESTFALL
French Official Publications

HOW TO FIND OUT IN
PSYCHOLOGY

A guide to the literature and methods of research

by

D. H. BORCHARDT MA, FLAA

and

R. D. FRANCIS FBPsS

PERGAMON PRESS
Oxford · New York · Toronto · Sydney · Paris · Frankfurt

U.K.	Pergamon Press Ltd., Headington Hill Hall, Oxford OX3 0BW, England
U.S.A.	Pergamon Press Inc., Maxwell House, Fairview Park, Elmsford, New York 10523, U.S.A.
CANADA	Pergamon Press Canada Ltd., Suite 104, 150 Consumers Rd., Willowdale, Ontario M2J 1P9, Canada
AUSTRALIA	Pergamon Press (Aust.) Pty. Ltd., P.O. Box 544, Potts Point, N.S.W. 2011, Australia
FRANCE	Pergamon Press SARL, 24 rue des Ecoles, 75240 Paris, Cedex 05, France
FEDERAL REPUBLIC OF GERMANY	Pergamon Press GmbH, Hammerweg 6, D-6242 Kronberg-Taunus, Federal Republic of Germany

Copyright © 1984 D H Borchardt and R D Francis

All Rights Reserved. No part of this publication may be reproduced, stored in a retrieval system or transmitted in any form or by any means: electronic, electrostatic, magnetic tape, mechanical, photocopying, recording or otherwise, without permission in writing from the publishers.

First edition 1984

Library of Congress Cataloging in Publication Data
Borchardt, D. H. (Dietrich Hans), 1916–
How to find out in psychology.
Includes index.
1. Psychological literature. 2. Psychology—
Research. I. Francis, R. D. II. Title.
BF76.8.B67 1984   150'.72   84–2827

ISBN 0-08-031280-2

The diagrams in this book are copyright save where acknowledgement is given to others for their authorship. Diagrams original to this book are the property of the authors and should not be reproduced without permission.

Printed in Great Britain by A. Wheaton & Co. Ltd., Exeter

Preface

SINCE antiquity scholars have recognized certain basic principles which must be observed when establishing a new theory. Among these is the necessity to ensure that a new view will harmonize with already accepted findings and tested facts even though it may conflict with existing interpretations. To this end it is essential that one knows where to find such opinions recorded and such facts listed.

It is the purpose of this work to guide students of psychology towards documented information and to suggest sources for the discovery of recorded data and the exploitation of such sources. Additionally there are sections describing aids to research methodology and to the presentation of the result of psychological research. What we have attempted to do in this book that is different from its predecessors is to arrange the above points in the form of an annotated guide that bears some relationship to the whole process of serious study and research.

We emphasize that we have not intended to present here a reading list in psychology. There are numerous introductory studies of this subject available today which include reading lists. Those who use them to further their studies should bear in mind that all such guides are naturally selective and bear more or less visibly the impression of the compiler's bias. This should not be considered a disadvantage; on the contrary it is preferable by far to know where one is going than to pay the fare without knowing the goal or the means of travelling. There are no teachers as dangerous as those who pretend to be "unbiased".

The work is divided into eleven chapters. The first two deal with what psychology is about and its major theories, and chapters III–VI deal with the bibliographic aids used by psychologists who want to find out about the literature of the subject. In general terms this part offers an explanation of the core of library search resources and of the way of using them. It must be added at once, however, that we have restricted ourselves to citing only works directly related to psychology, though that term has been given the widest possible interpretation. We have not dealt with general reference works, encyclopaedias, dictionaries and similar sources of information though they may well be excellent starting points for a broad outline of psychological concepts. Readers wishing to know about such general reference works are advised to consult Dr George Chandler's book in this same series, *How to find out*.

How one gathers and presents such material is the subject of chapters VII–X, which include guides to the principles and methods of research. The emphasis is on practical issues and an attempt has been made to enable readers to approach this part with their own problems of research and find suggestions for their solution.

Chapter XI is concerned with professional matters and includes information on psychological organizations, and on further training in psychology.

In culling the literature we have been obliged to make a choice between numerous works of seemingly equal excellence and to restrict our selection to some examples. Many of the titles finally included are of the early 1970s, and we stress that their listing was based on the criteria of well-known provenance, professional regard and tested usefulness. Other examples might have been selected by others writing on this same topic. However, the omission of one title or another in this book should not be construed as a criticism. Our aim was to be selective, not exhaustive, and to keep the book within a modest size; our cut-off date has been June 1982.

Instructors may wish to use this work as a teaching book. Our aim has been, of course, to present the material in such a way that will lend itself to this purpose as well as serving as an autodidact. Among our several goals is the education of the library user.

The writers are aware of the problems of sexist language. Insofar as it was consistent with style we have attempted to avoid it. Where masculine pronouns are used in the generic sense there was no intention to be male chauvinist. "Man" embraces "woman".

It remains to be added that while we claim to have chosen a new and particularly useful approach to the subject of this book, we are of course indebted to the extensive literature of this kind that has been compiled during the past 25 years. It is unquestionably our experience that there is a need to introduce students to the methodical exploitation of academic and general research libraries and to show them how to organize their own work, their notes, their reading and their experiments. This book is more than an updated review of the senior author's *How to find out in philosophy and psychology* (1969). It is a completely new approach to the same objective: to enable students to be better students through a systematic introduction to the literature of, and basic research techniques in, psychology.

This book is aimed at the psychology student who is proceeding with the formal study of psychology. It should be appreciated that different sections of this book will appeal to students at different years of their study. This work is meant to be retained as a reference source rather than to be acquired for a specific course and then discarded.

A number of students of the Chisholm Institute helped by testing some of the procedures recommended for the presentation of results and for following up literature searches; others provided assistance by reading sections of the book and commenting on the appropriateness of the presentation for undergraduates. The following deserve special mention: Joan Buzzard, Nic Eddy, Eric Kratzer, Coralee Lane, Bob Sinclair.

We are grateful for the skilful assistance received from Valerie Machin and Lorna McVeity who helped with the typing of the first draft, and to Nancy McElwee who was responsible for the preparation of the final draft.

Several of our colleagues have critically read one or more chapters of this book and we are much indebted to them for helpful comments. In particular we owe thanks to Professor Ray Over, Emeritus Professor Bill O'Neill and to Ray Choate, Head of the Library Reference Section at La Trobe University.

Appendix B (Report writing) is a substantially modified version of an article which appeared in the *British journal of educational psychology* in 1973. The contribution of R. D. Francis, J. K. Collins and A. Cassell is gratefully acknowledged.

Professor George Singer contributed to the section on careers for psychology graduates which appears in chapter XI.

Jean Hagger compiled the index and kindly checked the bibliographic references; she and Julie F. Marshall helped to proof-read the text, for all of which we thank them warmly.

Melbourne 1983 DHB
RDF

Contents

LIST OF ILLUSTRATIONS	xi
1. Definitions and Overviews	1
2. Historical and Theoretical Works	9
3. Reference Sources	23
4. Indexes, Abstracts and Union Lists	43
5. Computer-based Data Retrieval	53
6. Special Fields of Psychology	73
7. Preparations for Research	93
8. Citations and the Card File	109
9. Quantitative Psychology and its Methodology	119
10. Presentation of Results	127
11. The Profession	137
APPENDICES:	
A. A Guide to Library Searches	151
B. Report Writing: a Model for Empirical Psychological Reports	157
C. Self-testing for Authors of Empirical Reports	165
D. "A Reader's, Writer's and Reviewer's Guide to Assessing Research Reports in Clinical Psychology", by Brendan A. Maher	167
E. Psychological Societies	173
BIBLIOGRAPHY	175
SUBJECT INDEX	187

List of Illustrations

1	Broad divisions of knowledge	3
2	Catalogue entry examples	37
3a	Extracts from the APA *Thesaurus of psychological index terms*	57–58
3b	Extracts from the APA *Thesaurus of psychological index terms*	59
4	Meaning of terms	60
5	Rotated alphabetical terms	60
6	Illustration of "Relationship" terms	62
7	Illustration of Rotated alphabetic terms	63
8	PsycInfo subject coverage	65
9	Sample page from Orbit User's Guide	68–69
10	Notes of advice for users of *Psychological abstracts*	70–71
11	The Dewey system	98
12a	The DDC system: first summary	98
12b	The DDC system: third summary	99–100
12c	Expansion of DDC Classification numbers: three examples	101
13a	Library of Congress classification schedules	102
13b	Library of Congress classification schedules	103
13c	Library of Congress classification. Extract of schedules, BF: Psychology	104–105
14	Standard edge-punched reference card	113
15	Expansion of locatable categories	116–117
16	Summary of report outline—outline of an empirical psychological report	132
17	*Directory of European Associations*, 3rd ed, 1981; facsimile of p. 328	141

CHAPTER 1
Definitions and Overviews

PSYCHOLOGY is the term commonly applied to the sciences concerned with human mental life and behaviour. It embraces a large number of almost independent sub-disciplines; that is to say while psychology is an integral field and comprises numerous theories and practices, there are many areas of psychological study which are looked upon by some as being self-sufficient and clearly limited theoretical fields in their own right. To understand the present divisions and separate development of psychology it is helpful to examine the evolution of this quite old subject which has its roots in the teachings of Aristotle whence it also derived its name: psychology, i.e. the study of the soul or of the mind. The difficulty of translating "psyche" is well known and no apology is needed here for having cited at least two English equivalents which by their very nature indicate the difficulties this field of study has experienced in the period of its early development.

Modern psychology was born out of the rationalism and pragmatism of the eighteenth and nineteenth centuries. The long close association with philosophy, physiology, theology and the essential emphasis on human behaviour and performance, all contributed to mark it as a "dangerous" field where fools would rush in to disturb divine gifts, dispositions and, at times, invite retribution.

There is no need to recapitulate here the history of psychology, but since the source materials for the various branches of this discipline are specialized according to the subdivisions that have developed, it will be useful to identify briefly the major branches at least. To spell out this problem of the divisions of the subject, Henry Bliss wrote:

> When I—or better we—see a dog run and jump a fence and come to us panting, smiling, and wagging his tail, what in this complex object-matter is zoological, what is physical, what is physiological, what is psychological, what is objective, and what is subjective? For the subjective aspect may affect our perception of, and attitude toward, the object. The dog is of course by definition zoological. The fence and the dynamic jumping over it are rationally physical. The dog's panting is a

physiological action, and it is by no means a simple study. The smiling and tail-wagging are what? Well, they are complex behavior too, physical and psychological correlated. So psychology is very complex, a complication of mental and physiological and even physical elements. In the history of science psychology began as a philosophical and subjective study, close to mental philosophy and epistemology. Recently this study has become especially concerned with its endeavour to attain full status as a fundamental science. For this purpose more of objective study has been requisite, more experiment and induction from recorded findings and statistical data. The *objectivist* proceeds to measure the fence and the dog and the tail and the wag, and even the smile. But the objectivist also remembers that the dog has an inside and a nervous system, and an endocrine system, and even a mentality back of his emotion. His mentality is the basis of his behavior. Then, what is his behavior? It is the action of the dog; but one may argue that it is the dog in action, zoological–physical–physiological–psychological, not merely his physical action, that it depends on the physiological and psychological correlates. But let us not confuse the mental and the physical, the cause and the effect. The objective behavior is the physical and maybe physiological effect or correlate of the mental experience of motivation within the organism. It is the *mental* that is psychological. So the study of behavior is not psychology properly but only contributory to psychology; and psychology is more than the study of the behavior, it is the study of the *mental in life*, of mentality correlated with the behavior, and psychology studies the mental not only in the behavior but in other experiences and evidences.[*]

Any attempt to analyse or explain the story of the dog will illustrate adequately that the main streams now current in the science of psychology are concerned with physical and biological processes, physiological processes and reactions, sensory and cognitive processes and social or cultural settings. To understand the place of psychology as one of the several basic sciences developed by man, to explain his existence on this planet, we may try to fit it into the gamut of rationalizations which—as far as we know—are unique to our species. By arranging them in a circle, these attempts at theoretical interpretations of our existence are shown to be independent and of equal merit as the foundations of ontological explanations.

Indeed, psychology may be regarded as a middle-of-the-spectrum science. It is clearly not as molecular or analytical as physics nor so molar and synthetic as anthropology. At the one end of the spectrum the notions of physics incline to philosophical and in particular epistomological

---

[*]Bliss *Bibliographic classification*, 2nd ed. p. ix (by J. Mills & Vanda Broughton ... Class I: Psychology and psychiatry). London, Butterworths, 1978.

Definitions and Overviews

considerations about the nature of matter and the nature of evidence; at the other end of the spectrum some of the theories and postulates of anthropology are at a remove from the empirical domain. If one looks upon these fundamental and broad divisions of our knowledge of the world around us as forming a continuum, they may be diagrammatically presented by a circle (Fig. 1).

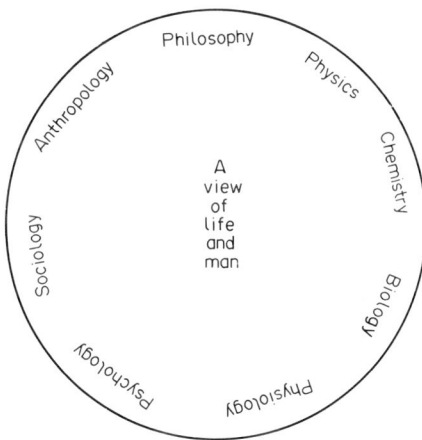

FIG. 1. Broad divisions of knowledge

In their attempts to provide answers in terms of these starting points—often taken as axiomatic rather than as empirical bases—psychologists have formed, wittingly and unwittingly, "schools" which it is customary to label according to some fundamental principle or after the name of the founder: behaviourism, Gestalt psychology (configurationism), "type" psychology, and psychoanalysis. In addition to those "labelled" schools there are areas of scientific inquiry which form, as it were, an extension of the core of psychology. Thus we have child psychology, clinical psychology, psychosomatic studies, industrial psychology, abnormal psychology, mental health, educational psychology, psychology of mental testing, etc.—all of which link fundamental psychological theory and principles to related fields of human behaviour.

The use of the term "classic" has been rightly and strongly criticized by T. S. Eliot in his famous lecture on the role of Virgil in the making of European literature, *What is a classic?* We have avoided using the term though it was tempting to apply it to the fundamental contributions by some of the great psychologists of this century. However, in the strict Eliotian sense, J. M. Baldwin's *Dictionary of philosophy and psychology*, with its two supplementary volumes by B. Rand, *Bibliography of philosophy, psychology and cognate subjects*, 1901–5 and reprinted in 1928, is a true classic. This work represents the quintessence of nineteenth century thought and knowledge on psychology and its philosophical origins. Students should not be put off by the complementary treatment of philosophy and psychology; that approach reflects the academic trend of the period and is appropriate for the turn of the century, and the perceptive reader will discover in Baldwin's definition and explanations a wealth of helpful ideas and interpretations. Nevertheless, its significance lies in the historical summing up of the link between philosophy and psychology; even though at the time of its first appearance scholars contributed to and witnessed the permanent separation of these two disciplines. The *Dictionary* proper, that is the first two volumes of this work contains, in one alphabetical sequence, concepts, names and terms that have bearing on, or are used in, philosophical and psychological discussions; to these are added explanatory passages of major schools and systems. Most of the articles are signed, and besides ample cross-references there are many brief bibliographic references. The editor's claims, set out on the title page, are, however, not fulfilled by the contents of this dictionary; references to the philosophy of the physical sciences are too meagre and the treatment of the biological sciences is mainly limited to the impact of neurophysiology on psychology. However, bearing in mind the date of first publication this criticism must be tempered by the perspective of time. From the point of view of the history of philosophy and psychology Baldwin's great work remains the starting point for any investigation of concepts at the beginning of this century; furthermore, his work provides us today with the *summa philosophica* of the nineteenth century. The bibliographical section of Baldwin's *magnum opus*, i.e. Rand's *Bibliography*, is discussed below.

Leaving this monument of an age we now turn, first of all, to a number of overviews which also deserve our special admiration because of the courage and dedication which have inspired the editors.

The most comprehensive guide to the state of the art and directions of research in all fields and aspects of psychology is the *Handbuch der Psychologie* (1966). Planned to consist of twelve volumes—some of which are made up of two physical tomes, the *Handbuch* has been edited by a team of German academics (K. Gottschaldt, P. Lersch, F. Sander and H. Thomae); the text has been contributed by scores of specialists, including some from English- and French-speaking countries, in translation, and the thousands of citations refer to the international literature on psychology. The subject-matter is divided over the twelve volumes as follows: general psychology (perception; learning, thinking and motivation); developmental psychology; psychology of personality; psychology of expression, tests and testing; social psychology; clinical psychology; industrial psychology; educational psychology; forensic psychology. The *Handbuch* began to appear in 1966 and it is the intention of the publishers to issue revised editions of separate volumes as the need arises.

Definitions and Overviews

Students and readers unfamiliar with German will have to make do with somewhat shorter expositions of terms, concepts and issues in psychology. The only English-language work conceived on a similar scale is S. Koch's *Psychology: a study of a science*. Intended to consist of seven volumes, six only have appeared between 1959 and 1963. The seventh, which was to be a summing-up of this extensive collection of essays on theoretical psychology, appears to have been abandoned. The work is divided into two major sections. The first three volumes are dedicated to conceptual and systematic studies, the other three volumes are concerned with empirical substructures and relations with other sciences. About ninety leading psychologists, mainly from the USA, have collaborated in this fundamental survey of the field. An updating of this work has not been envisaged.

An entirely different approach is represented by B. B. Wolman's *International encyclopedia of psychiatry, psychology, psychoanalysis, and neurology* which was published in twelve volumes in 1978. This is at present the most exhaustive treatment of the subjects listed in the title. In the introduction Wolman writes: "It is the collective effort of 2,000 authorities, bringing together the varied scientific data pertaining to human nature, its deficiencies, and their treatment." This is a scholarly work written for professionals who seek definitions and expositions on areas in which they are not experts; the encyclopaedia will help advanced students and researchers in the whole area of theoretical and applied psychology. It is not written for the layman. All articles are signed and a short biographical statement on every editor, associate editor and author can be found in the first volume. The index volume contains synopses of the topics treated (i.e. a list of the terms into which the main areas are divided), a complete list of articles arranged alphabetically under title, a name index and a subject index. Cross-references in the body of the work further help readers to find what they want.

Another comprehensive survey in English is Eysenck, Arnold and Meili's *Encyclopedia of psychology* of 1972. This three-volume work by international scholars contains dictionary-type definitions of terms as well as longer articles on complex topics; there are also biographical notes and bibliographies of major figures in the field. More specialized is Goldenson's *Encyclopedia of human behavior: psychology, psychiatry and mental health*, 1970.

All of these suffer from the unavoidable defect of relatively rapid obsolescence; advances in some fields of psychology are such that encyclopaedia entries tend to be out of date within five years or less. Nevertheless, the works mentioned offer reliable background information for students. Experienced scholars will, of course, keep up with the most recent developments through the journal literature of which much will be said below.

Besides encyclopaedic approaches to fundamental data, students are well advised to use appropriate dictionaries to ensure the safe handling of specialist terms. It is beyond the scope of this book to comment on the importance of general dictionaries of the English language for those who want to write for publication. It cannot be stressed enough that specialist knowledge is as much in need of a clear and unambiguous (not to mention grammatically correct) medium of expression as any other field of activity whose practitioners seek communication with a wider public. The proper use of one's own language is an indictor of one's own understanding of the subject under discussion; the tendency to hide fundamental ignorance behind the use of jargon is deplorable and brings discredit to every profession that allows it.

None should, therefore, be shy of seeking help from that unsurpassed guide to the use of English, the *Oxford English dictionary*, and the "Shorter" version at least should be at every writer's elbow. Those addressing themselves specifically to the North American literary market would be well advised to use *Webster's . . . international dictionary* to avoid misinterpretation of their message. As. G. B. Shaw pointed out decades ago, the British and the Americans are two great nations divided by a common language.

With regard to the special terminology of psychology, the following dictionaries offer reliable guidance. Of long standing, and tested by thousands of psychologists, is the broadly conceived work by H. B. and A. C. English, *Comprehensive dictionary of psychological and psychoanalytical terms*. This work is the successor to the senior author's *A student's dictionary of psychological terms*, which ran through four editions during 25 years. It may indeed be interesting to note how the terminology of the subject has changed and expanded over almost half a century of the subject's development. In its current edition the *Comprehensive dictionary* aims to include all the terms, both special and technical, that are in use by psychologists today. Illustrations and a brief commentary accompany many of the 12,000 terms in the dictionary. Somewhat more up to date and more broadly conceived is B. B. Wolman's *Dictionary of behavioral science* (1973). A large team of prominent psychologists, psychiatrists and scholars from related fields collaborated in this dictionary, which covers all areas of psychology, psychiatry and neurology, and also includes basic terms and concepts from genetics and pharmacology. Entries vary from very concise word equivalences to short notes of the encyclopaedia type; illustrations, short biographies and photographs make this dictionary especially attractive. The appendices include a statement on ethical standards for psychologists, drawn up by the American Psychological Association, as well as their classification of mental disorders devised by the American Psychiatric Association. This classification is revised from time to time and is at present available in a third edition known as DSM III (i.e. Diagnostic and Statistical Manual III).

Definitions and Overviews

There are also specialist dictionaries for different translation purposes, e.g. commercial or scientific. Not only do they vary in quality, and have a tendency to age rather quickly, but the more specialized dictionaries are often without the common words—ordinary everyday verbs, prepositions, and the like—but they do in fact presume a certain knowledge of the foreign language for whose specialist vocabulary they offer equivalent expressions in the user's native tongue. For the purpose of comprehending a foreign text they are usually adequate, provided the reader can grapple successfully with the foreign syntax. They are rarely adequate for the purpose of translating from one's own language into a foreign language—the obvious exception being of course those fortunate people who really master "like a native" the other language.

Useful in this context is Duijker & Rijswijk's *Trilingual psychological dictionary*, the second edition of which appeared in 1975. It consists of three volumes, in each of which the entries are arranged according to one of the three languages covered: English, French and German. Thus the series of entries 'abasement–abaissement–Erniedrigung' is changed according to the base language of each volume. On a narrower scale there exist French and German dictionaries of psychology which, besides their intrinsic merit for those who have enough command of French and German, include at least a large number of English equivalents in their explanation of terms. Piéron's *Vocabulaire de la psychologie* and Dorsch's *Psychologisches Wörterbuch* belong to this useful category. Both these works are recognized as fundamental texts and include features which are not to be found in their English counterparts, e.g. Dorsch's *Wörterbuch* has special appendices on psychological tests and testing, on the mathematical treatment of psychological problems, and has an extensive bibliography. Piéron, on the other hand, made a feature of describing the work of psychologists and their specific contribution, and besides mathematical formulae particularly important to psychology, there are also lists of relevant pharmacological terms and compounds.

Other dictionaries and encyclopaedias, compiled to ensure the proper understanding and use of words in specialized branches of psychology, will be dealt with in the appropriate sections of this book.

A new and intrinsically interesting approach to an explanation of psychological terminology is the construction and use of a thesaurus of the subject. The difference between a dictionary and a thesaurus should be well understood if each is to be fully exploited. While a dictionary helps us to understand the meaning of words by defining their boundaries and narrowing down the references to which they may apply, a thesaurus helps us to understand the meaning of a word by placing it into a wider context where it has greater generality or is related to other terms by great similarity of meaning. A thesaurus offers "alternatives" which are not necessarily exact equivalents but which, when used judiciously and in the appropriate context, may add shades of differences to a sentence and thus lend a wider or even a more precise meaning to the message that is to be conveyed. In other words, a thesaurus offers synonyms as well as opportunities for refinements of meaning. It may also include antonyms, as is the case with the most famous of general thesauri in the English language, Roget's *Thesaurus of English words and phrases*. Every writer should have it beside his desk!

For the purpose of this survey the *Thesaurus of psychological index terms* deserves a more detailed note. Sponsored and published by the American Psychological Association, it was specifically designed to help in the exploitation of machine-readable indexes to the literature of psychology. More will be found on this topic in Chapter V. Here it suffices to stress that a thesaurus has considerable intrinsic merits and is not necessarily and solely produced for the benefit of computer-based literature searches; indeed, its significance for the improvement of communications among scholars lies quite obviously in the fact that it constitutes a "treasury" of specific technical terms. These are so defined, and hedged with dos and don'ts, that misunderstandings due to loose usage of words are much less likely if the suggested terminology is adhered to. Let us also bear in mind that language is a live means of social as well as scientific and scholarly intercourse. It changes, abandons some words, adopts new ones. A thesaurus has to be brought up to date regularly.

CHAPTER 2

Historical and Theoretical Works

1. History and biography

THE history of psychology is intrinsically a fascinating field of study because it exemplifies in many respects the development of a modern field of science and demonstrates the effect scholastic tradition has had for a long time on one of the foundation stones of the social sciences in general. While many historians of the subject, such as D. B. Klein in his *A history of scientific psychology*, tend to stop in their analysis of the antecedents of modern psychology with the advent on the scene of William James and Wilhelm Wundt, others have courageously examined the evolution of current trends even though they themselves are inescapably a product, if not creators, of modern psychology. Outstanding in this respect is J. C. Flugel, whose *A hundred years of psychology, 1833–1933* is probably the best summing up of the current ramifications of the science; it has been brought up to date in 1964 by Donald J. West. Another classical study of the history of the subject is G. Murphy & J. K. Kovach's *Historical introduction to modern psychology*, first issued in 1928 and now in its 3rd edition (1972). For an understanding of the broader ramifications of psychology, readers are strongly recommended to consult R. I. Watson's *History of psychology and the behavioral sciences: a bibliographic guide* (1978). Of some value as a summing up of the infrastructure of modern psychology is R. Lowry's *The evolution of psychological theory*. Though rather conventional in its presentation, and now over ten years old, this survey is important even now because it clearly shows the continuity of psychological thought and theory.

Like other fields of science, but perhaps more than most, the history of psychology is intimately bound up with the lives of its eminent proponents. While we do not wish to argue the "Great man" versus the "Zeitgeist" approach, we do stress that a historical perception of psychology is inseparable from a biographical presentation of the major trends, theories and, let's face it, "schools". We might call this the milestone interpretation of psychology or of any other discipline. The two main weaknesses of this approach are that the great names tend to put everyone and everything off the centre of the stage, and that a "post hoc–propter hoc" interpretation attaches itself to the schools and theoretical structures which the great have created, and at times so designed that the edifices allowed no light to penetrate into the interior.

A. A. Roback's *History of psychology and psychiatry*, in spite of the author's own firm association with a particular school of psychology, and even after twenty years since its first publication, is still a very readable and instructive account. It is, in fact, not a listing but a series of close to 200 brief sketches of the major names in the psychological sciences—and we use the plural designedly because not all the persons included in this biographical dictionary (not alphabetically but chronologically and typologically arranged) would be considered psychologists in the strict sense of the word. There is a lot of wisdom on Roback's thumbnails.

A convenient and reliable presentation of the development of psychology in biographical terms, from earliest times to the present, is R. I. Watson's *The great psychologists from Aristotle to Freud*. Now in its 3rd edition, this is a useful textbook and though it is not exhaustive, it includes all the well-known great, and many of the lesser, lights. There are analyses and expositions of the principal contributions made by each psychologist included. In addition there is R. I. Watson's two-volume account of *Eminent contributors to psychology* (1974). Watson's book is a valuable guide to the literature of psychology in that it includes a bibliography of the published works of the leading psychologists. Volume one is a bibliography of primary references and volume two a bibliography of secondary references. The first volume covers more than 500 individual psychologists living between AD 1600 and 1967, and cites about 12,000 references. The second volume contains over 50,000 secondary references to the work of those same contributors. One of the singular merits of this work of Watson's is the genuinely international coverage.

A complementary publication, though in fact issued twenty years earlier, is *Readings in the history of psychology*, edited by W. Dennis. Quite obviously, this type of work does not lose its significance with age, but different scholars will see different contributions as a key to the edifice. R. J. Herrnstein & E. G. Boring edited a series of classical papers under the title *A source book in the history of psychology*, which is a very comprehensive collection. It was conceived to form part of a very large Harvard University Press project under the aegis of the American Philosophical Association, the History of Science Society and the American Association for the Advancement of Science. The work certainly comes up to one's expectations from so vast a body of organized learning and the great names of the editors. A concise overview has also been presented by W. M. O'Neill (1982). There exist other readers and edited readings, of course, but the ones mentioned here illustrate better than most the wide range of the discipline and its historical development.

The most interesting biographical exercises are, of course, autobiographies. They are, if we might be permitted to say so, ipso facto fascinating! Fascinating for what they reveal and for what they conceal—wittingly and unwittingly. If this is true of autobiography in general, how much more so (if there were degrees of truth) when the writer is a person highly trained in the analysis of the human mind, in the objective observation of human behaviour and in the scientific (i.e. inductive and measurable) analysis of the social world around him or her. There is a neat little story which illustrates the point we are trying to make here.

Carl Murchison, Edwin G. Boring and Karl Bühler realized as long ago as 1928 that the recent history of psychology could only be written by those individuals who had been creatively involved in its making:

> Since a science separated from its history lacks direction and promises a future of uncertain importance, it is a matter of consequence to those who wish to understand psychology for those individuals who have greatly influenced contemporary psychology to put into print as much of their personal histories as bears on their professional careers. (Preface to the series, vol. 1, p. ix; 1930)

The result of these considerations is the remarkable series entitled *A history of psychology in autobiography*. To date seven volumes have appeared; the first three were edited by Carl Murchison; the fourth and fifth by E. G. Boring and others; the sixth and seventh by G. Lindzey. The first contributor was none other than James Mark Baldwin, philosopher and psychologist, who helped to mould the North American academic scene at the beginning of this century and with William James established psychology as a scientific discipline in the leading universities of the time. The last volume contains such controversial people as H. J. Eysenck and C. E. Osgood—so different and controversial for such different but wholly academic reasons. While there is a slight preponderance of psychologists from the English operating world, the really great names from other linguistic groups are also represented. The series is being continued—a singular lesson in the evaluation of the relevant.

Whatever one may consider as the most outstanding achievement of psychology as a discipline, it has attained one broad objective which is perhaps a greater contribution to mankind than many of the great technical éclats so readily applauded by ordinary citizens: psychology has been the great leveller par excellence. It has taught us better, and more enduringly, than any ethical system that all kinds of man are equal when it comes to psychological facts, and that the perceivable differences are differences of scale and not basic constitutional and incompatible features.

This observation is important when one examines the reasons for the existence of national surveys of endeavours and achievements in the field of psychology. When psychologists speak of American, British, French, etc. psychology they do not, as a rule, wish to imply that the national character of the inhabitants of North America, the United Kingdom, France, etc. has produced a type of psychology—be it a "school" or a "system"—which could not have been produced anywhere else. Indeed, a study of the contributions to the discipline by the various linguistic groups that make up the scholarly community reveals that there have been contributions in many languages (and in that sense, from many national groups) to all major facets of the discipline.

It can perhaps be claimed, and justified on very simple grounds, that the originators of the main streams in psychological theory have had a greater following, and consequently a larger and possibly a more diversified body of literature, in their own country. When we speak of Italian psychology, Lombroso springs immediately to mind, and with him the phrenological approach to psychology, the measurement of stigmata—but there have also been, and there still are, important Italian contributors to psychoanalysis and to behaviourism. Again, the advent of politically hostile forces ejected the psychoanalytical schools out of Europe, and since the 1930s they are perhaps more at home in North America than elsewhere, and the literature of this branch of psychology is now predominantly in English. Many of its present-day followers cannot even read the German original texts.

In the few paragraphs that now follow we have restricted ourselves to the literature of national historical overviews. References to continuous current literature surveys and indexes will be found in Chapter VI on specialist fields of psychology and in Chapters IV and V on information and current awareness services.

Professional associations are another source of historical information. Perhaps the best known association, the APA, has only recently published such a survey with the title *American psychology in historical perspective, 1892–1977*, edited by E. R. Hilgard in 1978.

What is unique here is that it is a collection of 21 APA Presidential addresses, accompanied by a brief biography and chronology of the presidents of the APA between 1892 and 1977. For those interested in US psychology, and for those investigating specific substantive issues, this is a valuable source.

The histories of the achievements of national groups of psychologists should then, if they are to be of scholarly value, deal with the subject *per se;* above all they should not present it as if a particular nation had a lien on one branch (or perhaps all!) of the discipline. Fortunately—and properly, of course, in the light of what has already been said—there are national histories of academic standing and many of them provide a much more detailed account of the contributions to the discipline by the scholars of a particular country or linguistic group than can be provided by international attempts at bibliographic coverage. Among the better ones are the works by A. A. Roback on North America, L. S. Hearnshaw on the United Kingdom, M. Nixon & R. Taft on Australia. The latter is a composite work by twenty experts from a variety of fields of psychology.

There is one account of western psychology that deals not only with the conventional classics but which also contains a section on Islamic psychology—G. & L. B. Murphy's *Western psychology*, (1969). J. R. Kantor's *The scientific evolution of psychology*, 1963 is an earlier two-volume work which also contains a section on the Arab transmission of science.

The work of Latin American psychologists has been briefly summarized by R. Ardila in two accounts published in Latin American professional journals, but these are now almost fifteen years out of date. His later contributions, in the mid-seventies, set out in greater detail the state of the art in Colombia.

Western awareness of the work of Russian psychologists is all too often impeded by ignorance of the Russian language. We have therefore restricted these notes to books in English, and draw attention particularly to the endeavours of North American scholars to make Russian contributions available in translation and to present overviews of the progress of psychology in that country. A symposium on Soviet psychology, translated in English, was edited by N. O'Connor as long ago as 1961. This is the first comprehensive survey of Russian psychological literature in translation. Given the widespread ignorance of the Russian language this book is particularly important, and still serves a useful point of departure for students interested in the effects of dialectical materialism on psychology. The topics covered range from attention to psycholinguistics, and the influence of Russian psychologists since Pavlov's days will soon become evident to the reader.

A fascinating presentation of another world and another view of the history of science is J. Brožek & D. Slobin's *Psychology in the USSR, an historical perspective*, so typical of the many nationalistic surveys produced to commemorate the fiftieth anniversary of the Soviet revolution (the translation appeared in 1972). The East–West rapprochement during the 1960s led to the publication of the proceedings of several symposia at which Russian and Western psychologists participated, e.g. *Recent Soviet psychology*, edited by N. O'Connor, and *Psychology in the Soviet Union* edited by B. Simon.

Two relatively recent contributions to Russian psychology are John McLeish's *Soviet psychology: history, theory, content* (1975) and L. Rahmani's *Soviet psychology: philosophical, theoretical and experimental issues*, (1973). On a particular topic—Pavlov's typology of personality—there is of course Gray's book of that title which summarizes the field and comments on it.

The absence of a comprehensive retrospective bibliography of Russian psychology for the nineteenth and twentieth centuries further increases the difficulties of those who wish to become acquainted with the early growth of this science in Eastern Europe. The leading journal at the turn of the century, *Voprosy filosofiĭ i psikhologiĭ*, contained of course notes on current publications and reviews, and in 1939 A. P. Primakovskiĭ published a cumulative index to the *Voprosy* under the title *Ukazatel' statei retsenziĭ i zametok, napechatannykh v zhurnale "Voprosy filosopfiĭ i psikhologiĭ za 1889–1918 gg"*. This index was published "as a manuscript" and is practically unobtainable today except through photocopying. Though Russian psychology has not always been identical with Soviet psychology, it is an acknowledged fact that all current work in this discipline carried out in socialist countries is deeply affected by the methodology and investigations of the Marxist–Leninist schools in modern Russia. It is therefore pertinent to cite here the useful *Bibliographie der psychologischen Literatur der sozialistischen Länder* which has been issued since 1959 by the Deutsches Pädagogisches Zentralinstitut of the German Democratic Republic. The first volume of this annual survey bore the title *Vergleichende Pädagogik* but it is solely concerned with Soviet psychology. The second volume deals with Russian and Polish research in psychology and from the third volume on (1960), most Communist countries are dealt with in a nation-by-nation bibliography, with each national section further sub-divided into subjects. The first two volumes of this series contain extensive surveys of the "state of the arts" in Russia and in all issues Russian research and publications are clearly rated above those of other countries. There are no author or subject indexes.

A literature survey particularly related to the influence of Soviet psychological thought is R. & A.-L. S. Chin's *Psychological research in Communist China, 1949–1966*.

The French contribution to psychology has been summed up, for the years following on World War II, in the *Documentation sur la psychologie française* by D. Voutsinas. The sub-title, *Dix années de psychologie française*, indicates the scope of this survey which has been continued in annual review volumes. From the historical point of view it is important to note that the third volume contains a list of periodical articles by French psychologists published between 1843 and 1946, and that the sixth volume contains a bibliographic retrospect to 1746.

The very voluminous German-language contribution to the literature of psychology during the post-war years has been captured, bibliographically, by A. Wellek whose *Gesamtverzeichnis der deutschsprachigen psychologischen Literatur der Jahre 1942 bis 1960* appeared in 1965. The literature is arranged under year of publication and then according to a subject division, the scheme for which is outlined in the introduction. An important useful feature of Wellek's work is the introductory survey of the bibliography of psychology in Germany, and the list of serials, series and collective works which this bibliography covers. The introduction also refers to the gaps in the bibliography of German psychology caused by the political events in Germany of the thirties and the cessation of the *Psychological index*, to which Wellek contributed. Wellek's *Gesamtverzeichnis* includes, as the title suggests, the contributions by Austrian and Swiss scholars, but the work of the latter has also been covered retrospectively by a separate compilation entitled *Bibliographie der philosophischen, psychologischen and pädagogischen Literatur in der deutschsprachigen Schweiz, 1900–1940*, edited by E. Heuss. Its continuation, edited by H. Zantop, not only brings the listings up to 1944 but also includes all other linguistic groups of Switzerland.

2. Schools

We stressed earlier that a division of the psychological literature into national or linguistic groups cannot be very useful because this particular discipline is not amenable to such a basis for classification. The simple reason for this is, of course, that the subject under investigation is a topic remarkably unique—in both senses of the word. One may well question whether any true science can be justifiably treated from a nationalistic point of view, but it would lead too far to discuss this issue here. Yet to assume that all psychologists choose the same approach to answer all questions related to human behaviour would be simplistic in the extreme. Indeed, the differences in the several major lines of interpretations are obvious even to a layman, and the briefest examination of the literature shows that it is possible to discern the limitations of the fields which the various groups of psychologists have chosen. It is useful to refer to them as "schools" because there is a good deal of the master–disciple tradition in these groups.

This view of the "organization" of the discipline forms the basis of R. S. Woodworth's *Contemporary schools of psychology*, an admirably clear and concise exposition of the main European and North American trends and their representatives. Woodworth's account has been reprinted many times, and it has last been brought up to date by M. R. Sheehan in 1964. Popular and generally instructive as the book is, it should not be accepted without an awareness that there are not now, and probably never have been, strictly distinct compartments in the discipline. While Woodworth reflects accurately the "schools period", there are few present-day psychologists who would want to be so narrowly classified or circumscribed. We have, nevertheless stuck to the classification in order to present an easily comprehensible picture of the antecedents of current developments—antecedents which have become "classical" and intrinsically infertile within 75–100 years.

The evolution of modern psychology out of the "soul-searching" activities that dominated scholars from ancient times to the middle of the nineteenth century was aided, above all, by the physiologists who, in the spirit of the times, insisted on beginning their "soul-searching" with an analysis and measurement of nervous reactions through scientifically* controlled experiments.

From an historical point of view, therefore, it is justifiable to begin this bibliographic survey of the schools of psychology with the physiologists and experimentalists. One of the definitive works on the origins and growth of experimental psychology and its contributions to our understanding of human behaviour is E. G. Boring's *A History of experimental psychology*, which was first published in 1929. E. G. Boring was one of the many distinguished students of E. B. Titchener (1867–1927) who in turn had been a brilliant student under Wilhelm Wundt (1832–1920) who is commonly regarded as the father of modern experimental psychology. It will not escape the observant that Wundt was a German, Titchener an Englishman, and Boring a North American, and that Boring's account, dedicated to Titchener, was written by someone who has actually been involved in the development of this science. Boring's great historical survey and interpretation of the origins of experimental psychology has been reprinted and brought up to date several times.

These accounts of the findings of experimental psychology have been updated by J. W. Kling & L. A. Riggs in their work *Woodworth and Schlosberg's experimental psychology*, which has been last issued in 1971; the title is a tribute to the fundamental work by Woodworth published first in 1938. Closely related to experimental psychology and, indeed, to some extent its antecedent, is the study of physiology and neurology. Historically speaking this is the classical tradition which gave rise to modern psychology. A standard account of this development can be found in F. Fearing's *Reflex action: a study in the history of physiological psychology*. For those interested in the transmission of ideas and the growth of psychology, the century between 1850 and 1950 provides a repository of famous names of scientists whose influence upon each other has created an intellectual flowering similar to that of the late renaissance and of the second half of the seventeenth century.

One of the best textbooks on neuropsychology is still C. T. Morgan's *Physiological psychology* which first appeared in 1943 but has been brought up to date in 1965; however it is worth noting that the earlier editions of 1943 and 1950 contain more complete reference lists. The associated field of perception is covered by the accounts by Boring, Stevens or Osgood cited. Subsequent developments have concen-

---

* Aware of the ill use now so often made of the term "scientific", the authors wish to emphasize that here and hereafter in this book the term is to be understood to mean a scholarly attitude and method, irrespective of the field to which it is applied. Scientific means to us something that can be shown to stand up to logical explanation and to measurable processes. We emphasize that the term is not meant to be restricted to the natural sciences, or any other branch of human investigation.

trated on biochemical experimentation and the influence of pharmaceutical preparations on human behavior.

There are several other distinct schools of psychology whose origins are clearly founded in experimental psychology but whose creators keenly asserted that they were moving into a quite new direction. One such school is W. Köhler's Gestalt psychology, which from the 1920s on offered a new interpretation of man (as distinct from behaviourism and the introspective approaches then in vogue) and contributed substantially to later developments of psychological theories. Köhler's own fundamental treatise, entitled *Gestalt psychology,* first appeared in English in 1929 and in the 1930s a substantial literature grew around this school. K. Goldstein's *The organism: a holistic approach to biology derived from the pathological data in man* (1963) is probably the most important summing up of Gestalt theories in recent times.

Another derivative of experimental psychology is comparative psychology, which in its primitive formulation goes back to Aristotle. More modern applications can be seen in Charles Darwin, J. Loeb, C. L. Morgan and, in our own time, K. Lorenz.

Yet another attempt to interpret human actions and reactions was that by J. B. Watson, the founder of behaviourism whose grand exposition was first published in 1929 under the title *Psychology from the standpoint of the behaviorist.* Watson's teachings and the influence of comparative psychology have represented an important new approach which has dominated current psychology for some time.

A radically different view of man and his nature, and of the part nurture plays in shaping his behaviour, was taken by S. Freud, the founder of psychoanalysis. It must be stressed immediately that psychoanalysis, be it from the theoretical or from the practical point of view, has little to do with general psychology. It derived as a therapeutic process from the field of medical psychiatry and has subsequently been vested with a philosophical suit of considerable depth and importance. Like many other aspects of medicine it has had considerable influence on the science of psychology but, to repeat what is not obvious to many laymen, psychology can and does exist without psychoanalysis, and vice-versa. Nevertheless, there is an overlap and there are crossroads. Students should not close their eyes to those aspects of psychoanalysis which do have bearing on psychology; to read and study Freud is in itself an important part of one's education. No other author can provide as thorough an insight into psychoanalysis as its creator, and he is not that difficult to read. Some of his disciples have—as is the wont of so many pupils—confused and misinterpreted the original doctrine. The most reliable student and interpreter of the master was E. Jones, whose *The life and work of Sigmund Freud* offers the best account of the creator of psychoanalysis and of the achievements of this school.

Freud's influence has been enormous. In spite of the fact that his principal interests and teachings were not centred on, or derived from, a study of psychology, he greatly affected people's views of the human species, and incidentally every one of our interpretations of intellectual processes and many other activities besides.

As can only be expected with so strong a school, there soon grew up deviant disciples and strong opposition to the founder. The literature on psychoanalysis is very extensive and special attention will be paid to it in Chapter VI. Suffice it here to note that Freud's psychoanalytical interpretation spawned two major schools. One, headed by A. Adler, was dubbed by him "individual psychology"; the other founded by C. G. Jung did not adopt a specific title and aimed at a deep quasi-religious interpretation of the unconscious mind. The works by Adler and Jung respectively constitute the most important interpretation of their theories.

The most recent trends have been summed up under the catchword "Humanistic psychology". This approach to an interpretation of human behaviour owes a great deal to the philosophy of Heidegger and Husserl, and particularly their French disciples J. P. Sartre and M. Merleau-Ponty. Existentialist and humanist psychology are expounded by contemporary scholars such as I. L. Child, R. May and S. Strasser, but there exists as yet no major overview.

3. Theories

One of the explicit goals of psychology is to express its findings in generalized form. These laws, and the accounts that invest them with meaning—i.e. the theories, are derived from specific philosophical positions. Depending upon one's standpoint, psychology may be about the mind, about behaviour, about theoretical notions in the abstract: it may centre on either man or other animals. Commonly, of course, it centres upon more than one of these instances of subject matter.

Among the early contributors to the new science of psychology—albeit to a specific scientific aspect rather than to the philosophical infrastructure—was Sir Francis Galton (1822–1911), the inventor of sophisticated statistical techniques such as the correlation coefficient and improved questionnaire designs. He is, of course, best known for his work on heredity and eugenics but his contributions to statistical theories are highly significant for psychology. Several physiological problems also engaged his attention, and of particular relevance in this context are his studies of visual imagery. An overview of his highly original contributions may be gained from reading his *Memories of my life* (1908).

The earliest work of universal influence, and of the highest scientific importance, was the state of the art account published at the end of the nineteenth century by William James. His *Principles of psychology* is still unrivalled for its penetrating insight, for its wealth of information on the science of psychology which he as much as anyone helped to create, and for its exemplary prose style. It has been said that William James wrote textbooks like novels while his brother, Henry James, wrote novels like textbooks.

Many of the fundamental issues in the numerous theories of psychology are not peculiar to this discipline but are part of the whole framework of scientific inquiry. It is therefore appropriate to mention at least some of the works which try to explain in general terms the nature of scientific inquiry and to encourage students to acquaint themselves with the answers offered by a few leading philosophers of science to the perennial question: What is science all about?

Many philosophical problems in psychology are theories about theories (meta-theories) and have been documented in a number of places. Because it is not possible to divorce basic theoretical views about psychology from views about science in general, we recommend a work which is held in deservedly high regard, Sir Karl Popper's *The logic of scientific discovery*. It is claimed by Popper's disciples that it has now become almost an orthodoxy. There is a counter-view, which gives particular weight to the non-rational and creative aspects of science in A. Koestler's *The act of creation*, but this attempt to interpret the processes of scientific discovery does not compare with Popper's in vigorous analysis and clarity of purpose and style. Historical perspectives on the development of science have been examined by Kuhn (1963). His expressed view is part dialectical and part evolutionary. His earlier views formed a useful insight into the development of scientific thought. It should be borne in mind, however, that Kuhn was writing of the physical sciences.

A work published some time ago, but still with an important point to make, is Susan Langer's *Philosophy in a new key*. Langer argues persuasively that each age is characterized by a mode of thought and a means of conceptualizing insights, and that the predominant mode for each age finds expression in a variety of forms, of which science is but one.

Philosophical foundations of science are dealt with in the series of occasional volumes of essays known as *Minnesota studies in the philosophy of science*, which began in 1956. A recent issue (1978) is entitled *Perception and recognition: issues in the foundations of psychology;* the volume is edited by C. Wade Savage. Another series of essays and proceedings of meetings are the *Boston studies in the philosophy of science* which first appeared in 1963, though that first volume covers papers presented in 1961/62. The *Boston studies* also contain many volumes dedicated to philosophical problems as relevant to psychology as to any other discipline.

There are also works which deal with insights into scientific understanding and the psychological processes of theorizing. An important example is Hesse's *Models and analogies in science*, where it is convincingly argued that scientific explanations are in fact metaphors and analogies. Among the points made is the importance of metaphors for scientific understanding.

Indeed, according to Hesse, theory is a metaphor for the established world and science cannot but proceed by such analogies and metaphors.

When dealing in psychological systems and theories one needs a work that is a source of basic information about systematic and theoretical psychology. One such work is Marx & Hillix's *Systems and theories in psychology*. The major part of the work is by the authors, but there is an appendix on "non-American developments"—which include European, Soviet and Oriental psychology. The outlines in this book do not always accurately represent the origins of current theories; some of the views listed as American, e.g. Associationism, Gestalt psychology and Psychoanalysis, are all European in origin. It is, however, a very good American overview which affords brief definitional accounts of the various theoretical notions relevant to psychology.

Some of the problems in psychology have been dealt with in a series of classic articles, selected and published in the 1960s and issued under the collective title "Insight books". Each volume contains a collection of important writings on a specific topic, e.g. Teevan and Birney's *Theories of motivation in personality and social psychology*. The series is particularly useful because each volume is self-contained but there are now about twenty of them, and together they present an overview of the major issues in the field.

Theoretical psychologists write in diverse ways and sometimes in publications not ready of access. An example of this unfortunate practice is the series of commissioned works written by a set of distinguished authors who were requested to set down their philosophical standpoint in a very concise form, to be published in a seven-volume work by S. Koch entitled *Psychology: a study of a science*. Study One, incorporating the first three volumes, deals with conceptual and systematic issues; Study Two, incorporating volumes 4–6, deals with empirical sub-structure and relations with other sciences; volume 7 is a postscript to the study.

A more recently initiated British example is the *Psychology survey* series. Currently it is at No. 4. *Psychology survey* No. 1 (B. Foss, ed.) appeared in 1978; No. 2 appeared in 1979 (K. Connolly, ed.), No. 3 in 1981 (M. Jeeves, ed.) and No. 4 in 1983 (J. Nicholson & B. Foss, eds.). This series is designed to ease the problem of time spent on journal searches and, because of its modest price, to meet the needs of impecunious students, scholars, and libraries. Its aim is to let leading writers present authoritative accounts of developments in their own fields.

On the topic of differing ways of conceptualizing man, Stevenson's recent work *Seven theories of human nature,* captures the variety of orientations. The coverage is certainly comprehensive, ranging over Plato, Christianity, Marxism, Freud and his schools, Sartre and existentialism, Skinnerian conditioning and Lorenz and ethology. This is a serious and well-reasoned attempt to assess the ideological aspects of these approaches. We venture to suggest as an alternative, semi-serious, but delightful spoof on interpretation, the study by F. Crews entitled *The Pooh perplex*.

A work by a variety of authors and edited by Chapman and Jones, *Models of man*, sets out to express "the dilemmas and controversies confronting the student of behaviour". Its express purpose is to emphasize the plurality of psychology.

At a different level of abstraction one may find works that conceptualize psychological problems within a psychological framework. Two such works are Marx and Goodson's *Theories in contemporary psychology*, and Bolton's *Philosophical problems in psychology*. The former, in particular, is significant because it contains a series of philosophical examinations of the scientific basis of psychological theories such as the classic paper by S. S. Stevens on "Operationism and logical positivism", and McCorquedale & Meehl's equally important one on "The intervening variable and the hypothetical construct". Quite generally it illustrates the theme that "philosophical psychology reflects upon the aims and concepts of empirical psychology" and that empirical psychology must be founded on the language of rationality for actions, and that the reasons people give for their actions are at the heart of human behaviour.

Bolton's work is perhaps one of the best-known texts in the field since it successfully provides, in a single edited source, the basic information about action and psychology. It is a very good overview with the major concern being to join psychological insights to the philosophy of mind.

Another approach to psychological theory is to present its evolution, as was attempted by R. Lowry in his *The evolution of psychological theory*. This concise history is in three parts and conventional in content, but does show better than many other textbooks the continuity of psychological theory.

As well as books dealing with general theories there are also works dealing with theories in branches of psychology. One well-known instance is Lindzey's *Theories of personality: primary sources of research* (2nd ed.). The work is designed to give a "reasonable representation of contemporary theoretical contributions" as well as making them interesting and pertinent. It is particularly good on social and personalistic theories though weak on stimulus–response theories (why does Skinner get two chapters whereas Pavlov's typology not a mention?).

Nunnally's *Psychometric theory* is another well-regarded work in the field. This text is designed for higher-level students as a comprehensive work for courses in psychological measurement and its theory.

This chapter on theoretical aspects may read as if the level of abstraction made it irrelevant to problems in the practical world—but not so. Westland, for instance, has written on *Current crises in psychology*, wherein the usefulness of science, statistics, ethics, etc. is discussed.

There are, too, works whose titles indicate that they belong elsewhere. *Biology as a social weapon* is one such. It contains nine essays by different authors of directional practical relevance and includes such topics as race and IQ, aggression, and biological determinism.

It will be appreciated by the reader that we have simply outlined examples and seminal instances of the kinds of books that are available. Readers should regard these comments and references as points of departure rather than suitable destinations. Further, it is necessary to draw attention to the instances of a number of works on philosophy in the behavioural and social sciences which often appear under imprimaturs which are sociological. The purpose of this chapter then, it will be understood, is to point out the array of sources that might be culled for theoretical and philosophical information searches about psychology in particular and scientific issues in general.

CHAPTER 3

Reference Sources

1. Monographs

THE literature of psychology—like that of any other discipline—can be divided broadly into three distinct forms: monographs or books; periodicals or serials; and documents emanating from official bodies, professional organizations and the like. This latter group may, of course, also be divided into monographs and serials, but for the purpose of this discussion the division proposed will serve best because while librarians are dedicated to more precise definitions, library users are more concerned with finding their references quickly, using a simple and preferably habitual approach to manual data retrieval. In other words, library users who are not librarians, go to the "books section" or to the "periodicals section" of a library, or to the "government publications section" where such exists, to find among the books or periodicals or official documents whatever they are looking for. The finer distinctions between series, serials, periodicals, monographs, textbooks, etc. are, generally speaking, quite irrelevant to them. As a lesson in the psychology of professionalism, this is surely a good start.

The monograph literature related to psychology is quite considerable. Looking at the narrow field of psychology proper, several hundred new titles every year in English alone; once we extend our field of interest to the many associated and marginal disciplines that have bearing on, or are affected by, psychology, the number of books issued every year may well run to 2000 or more, and these include of course contributions in all major languages. To establish what has been written and by whom is no easy task, and it is as well to realize immediately that there is no international listing of the world's monograph literature on psychology and related disciplines. It is, however, possible to obtain fairly satisfactory partial answers by approaching the question from a national point of view.

Many, though by no means all, nations where a substantial publishing programme is in operation support the compilation of a current national bibliography, i.e. a list of books produced in the country. These lists may appear at weekly, monthly, quarterly or annual intervals, with appropriate cumulations; they may be arranged in alphabetical sequence of author and titles, or be in a classified order of subjects (usually following a standard system of classification) with guides to subjects covered or with detailed subject and author indexes. In some instances the lists are so slight that a complex system of classification is not warranted. It is quite beyond the scope of this book to examine in detail the national bibliographies of all nations. The literature in English, French, German and Spanish is unquestionably the most significant at present, and the sources of information on books in those languages, together with a note on Russian material, are set out below. For a listing of the national bibliographies issued by over 120 countries, readers may care to consult G. Pomassl's *Synoptic tables concerning the current national bibliographies*, compiled in the early 1970s but still substantially valid. More up-to-date but restricted in geographic coverage is the annotated directory of *Commonwealth retrospective national bibliographies* published in 1981 by the Commonwealth Secretariat, London.

For an annotated listing, we suggest that making the acquaintance of Sheehy's *Guide to reference books* will well repay the effort; and in the long run a thorough acquaintance with bibliographic reference sources in general will aid every researcher. Sheehy's *Guide* contains an annotated section on national bibliographies setting out the scope and coverage of each, including English-language and other sources.

The English-language literature on psychology stems from at least six major countries: the UK, the USA, Canada, Australia, New Zealand and South Africa. In addition, many English-language titles are issued in India, Scandinavia, the Netherlands, and a small number in a variety of other places. If one knows the author of a title and wants to identify the bibliographic citation the problem is not that difficult. The following current national bibliographies will help directly to answer that question:

Australian national bibliography 1961–
British national bibliography 1950–
Canadiana: Canada's national bibliography 1950–
New Zealand national bibliography 1967–
South African national bibliography 1960–

As will be noted from the above list, there exists no official, i.e. government-sponsored, national bibliography for the USA. The *Cumulative book index* published by the H. W. Wilson Co., New York, is the most comprehensive reporting service for monograph titles published in the USA and it is fairly reliable with regard to all commercially produced books. In fact it is, up to a point, a substitute for all of the national bibliographies listed above because the *CBI* is an international English-language bibliography which includes in its dictionary arrangement (i.e. entries for authors, subjects and titles are filed in one alphabetical sequence) references to the world literature in English. Though the output by US publishers is better covered than that of other countries the *CBI* does include the commercial publishers of the UK and of the British

Commonwealth, and the English-language books that appear on the European continent, Africa, Asia and the Middle East. There is, as the saying goes, no real substitute for the *CBI*—but its limitations should also be understood. It excludes all government publications, reports literature and most of the hundreds of symposia not commercially available. For researchers in the fields of psychology, that is an important and very extensive volume of publications, references to which cannot be retrieved through the *CBI*.

It remains to be added, in this context, that the national bibliographies referred to above offer directly or indirectly both an author title and a subject approach.

Besides the national bibliographies there exist also printed book form catalogues of national and other large research libraries. This type of reference work is particularly valuable for those wanting to prepare themselves for studies in other parts of the world, since consultation will throw some light on the holdings they may expect in the overseas institutions where they want to study. The importance of national library catalogues is enhanced by the fact that as libraries of legal deposit—a statutory requirement which obliges printers or publishers to supply to the national library of their country at least one copy of every book and journal printed or published—they will hold a copy of all books produced in their country. Legal deposit provisions have existed for a long time in Europe, and since the beginning of the nineteenth century it was enforced in every country where a national library had been identified. Consequently we may expect to find in the British Library or in the Bibliothèque Nationale every book on psychology published respectively in the UK or in France. Readers must be warned, however, that the book-form catalogues are always a few years behind the acquisitions records of the libraries whose holdings they list. Here, reference must be restricted to a few major examples:

> **British Museum.** Dept. of Printed Books. *General catalogue of printed books.* London, 1959–1966. 263 volumes.
> **Bibliothèque Nationale.** *Catalogue général des livres imprimés.* Anteurs, Paris, 1900–1974. 220 volumes. (in progress).
> **Harvard University.** Library. *Widener Library shelf list.,* Cambridge, Mass. 1965– (in progress).

It should be noted that the last named represents a classified book-form catalogue of one of the world's largest academic collections. These computer-produced shelf-lists, i.e. a list of the Widener Library's holdings as arranged on the shelves, with each volume devoted to a section of the classification scheme, represents a useful subject bibliography because of the wealth of the Widener Library. Supplements and updated editions appear from time to time. For our purpose volumes 42–43 are of particular importance because they show the Widener's holdings in philosophy and psychology.

Last to be mentioned in this context of major library catalogues is the *National union catalog: a cumulative author list,* a most important source of bibliographic data for an author approach. This great work, in several hundred volumes, lists the holdings of 700 major research libraries in the USA and Canada, showing full bibliographic details and locations. It has a complex listing and those wishing to use it should take care that they know its full potential as a reference tool.

Most of the catalogues of national libraries offer an author approach only, but both the Library of Congress and the British Museum (as it then was) have issued subject catalogues of their collections in book form. These are known as

Library of Congress catalog. *Books: subject.* Ann Arbor, Edwards, 1955– .

British Museum. Dept. of Printed Books. *Subject index of the modern works added to the library.* London, 1902–65 (no more published).

The Library of Congress volumes are fairly easy to use but the coverage tends to vary slightly from one quinquennial cumulation to another. The BM *Subject index* is more difficult to use because the subject headings shown are often general rather than specific and the arrangements within subject groups tends to be haphazard. Nevertheless, this is an important source of information for historical literature surveys.

Reference has already been made to Baldwin's *Dictionary of philosophy and psychology* (see p. 3) and its two complementary volumes *Bibliography of philosophy, psychology and cognate subjects,* compiled by B. Rand. In the first volume Rand arranged entries under the names of philosophers, psychologists, etc., including their journal articles, monographs and major criticisms of their work. The second volume is arranged according to major subject fields within each of which entries are listed in alphabetical sequence. Rand made a genuine effort to present a broad and comprehensive selection of the world's philosophical and psychological thought. It is not claimed that the bibliography is exhaustive, and users should be well aware of this. However, for the nineteenth century the work is undoubtedly the most reliable and extensive bibliographic guide in existence, and in particular it should be noted that this source of reference to monographs is unequalled for the period.

Another and somewhat more didactic approach to the identification of books on psychology is represented by reading lists made up for undergraduate students. There probably exist hundreds of such lists— maybe as many as there are academic teachers of psychology—and few of them will be exactly identical; the longer the list, the greater the divergence. Most of these lists are duplicated handouts to enrolled students, but Harvard University produced a printed form of this type of guide entitled *The Harvard list of books in psychology*. It is now unfortunately somewhat out of date, because the last (fourth) edition appeared in 1971. But anyone reading his way through the books listed would gain a very full insight into what psychology is all about.

Not to be forgotten, as useful and unpretentious sources of information on authors, titles and often also series, are the trade-oriented publications which provide data on books currently available from their publishers. "Books in print" is the collective name for these annual or biennial indexes, issued in the UK, the US, in Spain (*Libros en venta*), in France (*Les livres disponibles*).

It is not possible in this guide to sources of information for students of psychology to cite more than the basic reference tools commonly used by librarians to identify readers' requests. The works here mentioned are the obvious and most useful ones, for the layman in bibliography; those who want to make a thorough study of bibliographic services in general, or of the whole bibliographic apparatus related to psychology in particular, are advised to consult first of all Dr Chandler's *How to find out* and then to follow up his tips on specialist sources of information, or to study such in-depth analyses of reference tools as have been compiled by Malclés, Sheehy and Walford.

A totally different approach to finding references to the monograph literature is based on the practice of book reviews. There are few media wholly dedicated to book reviews; most reviews appear in the professional journals as an appendix or separate section—which is not to be taken as representing a lack of prestige attached to this form of current awareness services. However, the APA has for over 20 years published a journal wholly dedicated to book reviews and entitled *Contemporary psychology*. It was started in 1956 and now also covers films, tapes and "other media relevant to psychology". It is addressed to a broad readership of psychological literature, and its panel of expert reviewers discuss at some length between 600 and 650 titles per year and bring to the notice of readers another 300–400 books through short evaluative notes. A list of books received, which may or may not be reviewed or noted later, is printed at the end of each monthly issue; this list tends to include about 100 titles per month. In spite of the large number of titles mentioned one way or another, *Contemporary psychology* does not claim to list every book published on psychology.

As has been mentioned already, book reviews are well-established features in many journals. As students develop specialist interests they will want to identify their own choice of reading on the basis of expert opinions as expressed in scholarly reviews in the specialist journals. It is obvious, for example, that journals dedicated to the findings of the behaviourist school will review books on that same branch of psychology. There exist also, of course, several major generalist journals on psychology where books from the whole field may be reviewed. This pointer must suffice to draw attention to this source of information on current monographs.

The reading of book reviews is a minor art in itself. If a reviewer is excessively critical (in the negative or the positive sense) one should ask oneself whether there exists a hidden link (of hate or love) between the reviewer and the author. Scholarly reviews in general eschew all bias, but there may be many "scholarly" reasons for one author to hate another. If a reviewer has good and bad to say about a book, his credibility is unquestionably greater than when he leans too much towards appreciation or condemnation. Those comments may well be just common sense—but that commodity needs to be pointed up sometimes.

Last it should be noted that there exist some reliable lists of the general monograph literature on psychology. The best among these is probably *The Harvard list of books in psychology,* first published in 1938 and revised several times; the fourth edition appeared in 1971. The compilers, all on the staff of Harvard University, include the foremost scholars in this field. All entries are annotated and are arranged under the standard broad divisions of psychology. Anyone reading and working through the 700 recommended titles should be well prepared for taking an advanced course at a university. Emphasizing the background of the subject, W. Viney, and Michael and M. L. Wertheimer, compiled a very comprehensive and reliable guide to the sources of the history of psychology, published in 1979. The work contains thousands of entries, annotated and arranged under scores of headings. This is to date the best bibliographic history of the subject.

2. Periodical literature

Psychology is a live discipline whose theorists and practitioners are constantly in search of new interpretations and explanations of observed phenomena. Furthermore, the boundaries of the science are not static, and interdisciplinary relations continuously shed new light on the core topics of psychology. The quick and early publication of findings is of greatest importance, to announce new interpretation, to establish the reputation of scholars and to prevent waste of effort through duplication of research.

Current research results and achievements are traditionally first reported in the professional periodicals, which technically speaking include journals, serials and report literature, on the one hand to stake a claim, on the other to elicit responses and criticisms from colleagues. They therefore represent the primary sources of information on empirical, theoretical, methodological and logistic advances in the field. There exist today over 1000 journals dedicated wholly, or at least mainly, to research in the various fields of psychology. Tompkins & Shirley list over 400 titles in their *Checklist of serials in psychology and allied fields.* Issued in 1969, this list is sadly restricted to English-language publications and it omits a host of categories, e.g. "the material published by the United States government and the military". Even so it is strongly biased towards North America, but includes such odd (in this context!) titles as *AUK*, a famous ornithological magazine of venerable antiquity but scarcely of direct relevance to many students of psychology.

The study of psychology is, however, not a preserve of the English-speaking world and in many special fields the work of French, German, Italian, Russian or Spanish-speaking scholars may well be of greater significance. The Maison des Sciences de l'Homme, Paris, issued a *World list of specialized periodicals: psychology* which contains also approximately 400 entries but includes, of course, a high proportion of serials in languages other than English. The list was compiled in 1965 and is now also out of date.

There is no simple means of getting hold of a really current and comprehensive bibliography of psychology journals. Even the large library suppliers of serials do not list more than 200 at the most. For quite obvious reasons their sales catalogues, e.g. *Ulrich's international periodicals directory* and its companion volume *Irregular serials and annuals; an international directory*, are restricted to the core journals in the field. Few general institutions like university libraries subscribe to more than the basic 100–150 titles, if indeed they take in as many as that. It would be invidious to attempt to make a list of "core" journals in psychology but it may help to know that *Psychological abstracts*, the most important and comprehensive indexing service in the subject, lists well over 1000 periodicals directly related to psychology. More will be said presently about *Psychological abstracts*; at this point it is referred to merely to suggest that in the index issue of every volume there is, in the beginning, a list of the journals which have been used to compile *Psychological abstracts*. Again, most of the journals cited are in English—the old problem in a world where the physical means of communication are being constantly improved while the intellectual means tend to be neglected. To identify a wider range (at least linguistically), scholars have to consult the general international indexing services, such as the *Internationale Bibliographie der Zeitschriftenliteratur*, *Referativni Zhurnal* and the *Bulletin signalétique* (part 19 'Sciences humaines'), each of which lists the psychology journals which appear in the respective language group and, of course, major English-language journals as well.

It is useful to distinguish clearly between the several types of periodicals. There are first of all commercially produced journals which depend for their economic survival on subscriptions and advertising. Their publishers are often presses of world renown and much emphasis is laid on all contributions being refereed by experts before they are published. Editorial boards usually lay down and maintain an editorial policy which sets out the special fields in which contributions will be accepted and the intellectual or scholarly level required of contributors. However, some journals, almost indistinguishable from the commercially produced ones, are issued by societies and are based on a similar financial footing. The subscription price and advertisements must cover the cost of production, whether or not the subscription is included in the membership rates. It is interesting to note that the four major psychological societies in the English-speaking world: the American Psychological Association, the Australian Psychological Society, the British Psychological Society and the Canadian Psychological Association, publish between them twenty-seven journals.

Another category of periodicals is the house journal, i.e. a more or less regular communication medium designed primarily for a closed society. Into this category fall the bulletins, proceedings, Mitteilungen, etc. of the many national or specialized societies who use this means to advise their members of past or future events, of elections and awards, of obituaries and the like.

Some societies combine a scholarly journal with the function of a house journal but history shows that this is scarcely effective for long. A house journal may of course be produced by an institution and combine institutional news with articles of a scholarly nature. In general such articles tend to be research reports on activities undertaken within or under the aegis of the institution, be it a university department or an organization established for pure or applied research, in conjunction with or separate from a commercial enterprise—there are many possible combinations. It appears, however, that the research staff of such institutes often prefer to publish their scholarly contributions in the independent media—unless of course there is some contract which obliges them to issue their findings in employing institutes' reports series.

The vast majority of students and scholars will certainly not approach this question in the simplistic way: how many psychology journals are there and what's their name? For the serious student the "way in" to the current literature of psychology is through references to journal articles picked up from teachers and colleagues, books and the journals themselves. One discovery leads to another and those interested in experimental work will soon come across the *Journal of experimental psychology*, while others may find more material bearing on their particular interests in the *Journal of abnormal psychology*.

We have refrained from offering a selection of "most recommended" journals just as we have made no attempt to compile a bibliography of the most significant books in the discipline. However, to help with a general appreciation of the different categories we add below a typology of such journals.

Readers will recognize that journals are consulted for a variety of reasons; sometimes for browsing, sometimes for a specific article and sometimes for professional news and announcements. To recognize the reason for consulting a journal is to increase the prospect of getting value from it.

The accompanying table is a typology of journals designed to draw the reader's attention to function and usage. The restricted number of illustrations should not be construed to mean that we regard these as the "best"; they are, rather, presented, for the most part, as exemplars.

Type	Example
The house journal	*Bulletin of the British Psychological Society*
	APA Monitor
The book review	*Contemporary psychology*
(This is the only psychology journal devoted exclusively to reviews of books, though other journals have a section for book reviews.)		
General theoretical	*Psychological review*
	Psychological bulletin
General empirical	*British journal of psychology*
	Australian journal of psychology
Specialist	*Perception*
	British journal of mathematical and statistical psychology
International	*International journal of mental health*
	International psychologist
Journal/magazine	*Psychology today*
(This is the only general journal/magazine; *American imago* does a similar (though not the same) job but it is psychoanalytically oriented.)		

For a useful guide to information about psychology journals readers are recommended to consult Markle & Rinn's *Author's guide to journals in psychology, psychiatry and social work* (1977); however, this work is highly selective and serves, at any rate, a very special purpose to which further reference is made later.

Lastly we draw attention to a feature of some journals that is of special value to scholars. From time to time journal editors devote a whole issue to a series of articles on one topic; these are usually selected or invited and conceived as a set to be read as a unit. This not only produces a number of related papers within one set of covers, but has the further advantage that the contributions to the topic are usually up to date. Such journal issues have considerable reference value; frequently they may be purchased separately.

3. Government publications

Besides books and periodicals commercially produced, or sponsored and issued by non-profit-seeking private institutions and organizations, there exists a vast mass of printed materials sponsored and produced by government agencies of various kinds. These materials, embracing monographs—books and pamphlets—and serials, are variously referred to as government documents, government publications, official documents, official publications and sometimes even as official government documents or publications. Usage varies from country to country; we have chosen the term government publications.

As for the term government it does require a word or two of explanation. In most democracies, genuine or pseudo, there are at least two levels of government: the national government and the local government. At the national level we have the legislative, executive and judicial power of the modern state, while at the local level there is the grass-roots management of the living community, the organizations of the citizenry—in early times around the parish pump and now around more sophisticated basic supplies such as sewerage and water reticulation.

Countries organized on a federal system enjoy a further level of authority, wedged between the national and the local governments. Variously termed states, provinces, regions or cantons, this second level of government has a set of functions which may be justified on the basis of size, e.g. the USA, the USSR, or be the result of a long tradition, the abolition of which would be bloodily rejected even though its retention may no longer be warranted in terms of population size or geographic area, e.g. Switzerland. As a result another mountain of government publications is created to lie between the huge mass of material issued by the national government and the small pile of local government publications. In the last resort, the difference in the size of the piles is in direct relationship to the amount of tax money available to each of the three levels of public administration.

For a variety of reasons which need not concern us here, government publications tend to be the Cinderella of many library services. Even libraries in government departments are not necessarily giving this form of publication issued by their own departments the attention and priority it deserves. There are notable exceptions to this, and there are signs that more librarians take an interest in this material now than used to be the case.

What has all of this to do with the study of psychology? A great deal, even though it is not suggested, of course, that all government publications are related to psychological issues. Yet, it may surprise some to realize how many government publications have in fact bearing on questions in which psychologists are interested. The very simple reason for this is that a large number of government publications are of a statistical nature and report statistical data collected under the authority of national, regional or local governments.

Let us look at some examples of data of interest to psychologists contained in government publications. An obvious candidate for inclusion is the statistics of persons detained in mental asylums; another is the records of psychological tests used to classify or grade school children; the statistical results of social surveys of various minority groups which allow social psychologists to draw all sorts of conclusions from data collected by government authorities; the findings of a task force examining employment trends in relation to some social-psychological categories may be of considerable interest to psychologists working with courts of justice, social welfare departments, and parole boards. Not all the material published by a government need be of a statistical nature to be of interest to psychologists; thus the Australian Department of Ethnic Affairs has issued a pamphlet entitled *Please listen to what I'm not saying,* which deals with the communication problems of non-English-speaking immigrants. It will surely be of interest to those who are concerned with the assimilation processes of adult new Australians. It would be easy to extend this list but the point has surely been made that government publications as a category of published materials include many items of interest to the psychologist. Of special interest are the recorded numerical data of national censuses and surveys (see p. 123).

It will be obvious that government publications can also be divided into monographs and serials. The annual reports of government departments certainly are serials, but besides these some departments and authorities issue journals on a regular basis, containing research reports often but not always related to government-sponsored investigations, statistical data and general observations. Monographs are issued also; some represent the findings of commissioned research, others contain the reports of committees set up to investigate some problems.

The question arises firstly where to find references to the many publications emanating from government departments and authorities, and secondly how to get hold of the documents to which they relate. Again we have to stress that it would exceed the natural boundaries of this book if we were to present a comprehensive guide on access to government publications. There exist numerous such guides, each designed for one nation, which may be helpful and a few of which are listed below. We suggest that those who want to get the most out of the wealth of records emanating from public authorities will do well to acquaint themselves with the appropriate guide; the alternative is complete dependence on librarians skilled in the exploitation of this category of publications.

Here, then is a short list of the most useful guides to government publications arranged by country:

Australia	D. H. Borchardt (Ed.) *Australian official publications.* Melbourne, Longman Cheshire, 1979.
Canada	O. B. Bishop. *Canadian official publications.* Oxford, Pergamon, 1981.
France	G. Westfall. *French official publications.* Oxford, Pergamon, 1980.
UK	J. E. Pemberton. *British official publications*, 2nd ed. Oxford, Pergamon, 1973.
USA	L. F. Schmeckebier & R. B. Eastin. *Government publications and their use.* 2nd rev. ed. Washington, Brookings Institution, 1969.
	J. Morehead. *Introduction to United States public documents.* 2nd ed. Littleton, Col., Libraries Unlimited, 1978.

Though Australia, Canada and the USA are federations, Borchardt's volume alone deals with federal, state and local government publications; the other volumes deal only with the publications of the respective national governments. There exist other guides for other countries; two titles have been cited for the USA because the volume and coverage of that country's government publications justify at least two approaches to their description.

Armed, after a study of all or any of the above titles, with an understanding of the origin and scope of the publications of national governments, we now turn to the means of finding out what has been printed, and find that there are two different sources of information on current publications. One is the "commercial" listing provided by the country's government printer; the other is the bibliographic control of government publications provided by the country's national library.

In all the countries mentioned above, and in many others as well, the official printer or publisher to the government also produces a list of the publications produced by that organization on behalf of, or for the departments and authorities of, that country. It should be noted, however, that departments and authorities in many jurisdictions also publish independently of the central official printer and their publications are rarely listed by the official national printer. It will suffice here to name as examples the organizations for four of the five countries already referred to:

> Australia The Australian Government Publishing Service, Canberra, issues three different lists of its publications:
>
> > **Commonwealth** *publications: official list* (Weekly)
> > **Monthly** *catalogue of publications placed on sale*
> > **Annual** *catalogue of Commonwealth publications*

Some of the State Government Printers also produce lists of their publications, e.g.

Victorian Government Printing Office. *Monthly list of publications*

Canada The Canadian Government Publishing Centre, Ottawa, issues two lists:

Weekly checklist of Canadian government publications

Government of Canada publications . . . (quarterly, with an annual index)

Some of the provincial government printers also produce lists of their publications, e.g.

Ontario government publications; monthly checklist, which cumulates annually to become

Ontario government publications

UK Her Majesty's Stationery Office (known as HMSO), London, issues three lists of general interest:

Daily list of government publications. This is cumulated into the monthly

HMSO books catalogue: government publications of [month and year]. This is indexed and cumulated into the

HMSO annual catalogue: government publications, which contains a consolidated index; it also includes references to those publications by international and overseas organizations that are published in the UK.

USA The United States Government Printing Office (known as USGPO), Washington, issues only one list; with a semi-annual and an annual index:

Monthly catalog of United States government publications. A semi-annual and a cumulative annual index are issued relatively promptly.

For Australian, Canadian and French government publications the respective national libraries issue, either separately or as part of the national bibliography, a list of the publications produced by government departments and authorities. The titles of these three sources are:

Australian government publications. 1961– Canberra, National Library of Australia. (Three quarterly issues and an annual cumulation)

Canadiana; Canada's national bibliography. 1950– Ottawa, National Library of Canada. (Government publications are listed or indexed—the system changed over the years—in a separate section of the annual cumulations. It is necessary to study the introduction to each cumulation to ascertain how government publications have been treated). (Eleven times per year, with cumulated index)

Bibliographie de la France, première partie; Supplément II: publications officielles. 1950– Paris, Bibliothèque Nationale (Six times per year with an annual cumulative index)

The latter is complemented by the semimonthly *Bibliographie sélective des publications officielles françaises,* a compilation based on the acquisitions programme of five Parisian institutions (including the Bibliothèque Nationale).

On a very selective basis, the *British national bibliography* and the *Library of Congress catalog* also list some government publications. Furthermore it is pointed out that the Australian and the Canadian national bibliographies, as well as the LC just mentioned, include citations for the publications of several levels of jurisdiction.

Simple though the question of bibliographic control of government publications may appear to the uninitiated, the following points should be noted when using the reference sources referred to above.

(a) Not one of the catalogues and bibliographies compiled by the national libraries and normally based on the material received under legal deposit is complete, because a considerable proportion of government publications is not caught in the control net.

(b) Librarians have devised sophisticated rules to describe the authorship of government publications in order to avoid confusion in the public catalogues. It is not necessary to know these rules in detail in order to find one's way around a library but certain basic notions should be understood. In a broad sense the author of a government publication is the jurisdiction—country, state or local government authority—plus the name of the government agency. The entry in the library's public catalogue may be under the name of the jurisdiction, e.g. AUSTRALIA. Parliament, or UNITED STATES. Department of Health, Education and Welfare; or the entry may be directly under the name of the agency, e.g. NATIONAL Institute for Drug Abuse, or even under the name of the person who has prepared the document. Whichever type of entry has been selected for use, there should always be a reference in the catalogue from the form of heading not used. In addition, there will often be entries under the title of the work, the individual author, the series and the subject.

It is not possible to repeat here the detailed instructions on the cataloguing of government publications; if the desired title cannot be found in the catalogue, it will save a lot of time if you seek assistance from the library staff.
(c) The shelf arrangement of government publications varies from one library to another. If baffled ask the librarian to show you how they are arranged in the library you want to use.

Figure 2 shows six quite common examples of catalogue entries for a variety of government publications to be found in most libraries. Examples 1 and 2 show references to a publication entered under the jurisdiction, followed by the name of the particular agency responsible for the compilation of the published works. Examples 3 and 4 show instances where it has been considered more appropriate to enter the reference to the publication directly under the name of the agency which compiled it. Example 5 shows an entry under the name of the personal author of the report but additional references from the jurisdiction and agency will help library users to find it under that heading too. Example 6 shows an entry under the title which resulted from a conference; again there is a reference from the government department under whose aegis the conference took place.

VICTORIA. Parliament
The Parliament of Victoria and Parliament House.—12th ed.—(Melbourne): (Govt. Pr.), 1978
32 p.: ill.

UNITED STATES. Dept. of Health, Education, and Welfare. Departmental Task Force on Prevention
Healthy people: appendices: a task force report on disease prevention and health promotion/by the Departmental Task Force on Prevention.—(Washington): U.S. Dept. of Health, Education, and Welfare, 1978
305 p.; 28 cm.

NATIONAL INSTITUTE ON DRUG ABUSE
National directory of drug abuse treatment programs/National Institute on Drug Abuse.—Rockville, Md.: The Institute, (1976)
xi, 313 p.; 27 cm.—(DHEW publication; no. (ADM) 76–321)

HEALTH EFFECTS RESEARCH LABORATORY, Cincinnati
Health effects of human exposure to barium in drinking water/by G. R. Brenniman ... (*et al.*)
—Cincinnati, Ohio: Environmental Protection Agency, Office of Research and Development, Health Effects Research Laboratory, 1979
xiii, 127 p.: ill.; 28 cm.
—(Environmental health effects research series; EPA-600/1-79-003)

SYMPOSIUM ON SOIL AND PLANT TESTING
(1979: Melbourne, Vic.)
Proceedings of the Symposium on Soil and Plant Testing, Melbourne, March 16th, 1979/(edited by) K. I. Peverill and A. J. Brown.—Melbourne: Dept. of Agriculture, Victoria, 1980
67 p.; 30 cm.—(Agriculture note series; no. 50)

Fig. 2. Catalogue entry examples

In spite of two major wars directly affecting almost every nation on earth, and numerous other armed conflicts at regional levels, the twentieth century has witnessed a quite remarkable growth in international cooperation through the development of international government organizations. The creation of the United Nations Organization and its important specialized agencies, e.g. the World Health Organization (WHO), the United Nations Educational, Scientific and Cultural Organization (UNESCO) and the International Labour Organization (ILO) and other organizations such as the Organization of American States and the Organization for Economic Cooperation and Development (OECD) are evidence of concern for the need to have all nations work together if mankind is to survive in spite of itself.

All these organizations, and their subsidiary bodies, sponsor research in a great variety of subjects though predominantly, of course, on topics that will further the objectives of the organization involved. However, many of these objectives are directly or indirectly related to some aspect of psychology since human behaviour and the relationship between individuals and groups are at the heart of all efforts towards a continuing peace. All these organizations are much involved in statistical surveys, both of the social conditions of mankind and of the environment in order to provide facts and data on the basis of which ameliorative action can be taken.

Unfortunately, the volume of publications and mimeographed documents produced by these international organizations is so large and its bibliographic description so complex that few libraries will receive and maintain more than a token collection of particular interest to their clients. It is important therefore, to have access to the appropriate bibliographical tools which allow us to identify the material related to psychology and social issues hidden in that mass of printed documents. A useful introductory text on this topic is A. L. Atherton's *International organizations: a guide to information sources* (Detroit, Gale, 1976) which is precisely designed for beginners. Another useful handbook is the UN's own *Everyone's United Nations,* now in its 9th edition (1979).

Explanations of the system of publishing by the UNO and other international government organizations may be found in the following two titles, chosen from a large variety of such texts offering the most relevant data in the most assimilable form:

Dimitrov, Th.D. *Documents of international organisations: a bibliographic handbook covering the United Nations and other intergovernmental organisations.* Chicago, American Library Association 1973.

Winton, H. N. M. *Publications of the United Nations systems: a reference guide.* New York, Bowker, 1972.

Students and researchers are advised to acquaint themselves with these guides so that they will understand the complexities and shortcomings of the *United Nations document index*, (the latest title of which is *UNDOC*), the *UNESCO list of documents and publications*, etc.

4. Other types of Publications

Besides the three categories of publications so far discussed in this chapter, there exist other groups of documents which cannot easily be classed with monographs or periodicals. The most important among these is the vast range of higher degree theses which is produced annually in several thousand degree-granting colleges and universities. The quality of university degrees varies greatly and in the case of higher degrees—doctorates and masters—the thesis requirements determine to a large extent the standing of the academic qualification. There are also considerable differences in national standards and in examination practices over the ages. Fifty to a hundred years ago, a master's degree was a quite respectable distinction in any field except in Europe where the PhD had been established as the prime qualification for career academics since the middle of the nineteenth century. Then it became popular to aim at a PhD in the British and North American universities—perhaps by way of imitation?—and for the past 50 years a PhD has become the minimum qualification for an academic post. The entry requirements vary, but it is generally agreed that a thesis or dissertation for any doctorate should contain original work and deal with a branch or aspect of a subject not previously treated.

In some countries theses or dissertations—the two words will henceforth be treated as synonymous—have to be printed and published before they are accepted; in other places a typed copy (original) is accepted, or even a manuscript copy. What is important is that the originality of the thesis makes it an important contribution to knowledge. Theses are protected by a form of copyright which must be strictly observed; it is usually administered by the university library holding the deposit copy of the thesis.

Theses offer a rich source of inspiration for research and often contain, in the field of psychology, detailed accounts of investigations and experimental designs which may not appear in the printed literature for some time. For a number of reasons bibliographic control of dissertations has reached a reasonable level of competence, thus enabling candidates for higher degrees to make sure that the subject or topic of their choice has not already been treated, and showing research workers what dissertations have been presented on a special topic. The bibliographic control of theses also enables us to find out which university supported research on a specific topic—a point that may be of interest when deciding where to enrol for a higher degree.

Bibliographic control of theses exists at international, national and local levels. Every university or college worth its salt compiles an annual report or a research report in which are listed the successful candidates for higher degrees and the dissertations they have presented.

Many countries, but by no means all, maintain a national list of higher degree theses, both for doctorates and for masters. It is not necessary to spell out all of these since a list can be readily found in E. P. Sheehy's *Guide to reference books*, to which we have already drawn attention. Be it noted, however, that some national lists combine all higher degree theses in one listing—e.g. Australia's *Union list of higher degree theses in Australian universities and colleges*—while the US listings clearly distinguish between masters' theses and doctoral dissertations, as illustrated in the compilation for the American Research Libraries entitled *American doctoral dissertations* (1955/56–) and the *Masters abstracts* (1962–) produced by the well-known firm University Microfilms, Ann Arbor, Michigan.

There is a retrospective index to the *American doctoral dissertations* covering the years 1955–70. However, the best index to North American doctoral theses is the *Comprehensive dissertation index* which is computer-generated and retrospective to 1861. The *Comprehensive dissertation index* covers also the listing known as *Dissertation abstracts international*, of which more below. The *Index* includes some theses from universities outside the USA, including many Canadian institutions but there are few from other countries. The *Index* has a sophisticated system for the retrieval of data; main subjects are treated in individual volumes (psychology is listed in volumes 18–19) and within each volume theses are listed by keyword. Full citations can be found under the author entry as well as under the subject listing. However, and this is very important, the *Comprehensive dissertation index* is an INDEX, and an index only. Details of the contents of a thesis can be found in the *Dissertation abstracts international* which, since 1969, tries to include numerous universities outside North America.

The Association of Special Libraries and Information Bureaux (Aslib) issues, since 1953, an annual *Index to theses accepted for higher degrees in the universities of Great Britain and Ireland*. The Australian, Canadian and New Zealand counterparts appear as annual supplements to base lists compiled two or three decades ago. The Australian *Union list* already referred to can be interrogated on-line through AUSINET.

It is worth being aware of the existence of certain subject-related dissertation indexes and abstracts because the expensive larger reference tools cannot be found in all libraries. Thus we find an interesting UNESCO compilation *Theses in the social sciences: an international analytical catalogue of unpublished doctorate theses, 1940–1950,* obviously an effort to make good the lack of bibliographic control during the war years. Most of these limited subject area lists of dissertations are produced by associations and local-interest groups, and there exists no international listing of them but they can often be traced through the various national bibliographies or their surrogates. In the closely related field of education there are a number of indexing and abstracting services covering higher degree theses the most important of which is *Research studies in education* which began in 1953 and lists doctoral dissertations completed or under way.

Since dissertations are often sought via the interlibrary loan traffic, it is useful to know on what conditions, if at all, theses are lent by university libraries. Borchardt & Thawley's *Guide to the availability of theses*, 1981, provides information on this practical aspect of library services and contains some notes on the bibliographic control of theses in many countries.

For those interested in cross-cultural psychology comparisons there is a massive data bank on over 300 culture units. This resource is called the Human Relations Area Files (HRAF) and covers a wide variety of cultural data which are retrievable, including topics as diverse as aggression, marriage, scorcery, cannibalism, litigation, incest and humour. These data are cast into more than 700 subject categories grouped into 79 major topical sections. The cultures range as widely as the Zuñi Indians, the rural Irish and the Yoruba of Nigeria. The files, started nearly 30 years ago, are being constantly updated with the assistance of the staff from 21 universities and major research institutes. The data are available on microfiche and are excellently coded for ready retrieval; paper files on 5" × 8" stock are also available.

Useful teaching and usage guides are available in Lagacé's work, *The nature and use of HRAF files*, 1974 and in G. P. Murdock's description of the collection *Outline of cultural materials* (4th ed. appeared in 1972); though a little dated and incomplete, because of the continuous growth of the collection, both these guides make it possible to gain some idea of the structure of the files and how to exploit them.

There is a cognate publication which presents research and reference information in the field of cross-cultural statistical inquiry. This work was compiled by R. B. Textor under the title *A cross-cultural summary*; it appeared in 1967 and was published by HRAF Press.

An important and unique source of information on unpublished report literature is represented by an APA-sponsored catalogue of that type of material. The need for such a catalogue arose out of backlog of papers submitted for publication in the major psychological journals and the recognition of the usefulness of a retrieval mechanism that would help with the rapid communication between researchers. The volume of research-based contributions to all branches of psychology has been increasing at such a rate that it may take 12–18 months or more to get an article accepted and published, with the consequent delay in scientific communications, inconvenience to the authors and an ill effect on the development of research which depends so much on peer evaluation and helpful criticism. These considerations prompted the APA to set up a Journal Supplement Abstracting Service (JSAS) which would help researchers by centralizing data on unpublished research reports and by making them available—thus relieving authors and research institutes of the necessity to mail to their colleagues copies of their research results and similar reports. Since 1971 the JSAS publishes a quarterly entitled *Psychological documents* (from 1971 to 1982 it was known as *JSAS Catalog of selected documents in psychology*) which lists original psychology-related materials of all types, format and length. The papers or reports are not printed in full but abstracts accompany the citations. Paper and microfiche copies of the original documents are available on demand at very reasonable prices. There is a cumulative index and complete sets of documents may also be acquired at a special price. It is stressed that this journal is exclusively dedicated to unpublished reports and documents; by definition these contributions to the literature of psychology are not listed in *Psychological abstracts*.

Finally attention is drawn to an organization known as the Intergroup Consortium for Political and Social Research (ICPSR). The ICPSR is a wide partnership between the Centre for Political Studies in the United States and over 220 member universities and colleges. It is located in the Institute for Social Research at the University of Michigan, Ann Arbor. It is in close cooperation with various other organizations such as the European Consortium for Social and Political Research, the International Social Council, UNESCO, the Council of European Social Sciences, Data Archives and the International Federation of Data Organizations.

On its inception it was designed to serve a sub-set of political analysts; however, with growth and adaptation its services are now substantially wider. The Data Archives, for instance, receives, processes and distributes machine-readable data on social phenomena for over 130 countries and covers a wide range of information including such items as attitudes, records, international interactions, legislative programmes, etc. In addition to the domain of research, it also offers a service in training, methodology and research techniques and is therefore strongly recommended to readers who are engaging in enterprises involving social phenomena.

CHAPTER 4

Indexes, Abstracts and Union Lists

THERE arise, out of this ocean of data, two simple questions: how can one find an article in a journal on a given topic, or, in some cases, by a given author? and where can one find the journal containing that article? The answer to these questions will be found in the remainder of this section.

The easy but perhaps not the most economical way of finding an article in a periodical or serial is, of course, to look to the annual or volume index or to the contents page of issues not yet gathered into a complete volume. Obviously this method presupposes that one has direct access to the journals but, as has just been pointed out, there are some hundreds of journals on psychology and few libraries would hold more than a few score of these at the most. The core journals, and there are about twenty of them, will probably be available in most libraries of repute, and the strictly local ones will be found in institutions serving the interests of the profession in a region. While all serious students and researchers will need to have direct and easy access to the core journals, it is unlikely that these will suffice for those whose interest goes beyond the general problems of psychology. But even if one is lucky enough to be able to work in a library exceptionally strong in the literature on psychology, it is quite a task to trace a specific article in a journal or, much more difficult still, to identify the coverage of a particular aspect of psychology in the serials literature contained in several journals.

To assist scholars with the solution of this problem a number of comprehensive indexes to the journal literature have been developed during the past 85 years, and by 'comprehensive' we mean both the coverage of the large (and growing) number of journals as well as the depth of subject analysis reflected in the reference to the contents of those journals. The earliest indexes of this kind first appeared in the 1890s when one English, one French and one German publisher saw fit to offer such scholarly aids to the then recently emancipated study of psychology. While a number of journals began soon after that date to record in supplementary indexes the steadily growing volume of periodical and monograph literature, it was not until 1926 that a comprehensive abstracting service for the whole field of psychology was established. Chronologically arranged, these surveys cover the field as follows

L'Année psychologique, 1894–
Psychological index, 1894–1935
Zeitschrift für Psychologie, 1890–
Psychological abstracts, 1926–
Annual review of psychology, 1950–
Zeitschrift für experimentelle und angewandte Psychologie, 1953–
Psychological reader's guide, 1968–

For the general practitioner and researcher, *Psychological abstracts* is undoubtedly the most important of these, and more will be said about it below. *Psychological index* used to report and briefly analyse the periodical and monograph literature in all fields of psychology. Entries are arranged in classified order but there is neither a subject index nor a cumulative index, which fact greatly reduces its usefulness. However, almost half the entries of the *Index* are listed in *Psychological index: abstract references* which was compiled for the American Psychological Association by H. L. Ansbacher in 1941–42. It contains about 75,000 references to abstracts of 45,000 titles of the *Index*. The firm of G. K. Hall, Boston, issued in 1960 a combined list of all author entries in the *Psychological index* and in *Psychological abstracts* (volumes 1–33). Despite difficulties caused by an outdated classification and its selective approach, the *Psychological index* is an essential reference work for the period it covers.

The gap left by the cessation of the *Psychological index* in 1936 was not filled again until 1950 when the *Annual review of psychology* started to offer surveys of the field written by prominent specialists. However, the publishers of the *Annual review* adopted a very different approach. Like the *L'année psychologique*, the *Annual review of psychology* aimed at a selective and evaluative overview of the subject. Each year the publishers commission experts to review topics in their area of specialization. Such reviewers select, evaluate and summarize the literature to a specific recent date in their commissioned area and give an overview. This account may pay attention to some or all of methodological, theoretical and empirical issues and conclusions.

Not every topic is reviewed every year and, therefore, in instituting a search it is an appropriate strategy to start with the most recent volume and work from there backwards in time until one finds the most recent review. This will plainly use the previous review on the topic as a point of departure. By this means one locates not only the most recent review but also the most recent references.

Each issue shows the master plan of the topics under a series of main headings which sets out the subjects to be covered in successive volumes. Some main headings are covered in each volume and a number in each alternate issue. A few subjects such as psychology and the law have appeared but once to date. In 1975 a new section was introduced covering two special review topics. This section has a shorter copy deadline and, therefore, can include the most recent developments in these fields. The *L'année psychologique* has a great deal in common with the *Annual review of psychology* and the treatment of the whole field follows a similar approach, but is is well worth noting that the former is more international in scope and includes much more of the European schools of psychology than does the *Annual review*. Furthermore, the long continuity of the French survey makes it an exceptionally valuable work for retrospective literature searches.

The bibliographical supplement of the *Zeitschrift für Psychologie* (known from 1890–1906 as *Zeitschrift für Psychologie und Physiologie der Sinnesorgane*) started in the same year as the *Année psychologique* and the *Psychological index* and covers more or less the same ground but its entries are not accompanied by notes or comments, evaluative or otherwise. The *Zeitschrift* discontinued the literature survey during and immediately after World War I, but it was resumed in 1925 (volume 97). An extensive reviewing section which includes books in German and other languages, accompanies the bibliographical supplement which is based on German journals and serial publications. In 1938 the bibliographical supplement ceased again and was not continued in this journal. Instead a continuation is being published in the *Zeitschrift für experimentelle und angewandte Psychologie* since 1965. The gap 1942–60 has been closed by Wellek, whose work is discussed on p. 14.

The latest reference series to be established in the field of psychology is the *Psychological reader's guide*, which follows the pattern of the *Current contents* series which have been so well received in many other fields of scientific research. This is a monthly publication containing photo-reproductions (reduced in size where appropriate) of the contents pages of current issues of more than 200 journals in psychology. No summaries are given and there is of course no attempt at detailed indexing. Its coverage is international and multi-lingual. (There are no translations in English.) Each issue contains an author's address list and a list of journals cited; each contents listing is accompanied by a note showing name and address of editor, place of publication and price.

Today, the most important current bibliographical service for the whole field of psychology is *Psychological abstracts* published by the APA since 1926. As the title suggests, this retrieval tool to articles in about 1000 journals and report series provides abstracts of a strictly non-evaluative nature based on the original abstracts published in many of the journals cited and on summaries prepared by a panel of experts or the authors themselves.

The *Abstracts* appear bi-monthly and contain now over 18,000 articles per year covering books, periodicals, and dissertations. Though the vast majority of references comes from English and American sources, some of the more important periodicals in other languages are also abstracted; titles not originally in English are translated and cyrillic characters are transliterated, but despite the size and range of *Psychological abstracts*, material in languages other than English is not as comprehensively covered as it might be.

As earlier mentioned, there are combined cumulative author and subject indexes to *Psychological index* and *Psychological abstracts*—in the case of the latter covering volumes 1–33 in the first place. These indexes have been extended for *Psychological abstracts* for another two decades (1961–1981), and further issues of cumulative indexes are progressively being prepared.

As with any highly specialized reference tool, it pays in terms of time and labour to make oneself thoroughly acquainted with the organization, scope and capabilities of *Psychological abstracts* if one wants to get the maximum benefit from it. It is useful, for instance, always to begin looking at the most recent issues and working back. Recent research will take account of earlier knowledge of a particular subject. The subject index in the most recent cumulated issue should be consulted first. Monthly indexes more recent than the latest cumulated issue should also be consulted. The numbers listed after the subject index term indicate abstract numbers, not page numbers, and relate to abstracts in that volume.

When searching the abstracts, location of the appropriate key word or concept is obviously vital. If one is interested in, say, "isolation" a perusal of the index will show that "isolation (social)" is given as a cross-reference. The more analytic approach is to be found under "sensory deprivation" which is not cross-referenced from "isolation" (at least not in the 1978 index).

Clearly the compilation of a search list of key words and concepts is an essential prerequisite to a thorough search. The time spent in compiling this list is well repaid. Further, in addition to searching by topic or theme, one may of course also search by author. If it is known, for example, that Jourard had an enduring interest in the development of personality theory then a search using that name should yield articles which in their reference lists will yield further articles.

A word of caution is necessary in the selection of terms. If one searches an author's name it is highly improbable that it would have changed, although it could happen. If one searches terms there is a greater likelihood that the preferred terms will change over the course of years. One obvious example of that is that three decades ago television was not accorded the importance that attaches to it today. In looking for relevant terms there is no substitute for the *Psychological abstracts* itself for the relevant period.

Since 1967, the data contained in *Psychological abstracts* have been stored in machine-readable form. This change has imposed on the computers a vigorous demand for standardization in the subject terms used and has led to the development of the APA's *Thesaurus of psychological terms* which has been commented on in some detail on p. 56. More importantly, however, this development has opened up the range and depth of literature searches in the whole field of psychology and, indeed, in a number of related subject fields. It has in particular made it a great deal easier than ever before to relate the data of psychology and those of other disciplines, notably in the biological (including medical) and social sciences.

While the necessary standardization of the use of language has been aided by the construction of a thesaurus, the need for standardized bibliographic citation has also to be recognized. This question is briefly touched upon in the chapter on report writing.

The computerization of the data base on which *Psychological abstracts* rests has brought in its train the need for guidance to the whole data retrieval system that is not available to the researcher. The above brief notes on *Psychological abstracts* are primarily related to the standard manual retrieval methods. Computer-assisted retrieval is fully described in *PsycINFO,* the latest edition of which appeared in 1981. This very helpful "Users Reference Manual" contains a full description of the procedures best suited to obtain bibliographic data (i.e. reference to the literature of psychology) from the printed version of *Psychological abstracts* as well as from either the DIALOG or the ORBIT system through which the PsycINFO data base can be exploited.

To summarize, then, *Psychological abstracts* may now be searched manually or by computer; the latter costs more, and cost–benefit ratios should be considered when contemplating a machine-based search. It ought to be absolutely clear to students that the purpose of using a computer is merely to save time. There is no intrinsic virtue in computers and they can only regurgitate what we have put into them. But they can perform combinations and permutations more quickly, and consequently execute machine-readable searches many times faster, than can be achieved manually. This fundamental notion must be fully grasped by students in order to make it clear beyond reasonable doubt that by using computers we must accept the consequences that:

(a) bibliography citations must be standardized and even psychologists may have to conform to a system new to them;
(b) computer-based approaches to reference retrieval are not in essence different from manual approaches to data bases;

(c) the availability of machine-readable references in many different fields does not in any way imply that all these fields or all the references are of interest to all who have access to a computer terminal.

What is still lacking, above all, is an economical and efficient system for computer based document retrieval.

The limits of the discipline of psychology have ever been very elastic, and if it is correct to refer to it—as we have in the introduction as a middle-of-the-spectrum science—it is by the same token influenced by and affecting many other fields of research. None should therefore ignore the potential use of the abstracting and indexing services in cognate disciplines. It is impossible, quite obviously, to cite here all the reference services that might have bearing in the study of psychology; so much, indeed everything, depends on the interests of the researcher, and no pretence is made to include in this book a general guide to the reference collections and services of a good academic library.

Those working in the field of industrial psychology, for instance, may well have to consult and rely heavily on the *Engineering index,* while medical practitioners concerned with the effects of drug abuse may need to refer to the appropriate section of *Chemical abstracts* to check the literature of certain components or the molecular structures of hallucinogenic substances.

Then again there are quite obvious crossroads where research has already developed a traditional pattern of mutually dependent approaches. A typical example would be the field of educational psychology where several special fields (child psychology, psychology of learning, developmental psychology, physiological psychology) help to create the necessary background for fruitful research.

If we proceed from the general to the particular, reference should first be made to the *Social science citation index* which offers an author and subject approach to the literature of the social sciences. Primarily conceived as an index of the most-cited authors—and based on the philosophical assumption that frequency of citation confers standing and value on the author and consequently authority to his utterances—*SSCI* consists of four separate but related sections: the Citation Index, arranged by author; the Permuterm Subject Index in which every significant word in a title is paired with every other significant word used in a title; the Source Index which provides a bibliographic description of the sources of citation listed in the citation index; a Corporate Index, divided into a geographic section and an organization section. This is a very sophisticated retrieval system based on about 10,000 source items (i.e. journals and books) and it requires experience to exploit it fully. Again it must be stressed that its coverage is considerably stronger for English-language literature than for other languages, but apart from that limitation *SSCI* is one of the most comprehensive indexing services now in existence—always provided that the criteria for inclusion are recognized as valid. It is also stressed that the *SSCI* is not an abstracting service; the references cited are not enlarged by evaluative or descriptive notes. The *SSCI* may or may not be the perfect system, but as long as its limitations are fully understood it is probably as comprehensive and useful a system as can be constructed at the price and the better one is acquainted with its sophisticated structure the more one is likely to get out of it. First-time users in particular should study the booklet produced in 1977 by the publishers, *SSCI: guide and journals list*.

Another social science index, with relevance for students of psychology, is the annual *Recent publications in the social and behavioral sciences*. This is a continuation of the *ABS guide to recent publications in the social and behavioral sciences* of 1965. The series is part of the publications programme of the *American behavioral scientist*, a bi-monthly journal which includes extensive notes on the current literature in the behavioral sciences. *Recent publications* is particularly useful for its coverage of English-language monographs.

The physiological basis of psychology is broadly covered by the famous and traditional reference service entitled *Index medicus*. Founded in 1879, the name of the index was changed several times between 1927 and 1960. This bibliography of the literature of medicine is currently based on 2600 journals. The monthly issues are arranged alphabetically by subject; there is an annual cumulated author and subject index, and there is a separate bibliography of medical reviews. The cumulated edition is styled *Cumulated index medicus*. The treatment of the terms psychology and psychiatry is fairly extensive but limited, of course, to the medical angle. However, the effects of biochemical research on the study of psychology have to be approached through the appropriate biochemical subject terms.

Another reference source for the physiological background to psychology is *Biological abstracts* which covers approximately 9000 current journals in the life sciences and closely related disciplines. *Biological abstracts* appears twice a month and each entry contains a complete bibliographic citation including the author's address and the language of the original, followed by a concise summary. Each issue consists of an author index, a biosystematic index (by taxonomic categories), a generic index (by genus–species names), a concept index by broad subject fields, and a specific subject index. A monthly supplement entitled *Biological abstracts/RRM* lists reports, reviews and meetings related to the life sciences. Semi-annual cumulative author and subject indexes help to make *Biological abstracts* a highly sophisticated reference tool. Though major journals in languages other than English are included, the preponderance of entries comes from the English-speaking world.

The continuing specialization in psychology has quite naturally led to indexing and abstracting services for several branches of the discipline. Thus education and the study of children in general have always been closely associated with psychological studies. There exist three well-known indexes to the field of education: *Education index* published by the H. W. Wilson Co. of New York since 1929; the *Australian education index* produced since 1958 by the Australian Council for Educational Research, Melbourne, and the *British education index* issued since 1954 by the Library Association, London.

Besides these three indexes there are two abstracting services: *Current index to journals in education* which was first issued in 1969 and *Resources in education* which started to appear in 1966. The former, though called "Index", contains brief abstracts of articles in almost 800 educational and education-related journals. The latter is a listing of official publications and report literature in the same field. Both these are important products of the Educational Resources Information Center (ERIC) which was established by the US Department of Education for "acquiring, selecting, abstracting, indexing, storing, retrieving and disseminating" education-related literature. The semi-annual indexes offer the best possible access to the English-language material in this field, and in the context of this booklet it is noteworthy that they include references to mental health, child development, cognitive psychology, clinical psychology—to name but a few of the major areas of psychology. Further reference to the ERIC services is made in the context of computer-based retrieval services, among which ERIC plays a leading role. Furthermore, it must be noted that there are specialized indexes and abstracting services for several major branches of psychology, e.g. psychoanalysis, child psychology, industrial psychology; these will be discussed in some detail below.

The professional associations of some countries have found it useful to publish an indexing and abstracting service for their own members and related specifically to the professional literature of their own country. Distribution of these services is often restricted to association members. Two such publications are for sale, however, and are worth noting here. One is the *German journal of psychology*, the other is the *Indian psychological abstracts*. Both are in English in order to attract a wider readership; and both are scheduled to appear quarterly.

We have so far, in this chapter, pointed out how one can trace references to the journal-based literature in psychology, and have noted early on that most research libraries will hold less than a few score of journals in the field in psychology. There are notable exceptions, but even the largest university or national libraries will not contain all the journals which have bearing on research in psychology, and the same goes for research institutes dedicated to psychology. The question arises, therefore, how one can identify the location of periodicals not held locally, i.e. in the library where one normally works.

Librarians have been involved for centuries in the solution to this question and have devised union lists of regional holdings to this end. Union lists are inevitably based on the cooperation of a number of libraries who are willing to help each other, and thereby their clientele, with the supply of literature. These union lists contain, normally, standardized entries for library materials—books or journals—with a location symbol and a precise indication of the holdings of the institution represented by that symbol.

There are union lists of library materials according to bibliographic form, e.g. manuscripts, audiovisual materials, journals, series, or according to discipline, e.g. French literature, economics, law, psychology. In addition there may be union listings restricted in coverage by combining a criterion of the first with another of the second division of types, e.g. a union list of printed French drama or a union list of theses for higher degrees in psychology.

There are hundreds of such union lists of varying quality and it is beyond the scope of this book to deal with them in detail. Students in North America will be particularly interested in the *Union list of serials in libraries in the United States and Canada*, 3rd ed., 1965, which is being kept up to date by the Library of Congress listing entitled *New serial titles; a union list of serials commencing publication after Dec. 31, 1949*. This latter is issued monthly, with quarterly and annual cumulations; the entries for 1950–70 have been converted into a computerized data bank and the Library of Congress is ensuring that subsequent listings are added to that data bank. A two-volume subject guide to *New serial titles 1950-1970* has also been issued; it is arranged according to the Dewey Decimal Classification. Its several indexes make it easy to use.

Students in the United Kingdom have at their disposal the *British union-catalogue of periodicals . . .* ; its four base volumes appeared in 1955–58 and a *Supplement to 1960 . . .* was issued in 1962. Since 1964 a quarterly updating service, with annual cumulations, has been issued with the subtitle *New periodical titles*. Other union lists in the English-speaking world are the *Union list of serials in New Zealand libraries* (3rd ed., 1969–70 in six volumes and the warning that entries for conferences, symposia, etc. need to be checked in the 2nd ed.), the one-volume list styled *Periodicals in South African libraries*, 2nd ed., 1972–73; while in Australia there are two complementary lists, each consisting of several volumes, entitled respectively *Scientific serials in Australian libraries* and *Serials in Australian libraries social sciences and humanities; a union list*. These two retrieval tools have been issued in loose-leaf form in 1958 and 1968–74 respectively. Both are being kept up to date with microfiche supplements.

Besides providing all important data on where to obtain the serials required but not held in the library service of the institution to which one is attached, these union lists offer the additional boon of citing all the important journals in their country of origin and of referring to them in a reliable and standardized form of bibliographic citation. Though none of them is designed to provide subject approaches to serials, questions related to this aspect can be answered by the lists of psychology journals referred to on pp. 28 and 185. Larger university and research libraries will have all the union lists cited, and their reference staff will be adept in using them for interlibrary loan services.

There exists nothing quite like these union catalogues of the English-speaking world in other countries. Above all, there are but few published union lists which are being kept up to date. An overview of union lists can be gleaned from the American Library Association's *Guide to reference books*, the 9th edition of which, and its *Supplement*, have been edited by Eugene P. Sheehy.

CHAPTER 5

Computer-based Data Retrieval

THE phenomenal growth of recorded data over the last 60 years or so has made the collecting, sifting and sorting increasingly difficult, and the development of computer-based search services now plays a significant role in data retrieval. It cannot be emphasized enough that the intrinsic merit of a machine-readable data base rests on its technology. The intellectual content of such a data base has been created by people, the keys necessary to obtain access to the content of the data base and to the combinations of groups or configuration of data have also been devised by people. The whole process is person-devised, and it is only the greater speed of electronic circuits that make these processes genuinely advantageous. They have, at the same time, the disadvantage that their power of selection and discrimination must be wholly predetermined. Machines cannot make a choice unless they have been programmed to do so, and consequently they cannot lead us to new discoveries directly. At best they can make us very quickly aware of combinations which it would take hours, days or even months to recognize in a manual system and by means of consulting printed records.

There are some general observations on computer-based data banks which are worth making at this point. One is that most of these data bases are of fairly recent vintage and they do not contain references to material before they were set up, though some owners of data bases make an effort to incorporate references to earlier materials as time and financial resources allow.

Next, it is worth making at least this brief comparison between computerized and manually operated data banks. *Psychological abstracts* in its printed form is a data bank which must be used, can only be used, in a manual mode, i.e. the searcher picks up a volume or an issue and finds what he wants through the indexes (see chapter IV). It naturally takes some time for literature references to appear in the printed version of *Psychological abstracts* while it is relatively quick and easy to add a reference to the computerized version of *Psychological abstracts*. Consequently, a computerized data bank tends to be more up to date than a manual one. On the other hand, there appears to be a tendency for computerized data banks to be fed with references to standard journals and possibly monographs, leaving aside pamphlets, report literature, and many other ephemera. Such ephemera are more readily found, some time after publication, in the comprehensive printed "data banks". It is difficult to prove this but experience with several data retrieval services suggests this pattern.

Thirdly, it is important to distinguish between "on-line" and "off-line" interrogations of computerized data banks. "On-line" interrogation means a direct dialogue between the searcher and the data bank; questions are transmitted to the data bank and responses are sent back, very quickly—in a matter of seconds—based on the material stored in the data bank. "Off-line" interrogation, by contrast, consists of transmitting a carefully worked-out prolific set of questions, and waiting in a queue for the answers to be sent back, maybe 24 hours later.

At this point it is worth adding that computer-based searches, like any other literature survey, may be retrospective or current, generating lists of monographs, articles or reports on a particular topic. In addition to such searches these electronic data processing systems can also offer a service known as "selected dissemination of information" (SDI). Such a service, which may also be referred to as a current awareness service, provides subscribers with printouts of material in certain designated areas as such material is added to the main system's data base. An SDI service may be offered by special institutions, by universities through their libraries or research centres, or by companies who do so on a commercial basis.

Last, it should be noted that while practically all tax-supported institutions such as state, university and public libraries allow free and gratis access to such printed reference sources as they possess, many charge their clients for the use of computer-based searches. This is not the place to examine the effects of this practice and it is possible that during the next decade a different practice may evolve. For the present, however, the extra speed offered by the computer and such other advantages as modern technology may offer, have to be paid for separately and in addition to the tax monies that are used to support traditional library and information services.

Bibliographic searches using computer-based data retrieval systems are generally faster, but disregarding staff time and costs they are rarely cheaper than manual searches of printed indexes and abstracts. However, the response to an inquiry addressed to a computerized data bank may result in a number of unnecessary references being produced because the computer can select only what it has been told to select. It does not—and this cannot be emphasized sufficiently—it does not, on its own, distinguish the relevant from the irrelevant. To avoid the arduous task of sifting through large volumes of extraneous information it is necessary that the user of a computerized data bank be very specific in the choice of subject terms. Time is another factor for consideration, and it may sometimes be more expedient to do a manual and limited search than formulate the subject terms and wait for the requested information from the computerized data bank. There will, of course, be exceptions—and those users who have access to on-line terminals are well advised to plan their search strategy with great care.

It is convenient and important to ask oneself the following six questions before embarking on a computer-based literature search:

(1) Is the job large enough to warrant it? For an undergraduate it may not be; for a thesis or a research paper it could be.
(2) Do I need to be certain of getting all references? If yes, omissions are less likely if a computer-based search is used—bearing in mind the limitations referred to earlier.
(3) Do I need a quick response to a well-defined question? For quick searches the computer-based search is unrivalled—provided one is able to interrogate "on-line". For smaller "off-line" searches there may be no advantage due to delays in the mail system.
(4) For "on-line" searches is there local access to a suitable terminal?
(5) How does the cost compare when one puts the direct money cost against the cost of a person searching the relevant abstracts?
(6) Does the computer-based search give access to file information not otherwise available?

Quite obviously all the answers need not be in the affirmative before the use of a computer is recommended. It is the mix that matters, and the full awareness of the limitations of the machine as compared with the human brain. The economics of a literature search are therefore determined by three fundamental factors:

(a) speed with which the information is needed;
(b) coverage that is required of the search;
(c) availability of the information other than by computer-based search.

When conducting a search using computer-based retrieval systems it should be clearly understood that no search will improve upon the key words used to designate the search. We have referred briefly in Chapter II to the importance of using the appropriate vocabulary when discussing psychological issues, if for no other reason than to ensure that all concerned are talking or writing about the same concept, idea or thing. When it comes to using a computer to retrieve references to such data, the use of a uniform terminology is obviously essential. A computer cannot easily evaluate shades of meaning, even though it is granted that shades of meaning can be incorporated in computerized responses to certain inquiries; the program necessary to achieve this would have to be so complex, and the computer's power so great, that all economies otherwise attainable through machine-readable retrieval services would be lost. The originator of the search will therefore need to be very clear about the words and concepts—and their connections—before commissioning the search. Getting the right degree of specificity is an art: too narrow a focus may miss crucial references; too wide a focus will generate a list with many redundancies.

The best source of key words and concepts for research in psychology is the APA's *Thesaurus of psychological index terms,* and because a machine-based search without it is virtually impossible, it is very important to be well acquainted with it and to have access to it before planning one's search strategy. The *Thesaurus* has already been updated twice; it is obviously important to use the latest edition and at the time of writing that is the 3rd edition of 1982.

The APA's *Thesaurus of psychological index terms* is used to classify all the specific terms used in psychology and to show them in their sub- and super-ordinate relationship. Its relevance to research in psychology, or to any other subject for which it may have been constructed, lies in the fact that a literature search can be no better than the search terms used. Thus to examine an index to a journal or a book under terms such as "emotions" or "brain diseases" may produce no result because the authors (or the indexers) have used other, often more precise, terms such as anger, laughter, cerebral palsy or brain dysfunctions.

The first edition of the *Thesaurus* appeared in 1974. It was designed to offer a controlled vocabulary which afforded a means of structuring the subject matter of psychology and also to serve, as has been suggested, as a tool for information retrieval. A second edition was issued in 1977; it was a major revision and included approximately 200 new terms and omitted about 180 now-unused terms. The latest edition of 1982 is a further update which includes many new terms, omits other terms found to be redundant, and adds, as an important innovation, the date of first usage of a term.

The *Thesaurus* is divided into two major sections setting out respectively "Relationships" and "Rotated alphabetical terms". The first of these comprises the bulk of the work and represents a hierarchical approach to psychological terminology. The editors have explained this in detail in the introduction to the original edition of the *Thesaurus:*

> The major relationships denoted are: synonymous, broader, narrower, and related. Synonymous relationships refer to different terms, or variations in the spelling of a term, used to represent a single concept. In this listing, the preferred term for representing the concept is denoted along with nonpreferred synonymous terms. Terms representing broader and narrower concepts, in the sense of genus-species relationships, are also denoted. Finally, terms representing concepts that are

frequently associated with the concept represented by the listed term are displayed. Secondarily, two additional relationships are noted: extremely broad conceptual areas are displayed as array terms; and extremely specific descriptors, name of a person, place, test, and document type are displayed as identifiers. Array terms are identified by a slash (/) following the term.

Figures 3a and 3b show facsimiles of sections of the Introduction to the third edition of the *Thesaurus*, while the layout of postable terms is illustrated by the excerpt shown in Fig. 4.

INTRODUCTION

THESAURUS HISTORY

Psychology has multiple roots in the older disciplines of philosophy, medicine, education, and physics. As a result, the vocabulary of psychological literature is characterized by considerable diversity. As the field has grown, each new generation of psychologists has added to the vocabulary in attempting to describe their studies and perceptions of behavioral processes. This uncontrolled evolution of the psychological vocabulary has contributed to complex literature search and retrieval problems.

In response to these problems, the American Psychological Association developed the first edition of the *Thesaurus of Psychological Index Terms* in 1974. This controlled vocabulary was designed to provide a means of structuring the subject matter of psychology and to serve as an efficient indexing and retrieval tool. Since the publication of the first edition, the *PsycINFO* indexing staff has charted trends and newly emerging areas of interest reflected in the psychological literature as a way of updating and revising the *Thesaurus*. The present edition represents a concerted effort to provide a more valuable tool for researchers, practitioners, students, information service providers, and others interested in psychology.

First Edition (1974). Term selection was the first step in the development of the 1974 edition. The 800 index terms used by *Psychological Abstracts* (*PA*) prior to 1973 and a list of the frequencies of the occurrence of single words in titles and abstracts in *PA* over a 5-year period were taken as the starting points. In addition, phrases and terms were obtained from key-word-in-context (KWIC) lists produced from 10,000 titles of journal articles, books, separates, and dissertations. Inclusion/exclusion rules were developed, with a resulting list of about 3,000 potential terms reviewed by subject-matter specialists for final selection. These terms were arranged to express interrelationships, including *use, used for, broader, narrower*, and *related* categories.

Second Edition (1977). The first major revision of the *Thesaurus*, which included approximately 200 new terms, was published in 1977. Approximately 180 never-used terms from the original Thesaurus were deleted, and a rotated alphabetical-term section was added for more accurate selection of multiple-word index terms.

DEVELOPMENT OF THE THIRD EDITION (1982)

New Terms. Since the publication of the second edition, both *PA* and *PsycINFO* users and the indexing staff have proposed additional terms for inclusion in the 1982 edition. Based on these suggestions, 240 new postable and 143 nonpostable terms were developed to fill gaps in the second edition and represent new concepts and terminology expressed in psychological literature. The criteria for term inclusion were the frequency of that term's occurrence, its potential usefulness in providing access to specific information, and its relationship or overlap with existing *Thesaurus* terms. New terms were extensively researched so that they could be integrated into the Relationship Section and so that scope notes could be developed. *Appendix A* is a list of all the new postable terms.

Discontinued terms. In a continuing effort to increase precision, decrease overlap and the inconsistent use of terms, and reflect current terminology, 45 terms were changed from postable to nonpostable status. Although these discontinued terms appear in the *Thesaurus* as nonpostable, and hence are no longer used, each is accompanied by a scope note designating the period during which it was used, and each is searchable online for that period. *Appendix B* contains a list of these discontinued terms.

Because of insufficient use (zero or one posting in nine years), six terms were removed from the *Thesaurus* altogether. *Appendix C* is a list of these terms.

Dating of Terms. The index terms that make up the *Thesaurus* were added at different times, corresponding to the publication of its first edition and the subsequent revisions. Therefore, each postable term appears in the Relationship Section and in the Postable Term Codes Section with a two-digit numerical superscript to indicate the year of that term's inclusion in the *Thesaurus*. The following years may be specified by superscripts: 1967, 1971, 1973, 1978, and 1982. The superscript "67" indicates that the term was part of the original list of 800 terms used to index *PA* and *PsycINFO* records since 1967 and can be used to search for references across the entire time span of the *PsycINFO* database. Terms appearing with a superscript other than "67" permit access to references from the year indicated and forward.

In 1971, approximately 20 terms were added to the original 800-term list, and these appear with the superscript "71." The approximately 3,000 postable terms with the superscript "73" appeared in the first edition of the *Thesaurus* (1974). Terms added in 1978 were incorporated into the second edition (first revision) published in 1977. Terms appearing for the first time in the present edition (second revision) have the superscript "82."

The current edition of the *Thesaurus* also involved extensive revision of the hierarchical relationship of terms to make them more complete and/or consistent and to reduce misleading or redundant relationships.

Scope Notes. For the first time, approximately one-third of the postable and nonpostable terms are accompanied by scope notes, brief definitions or statements of the term's meaning or use in the *PsycINFO* indexing system. Scope notes have been added to most new and all discontinued terms, terms with ambiguous meanings, terms that have applications unique to the *PsycINFO* database, and terms whose usage has changed over time. The scope note always refers to the one term with which it is associated and does not necessarily have implications for the terms displayed in its hierarchy. The following are examples of some of the scope notes from the Relationship Section:

Definition and usage   **Social Isolation** [87]
                                        SN Voluntary or involuntary absence of contact with others. Used for human or animal populations.

FIG. 3a. Extracts from the APA *Thesaurus of psychological index terms*

USERS GUIDE

Word Form Conventions. Conventions dealing with singular and plural word forms, direct and indirect word entries, abbreviations, acronyms, homographs, and punctuation have been used to ensure standardization of the *Thesaurus* vocabulary. For example, noun forms are preferred entries, with the plural used when the term is a noun that can be quantified (e.g., *Computers, College Students*, or *Employment Tests*) and the singular when the term refers to processes, properties, or conditions (e.g., *Learning, Grief*, or *Rehabilitation*). Direct entry or natural word order is preferred when a concept is represented by two or more words (e.g., *Mental Health* vs "health, mental" or *Artifical Intelligence* vs "intelligence, artificial"). Some terms that would exceed the 36-character limit if completely spelled out are abbreviated (e.g., *Minn Multiphasic Personality Inven* and *Rotter Intern Extern Locus Cont Scal*). A selected number of acronyms are also used, such as *DOPA, REM Sleep*, and *ROTC Students*. In cases where ambiguity may occur and to clarify the meaning of homographs, qualifying expressions are included in parentheses [e.g., *Culture (Anthropological), Recall (Learning)*, and *Chronicity (Disorders)*)].

Term Relationships. The terms in the Relationship Section are displayed to reflect the following relationships:

Use. Directs the user from a term that cannot be used (nonpostable) to a postable term that can be used in indexing or searching. The **Use** reference indicates preferred forms of synonyms, abbreviations, spelling, and word sequence:

Language Handicaps
Use Language Disorders

UF (used for). Reciprocal of the **Use** reference. Terms listed as **UF** (used for) references represent some but not all of the most frequently encountered synonyms, abbreviations, alternate spellings, or word sequences:

Language Disorders [82]
UF Language Handicaps

B (broader term) and **N (narrower term).** Reciprocal designators used to indicate hierarchical relationships:

Achievement [67]
N Academic Achievement

R (related term). Reciprocal designators used to indicate relationships that are semantic or conceptual but not hierarchical. Related-term references indicate to searchers or indexers terms that they may not have considered but that may have a bearing on their interest:

Achievement Motivation [67]
R Fear of Success

Array Terms. Index terms that represent conceptually broad areas are designated array terms and are identified by a slash (/) following the term. These terms are used in indexing and searching when a more specific term is not available. Array terms are displayed in the *Thesaurus* with only selected related terms:

Communication/ [67]
R Animal Communication
Censorship
Communication Systems

RELATIONSHIP SECTION

Each *Thesaurus* term is listed alphabetically, cross-referenced, and displayed with its broader, narrower, and related terms. In addition, scope notes provide definitions and information on proper use of terms. The date of the term's inclusion in the *Thesaurus* appears as a superscript.

Index term (postable) with date of entry		**Afferent Pathways** [82]
Scope note	**SN**	Collections of fibers that carry neural impulses toward neural processing areas from sensory mechanisms or other processing areas.
Used for term (nonpostable)	**UF**	Sensory Pathways
Broader term	**B**	Neural Pathways Peripheral Nerves
Narrower term	**N**	Spinothalamic Nerves
Related term	**R**	Efferent Pathways Sensory Neurons

ROTATED ALPHABETICAL TERMS SECTION

Because many terms represent concepts not expressed in a single word, postable *Thesaurus* terms are listed in alphabetical order by each word contained within them. Thus, a *Thesaurus* term containing three words will appear in three locations in the Rotated Alphabetical Terms Section as illustrated below:

Academic Underachievement
College **Academic** Achievement
Ac**a**lculia
.
.
Achievement Potential
College Academic **Achievement**
Mathematics **Achievement**
.
.
Collective Behavior
College Academic Achievement
College Dropouts

In some cases, unusual spellings of *Thesaurus* terms were caused by a limitation of 36 characters per term, e.g., Mental Retardation (Attit Toward). The shortened word contained in these terms will appear in alphabetical order as if the word was spelled out completely:

Marriage **Attitudes**
Mental Illness **(Attitudes Toward)**
Mental Retardation (Attit Toward)
Middle Class **Attitudes**
Occupational **Attitudes**

POSTABLE TERM CODES SECTION

Each postable *Thesaurus* term is listed in alphabetical order to facilitate rapid selection of search terms and verification of spelling. The numeric codes preceding each term provide additional access points for online searching. The superscript gives the date of term entry.

00010 Abdomen [73]
00020 Abdominal Wall [73]
00030 Abducens Nerve [73]
00040 Ability Grouping [73]
00050 Ability Level [78]
00070 Ability/ [67]

APPENDIX B: DISCONTINUED TERMS

Subject Code	Discontinued Term	Period of Use	Now Use
00410	Acculturation	1973-1981	Cultural Assimilation
02760	Animal Innate Behavior	1973-1981	Instinctive Behavior
02770	Animal Instinctive Behavior	1967-1981	Instinctive Behavior
03150	Antiepileptic Drugs	1973-1981	Anticonvulsive Drugs
03200	Antipsychotic Drugs	1973-1981	Neuroleptic Drugs
03210	Antischizophrenic Drugs	1973-1981	Neuroleptic Drugs
04004	Asian Americans	1978-1981	Asians
08020	Caucasians	1973-1981	Whites
11010	Concept Learning	1973-1981	Concept Formation
11210	Conference Proceedings	1973-1981	Professional Meetings and Symposia
13850	Developmental Differences	1973-1981	Age Differences
15250	Drug Adverse Reactions	1973-1981	Side Effects (Drug)
15300	Drug Effects	1967-1981	Drugs/
15340	Drug Potentiation	1973-1981	Drug Interactions
15370	Drug Synergism	1973-1981	Drug Interactions
15430	Drug Withdrawal Effects	1973-1981	Drug Withdrawal
15810	East German Democratic Republic	1967-1981	East Germany
15830	Eating Patterns	1973-1981	Eating
26050	Interest Patterns	1973-1981	Interests
27480	Korea	1973-1981	North Korea South Korea
30770	Mental Health Consultation	1973-1981	Professional Consultation
33250	Negroes	1967-1981	Blacks
33928	New Guinea	1973-1981	Papua New Guinea
34470	North Vietnam	1973-1981	Vietnam
34540	Novocaine	1973-1981	Procaine
36310	Paralydehyde	1973-1981	Paraldehyde
39860	Practice Effects	1973-1981	Practice
40690	Professional Contribution	1973-1981	Professional Criticism
41960	Psychosocial Resocialization	1973-1981	Psychosocial Readjustment
42610	Race Attitudes	1973-1981	Racial and Ethnic Attitudes
42615	Race Relations	1978-1981	Racial and Ethnic Relations
42620	Racial Differences	1973-1981	Racial and Ethnic Differences
42630	Racial Discrimination	1973-1981	Social Discrimination
42640	Racial Integration	1967-1981	Social Integration
45660	School Integration (Racial)	1973-1981	School Integration
48690	Somnambulism	1973-1981	Sleepwalking
48790	South Vietnam	1973-1981	Vietnam
48845	Spanish Americans	1978-1981	Hispanics
49440	Stammering	1973-1981	Stuttering
53350	Tobago	1973-1981	Trinidad and Tobago
54290	Trinidad	1973-1981	Trinidad and Tobago
54810	Union of South Africa	1973-1981	South Africa
54830	United Arab Republic	1973-1981	Egypt
56640	West German Federal Republic	1967-1981	West Germany
56660	West Pakistan	1973-1981	Pakistan

FIG. 3b. Extracts from the APA *Thesaurus of psychological index terms*

```
Index term (postable)   Afferent Pathways[82]
with date of entry

    Scope note       SN  Collections of fibers that
                         carry neural impulses to-
                         ward neural processing
                         areas from sensory mech-
                         anisms or other pro-
                         cessing areas.

    Used for term    UF  Sensory Pathways
    (nonpostable)
    Broader term     B   Neural Pathways
                         Peripheral Nerves
    Narrower term    N   Spinothalamic Nerves
    Related term     R   Efferent Pathways
                         Sensory Neurons
```

FIG. 4. Meaning of terms

The other major section is the "rotated alphabetical terms" so a term not expressed in a single word will be listed in its appropriate locations. Figure 5 is an example of how the "User's" guide explains this.

The 3rd edition also contains a list of document-type identifiers as well as an Appendix showing a content classification set of categories and codes used in the *PsychINFO* data base.

Because many terms represent concepts not expressed in a single word, postable *Thesaurus* terms are listed in alphabetical order by each word contained within them. Thus, a *Thesaurus* term containing three words will appear in three locations in the Rotated Alphabetical Terms Section as illustrated below:

    Academic Underachievement
  College Academic Achievement
    Acalculla
     ·
     ·
     ·

    Achievement Potential
  College Academic Achievement
    Mathematics Achievement
     ·
     ·
     ·

    Collective Behavior
  College Academic Achievement
    College Dropouts

FIG. 5. Rotated alphabetical terms

Let us suppose that one is interested in searching the concept of appetite control. On checking the relationship section under "Appetite" we find that the *Thesaurus* contains no reference under "Appetite control" but refers us under "Appetite" to "Appetite depressing drugs" and on checking a little further we note that "Appetite depressing drugs" is a major term in its own right. We also note below it "Appetite disorders" as another related term. Figure 6 illustrates this point, and it is also observed that "Appetite depressing drugs" does not appear under "Appetite disorders", though there we have been given another useful clue by the reference to the term "Nutritional deficiencies".

The rotated alphabetical terms section shows our topic under three headings at different points of the alphabetical sequence, as illustrated in Fig. 7; the bold print represents the filing medium, but the three words remain in the same order, thus indicating the term which is critical for reference retrieval in *Psychological abstracts* (Fig. 7). As may be seen, our topic "appetite control" can be approached through a variety of related terms, offering varying degrees of precision and offering, at the same time, other relationships. On following up some of these one reaches, e.g. "biochemistry", "eating", "food" and "metabolism disorders". The point being made here is that there are multiple points of entry and an open-ranging mind will produce a more useful result than any attempt to follow a mechanical process.

There is also a third (minor) section of the *Thesaurus* called the "Postable terms code", which gives a five-integer identifier for each psychological term; the terms are arranged in alphabetical order. This system of code numbers provides additional access points for on-line searches.

We have dealt with the thesaurus concept at some length because it is of fundamental significance when literature searchers are transferred from manual practice to mechanical, i.e. computer-based modes. The employment of non-discriminating devices such as a computer—and even the so-called "intelligent computer" can as yet do no more than react to predetermined stimuli—imposes on the user a strictly defined set of questions or forms of input. The computer will react, simply because it has been so constructed and geared, and regurgitate all data held on, say, DYSTHYMIA but it will not produce any reply to a search for "Emotional depression". The inquirer must adhere to the vocabulary to which the computer has been set. Only when this fundamental limitation of computers has been understood can this quite remarkable and powerful machine be exploited to its full capacity.

The best known computer-assisted retrieval system for psychologists is PASAR (Psychological Abstracts and Retrieval) which is based on the data base created by *Psychological abstracts*. This service has been in existence since 1967 and provides worldwide coverage of psychology and

Appetite Depressing Drugs[73]
UF Anorexigenic Drugs
N   Amphetamine
    Dextroamphetamine
    Phenmetrazine
R   Appetite
    Drugs/

Appetite Disorders[73]
B   Symptoms
N   Anorexia Nervosa
    Hyperphagia
    Obesity
R   Aphagia
    Appetite
    Nausea
    Nutritional Deficiencies
    Underweight

Eating[67]
SN Use EATING or EATING PATTERNS to access references prior to 1982.
UF Eating Patterns
B   Food Intake
N   Diets
R   Appetite
    Food

Eating Patterns
SN Use EATING PATTERNS or EATING to access references prior to 1982.
    Use Eating

Nutritional Deficiencies[73]
UF Deficiency Disorders (Nutritrional)
    Malnutrition
N   Kwashiorkor
    Pellagra
    Protein Deficiency Disorders
    Starvation
    Vitamin Deficiency Disorders
    Wernickes Syndrome
R   Alcoholic Psychosis
    Alcoholism

FIG. 6. Illustration of "Relationship" terms

Thematic Appperception Test
Appetite
Appetite Depressing Drugs
Appetite Disorders
Job Applicant Attitudes

Depersonalization
CNS Depressant Drugs
Appetite Depressing Drugs
Depression (Emotion)
Anaclitic Depression

Antispasmodic Drugs
Antitremor Drugs
Antitubercular Drugs
Appetite Depressing Drugs
Cholinergic Drugs

Fig. 7. Illustration of Rotated alphabetic terms

related behavioural sciences. A user's reference manual entitled *PsycINFO*, last issued in 1981, contains details of the contents and services of the PASAR system; the fees charged; a list of index terms; and an explanation of the service systems BRS, "DIALOG" and ORBIT in so far as they are relevant to the interrogation of the PASAR data bank. Because the *PsycINFO* data base is obviously the most important data base for psychological research, we have included, as Fig. 8, a facsimile of the content classification categories used in that base. It will be noted that there has been a change in the code numbers in 1976. The simple reason for the expansion of the number system used from 1967 to 1975 was the growth in the volume of data to be stored.

Social sciences citation index, the printed version of which has been described on p. 48, has been computerized since 1972; as resources permit previous years of this *Index* will be computerized, working backwards from 1970-71. The name of this data base is "Social Scisearch" and it covers the same range of important social science journals, supplemented by social science articles from physical and biomedical journals, as the printed version. Beginners are warned once more that the *Social sciences citation index* is an index to terms only, and does not contain summaries of the articles or documents referred to as is the case with *Psychological abstracts*.

Additional to these two main data bases for psychological research there are a number of other computer-based retrieval systems of value to psychologists. These include the data bank created in 1966 by the Educational Resources Information Centre and commonly known as ERIC. It covers the broad field of education, including educational management, teacher education, education of exceptional children, career education, pre-school education, higher education and, of course, educational psychology with all its ramifications. References are selected from the literature of research reports, conference proceedings, theses, pamphlets, etc. and approximately 700 journals in education and related fields. Most of the citations come from the English-speaking world and there is a dominance of North American literature.

MEDLARS (Medical Literature Analysis and Retrieval System—based on the data banks of *Index medicus*, *Index to dental literature* and *International nursing index*) and BIOSIS (Biological sciences information system—based on the data bank created by *Biological abstracts* services) offer access to the medical and biological aspects of psychology; reference to the importance of these data banks has already been made on p. 49. Suffice it here to say that these systems are among the best developed, most comprehensive and most sophisticated reference retrieval services now in operation.

Exceptional child education abstracts, as its name properly suggests, deals with both handicapped and gifted children, and is a useful supplement to ERIC. The computer-based file dates from 1966. In a

PSYCINFO
DIALOG INFORMATION RETRIEVAL SERVICE

11

FILE DESCRIPTION

The PSYCINFO (Psychological Abstracts Information Service) database covers the world's literature in psychology and related behavioral and social sciences such as psychiatry, sociology, anthropology, education, pharmacology, and linguistics. Over 950 periodicals and technical reports, and monographs are scanned each year to provide coverage of original research, reviews, discussions, theories, conference reports, panel discussions, case studies, and descriptions of apparatus. PSYCINFO, produced by the American Psychological Association (APA), includes all material from the printed *Psychological Abstracts* and additional material from *Dissertation Abstracts International* and other sources.

Informative abstracts are included for most of the records in the file.

SUBJECT COVERAGE

The following general fields are covered:

- Applied Psychology
- Communication Systems
- Developmental Psychology
- Educational Psychology
- Experimental Human and Animal Psychology
- Experimental Social Psychology
- General Psychology
- Personality
- Physical and Psychological Disorders
- Physiological Intervention
- Physiological Psychology
- Professional Personnel and Issues
- Psychometrics
- Social Processes and Issues
- Treatment and Prevention

SOURCES

Material included in PSYCINFO is drawn from approximately 1,050 primary sources, both domestic and international, including the following: periodicals, technical reports, monographs, and *Dissertation Abstracts International*.

DIALOG FILE DATA

Inclusive Dates: 1967 to the present
Update Frequency: Monthly (approximately 2,700 records per update)
File Size: 352,300 records as of March 1981

ORIGIN

PSYCINFO is produced by the American Psychological Association. Questions concerning file content should be directed to:

PsycINFO Telephone: 800/336-4980 (U.S. except Virginia)
User Services Department   202/833-5908 (in Virginia)
American Psychological Association
1200 Seventeenth Street, N.W.
Washington, DC 20036

Database copyrighted by the American Psychological Association. Buyer agrees not to use data retrieved for the purpose of replacing all or any part or as a substitute for license, lease, or purchase of any of the data base.

DIALOG is a Trademark of LMSC, Inc. Reg. U.S. Pat. & Trademark Office.
©LMSC, Inc., 1981.

(Revised April 1981) 11-1

FIG. 8. PsycInfo subject coverage

related field *Child abuse and neglect,* which began in 1965, is a very recent file concerned mainly with current projects. Its major drawback is its restriction to English-language projects in the USA.

Of marginal interest except to the specialists are LLBA and NTIS. The former, known as *Language and language behaviour abstracts (LLBA),* provides selective access to the journal literature on this aspect of communication behaviour from various parts of the world. It encompasses literature on linguistics, interpersonal communication and learning disabilities. It has been in computer base from 1973. *National technical information service (NTIS),* which began in 1964 is a broad interdisciplinary file which includes the behavioural and social sciences, economics and business, urban technology, environmental pollution and control, and various other physical science and engineering subjects.

The fact that computerized data bases exist is one thing; how to make use of them is another. In some countries children are introduced to the use of computers in secondary schools and those fortunate few come to appreciate the potential of computer-based retrieval methods even before they can make proper use of them. Since at this point in history there are still many, many students entering tertiary education without the benefit of having had their multiplication table replaced by an electronic adding machine, a few notes on the basics of machine-readable retrieval systems will surely be appropriate. It is, above all, important to realize that mechanical things are mechanical; however sophisticated the mechanism there is no way in which a mechanical apparatus can make value judgements. To use a mechanical retrieval system does not absolve those who do so from the necessity of using the one and only computer which cannot be manufactured by human hands: man's brain.

It is, of course, not practical to embark upon a computerized literature search unless one is connected (electronically) with a computerized data bank. A "hook-up" may be effected either by a land line or by radio link. The latter is very common, now, and enables countries such as Australia, South Africa and India to exploit these data bases in other continents.

More importantly, perhaps, there are two distinct procedures which, though they enable researchers to have equally thorough access to data banks, differ greatly in cost and strategy. One is the off-line batch procedure which consists basically in asking the data bank to provide, at a time convenient to its operators, a printout of all the references that meet a particular qualification. The more specific the request, the greater the chance of finding relevant references among those identified by the computer. The cost for this type of search is relatively small but delivery may take some time (days) and there is no possibility of restructuring the request while the computer is chugging away. If the result of the search is unsatisfactory, a lot of money may be wasted and a new search may have to be formulated, transmitted and paid for.

As an alternative, on-line interrogation of a data bank—i.e. a "face-to-face" questioning of the data bank by the researcher via a terminal—has the advantages that the searcher can evaluate the replies received, can ask for a print only of those which seem relevant, and can introduce new questions, change the parameters of his inquiry, or ensure that the thesaurus terms are permuted in a new manner. The only disadvantage is that if the investigator is not thoroughly prepared this type of search tends to be very expensive.

Owners (i.e. in many instances the creators) of data banks, as well as the service systems (i.e. the companies that provide the linkage between the searcher and the data bank), charge x dollars per minute or hour of on-line connection plus a hit-fee (i.e. y dollars for every reference that matches the researcher's specification). The charges made by the operators of service systems vary greatly. The really large operators, e.g. *The Lockheed Information Systems* (Dialog) of Palo Alto, California, USA, or *The Systems Development Corporation* of 2500 Colorado Ave., Santa Monica, California 90406, USA, will, if requested, search several data bases and produce one integrated reply from them. This service tends to be costly.

In order to obtain the most economical service—both in terms of real costs and in relevant references taken from the most suitable data bank—researchers would do well to examine carefully the guides produced by the data base operators. The large systems such as DIALOG, ORBIT or EURONET issue quite detailed catalogues and instruction manuals; these are supplied free to institutions who contract to make use of the services offered (see Figs 9 and 10). In addition to these large international networks, there exist in some countries national data base services to complement them and to service local data bases which are unlikely to be much in demand in other countries. An example of such a national data base service is the Australian computer-based network called AUSINET.

Computer-based retrieval of information is a process which makes use of already prepared data and references. However, students and researchers may wish to use computers to assist them in the handling and retrieval of data they themselves have collected or created. Such a need arises in projects where one has a vast array of reference material derived from publications, reports, etc. or large quantities of data resulting from experiments. The data are put onto the memory bank coded by author, title, key terms or concepts, year, type of publication, or any of the criteria which were used to derive the experimental data in the first place. One of the singular merits of a computer-based system is that material may be entered at any time in any order and retrieved in any bloc or sequence required by the operator. The only catch is that the construction of the necessary software package requires special competence not normally met in students of psychology. It is therefore recommended to search for some ready-made package.

Among the many programs or software packages available on the market there is one which seems to merit special recommendation. It is known as "Famulus" and will enable researchers to do just that. The "Famulus" documentation system organizes files and controls data management, file manipulation, information retrieval, thesaurus construction and a host of other functions. The package was constructed in 1972 by the Computer Centre of University College, London and is an excellent example of what can be done by the orderly electronic mind.

SAMPLE RECORD

```
AN  - 59-08837(04)
TI  - The possible use of sociodrama as a training technique for the
      moderately mentally handicapped in school, half-way training
      centre, and sheltered workshop
AU  - Foster, S. E.
OS  - Mt Gravatt Teachers' Coll, Brisbane, Australia
SO  - Exceptional Child; 1975 Mar Vol 22(1) 38-44
DT  - J (Journal)
LA  - Engl
CC  - 3570 (Special & Remedial Education)
IT  - SHELTERED WORKSHOPS (47180); EDUCABLE MENTALLY RETARDED (15960);
      SOCIAL SKILLS (48395); CHILDREN (08830); ROLE PLAYING (44860)
ST  - Sociodrama, development of social skills, moderately mentally
      handicapped children in school & halfway training center &
      sheltered workshop
AB  - Discusses sociodrama as a technique to help children with moderate
      mental handicaps develop social skills in which they often become
      deficient. With a modification of the procedure toward the
      practicing of response patterns and away from problem solving,
      sociodrama would provide opportunities for learning both by
      conditioning and through cognitive modification for all but the
      most profoundly retarded. Its dramatization process of role
      playing involves movement, language, and convergent and divergent
      thinking. Sociodrama provides the individual with a picture of
      how he operates in real life situations, and such feedback could
      be increased through the use of videotape. The behavioral
      outcome of acquiring and developing personal interrelationship
      values through dependency learning is described as an example of
      how the social skills of the retarded could be enhanced by
      participation in sociodrama. (W. E. Lindsey)
```

FIG. 9. Sample page from Orbit User's Guide

SEARCHING TIPS

ELEMENT NAME	NOTES	USER:
Basic Index	Single words derived from Titles, assigned Index Terms, Supplementary Terms and Abstracts. No qualifier required.	PATTERN AND RECOGNITION
Index Terms	Use /IT to search single-word controlled vocabulary terms. /IT qualifier is optional for multi-word terms. Subject Codes equivalent to Index Terms are searchable as they appear with or without qualifier.	RECREATION THERAPY ALCOHOLISM/IT 51920
Index Term Words	Use /IW to search single words derived from assigned single- and multi-word Index Terms.	CLINICAL/IW AND ALL PSYCHOLOG:/IW
Title Words	Use /TI to search single words derived from Titles.	LANGUAGE/TI AND LEARNING/TI
Authors	Variable format; use truncated entry.	WELLMAN, H:/AU
Organizational Source	Search with /OS appended to each single word.	U/OS AND WISCONSIN/OS AND MADISON/OS
Journal Citation Name	Enter full name, up to 33 characters, with /JC.	SOCIAL PSYCHIATRY/JC
Document Type	Search with /DT (B=book; J=journal; R=report; S=separate; and U=unconventional medium.)	5 AND B/DT
Category Codes	Search 2-digit codes (1967-1976) or 4-digit codes (1976-) with /CC. (See user manual for complete list.)	5 AND ALL 25:/CC

FIG. 9 (Cont.) Sample page from Orbit User's Guide

PSYCHABS

GENERAL DESCRIPTION

SUPPLIER	American Psychological Association, Inc. 1200 Seventeenth Street, N.W. Washington, D.C. 20036 (202) 833-7624
PRINTED PUBLICATION	*Psychological Abstracts*
CONTENT COVERAGE	Provides comprehensive coverage of literature in psychology and other behavioral sciences. Includes the areas of psychometrics and statistics, perception and motor performance, cognitive processes and motivation, neurology and physiology, psychopharmacology and physiological intervention, animal psychology, developmental psychology, cultural influences and social issues, communication and language, personality, physical and psychological disorders, treatment and prevention, education, psychology and applied psychology.
PERIOD OF COVERAGE	1967 to date
UNIT RECORD	Citation, assigned controlled vocabulary, and abstract
SIZE OF FILE	Approximately 24,000 records per year of coverage
UPDATING FREQUENCY	Monthly

FIG. 10. Notes of advice for users of *Psychological abstracts*

Computer-based Data Retrieval

PSYCHABS RECORD DESCRIPTION

SEARCH QUALIFIER	ELEMENT NAME	PRINT/STRS QUALIFIER	STANDARD PRINT COMMANDS		
			PRINT	TRIAL	FULL
--	Basic Index (*single words from TI, IT, ST, and AB*)	--	-	-	-
/IT	Index Terms	IT	-	X	X
/IW	Index Term Words	--	-	X	X
/TI	Title	TI	X	X	X
(IN BI)	Supplementary Term Phrases	ST	-	X	X
(IN BI)	Abstract	AB	-	-	X
/AN	Accession Number	AN	X	X	X
/AU	Authors	AU	X	-	X
/OS	Organizational Source	OS	X	-	X
/JC	Journal Citation Name	--	-	-	-
Ranging	Publication Year (PY)	--	-	-	-
/DT	Document Type	DT	-	-	X
/LA	Language	LA	-	-	X
/CC	Category Codes	CC	-	X	X
/UP	Update Code	--	-	-	-
STRS ONLY	Source (*includes JC, PY*)	SO	X	-	X

FIG. 10 (Cont.) Notes of advice for users of *Psychological abstracts*

CHAPTER 6

Special Fields of Psychology

It has been repeatedly remarked that during the past 50–75 years the study of psychology has greatly increased in specialization and sophistication. Many traditionalists tend to see in this development a danger of weakening research efforts in the fundamental aspects of psychology, and some have not hesitated to refer to certain marginal fields as breeding grounds for charlatans. It is not our intention to pass judgement on these views, nor do we propose to criticize or justify the divisions that have occurred in the professional associations. Certain specialist schools of psychology have inspired a substantial quantity of literature which in turn has necessitated certain forms of bibliographic control. The special fields discussed below are of necessity a mere selection of the many specialized areas of psychology and of some of the particular approaches to the interpretation of human behaviour that have grown into established schools through the vigorous and persuasive teachings by one person. There exist scores more of cliques which have sprung up around some forceful visionary, and which tend to interpret man and his social environment in terms of that leader's teachings. It is not possible to deal with all of them here, nor is it likely to be useful to dissect the whole field of psychology into its constituent parts as they are traditionally treated in the better textbooks. We have instead concentrated on those topics and approaches which have already benefited from a literature survey of some substance, and restricted ourselves to point to the references to other specific areas of psychology as they have been summed up in particular bibliographies.

Furthermore, it is emphasized that in Chapter 2 we have already referred to a number of historical accounts of the major fields of psychology. In that context we did not include references to literature surveys which are our particular concern here. We have also paid attention, in our selection of literature surveys, to the need for current data. For that reason we have tended to omit in particular those bibliographies which have been compiled many years ago and which were strictly limited with regard to the period covered. A list of books published on animal psychology during the years 1920–25 is just no longer of much relevance; it will have been superseded or the contents absorbed in more recent publications.

Physiological psychology

The relationship between mind and body has been a preoccupation of the medical profession since antiquity; the theologians of the middle ages and the students of the incipient era of rationalism spent much time thinking and writing about the control of the mind over the body and the effects of bodily functions on the mind. In the nineteenth century these studies were continued at an experimental level and subjected to scientific scrutiny. The investigations by Helmholtz and others helped to pave the way for a new approach on the link between physiology and psychology, as treated by W. Wundt, W. James, G. T. Ladd, C. S. Sherrington, E. B. Titchener and others. A summing up, with a substantial bibliography, was presented by L. T. Troland in his *Principles of psychophysiology* (3 vols) which first appeared in 1929 but was reprinted in 1969. The contributions made by the school of Ivan P. Pavlov and S. L. Rubenstein are discussed in the two works by John McLeish (1975) and by L. Rahmani (1973) already referred to on p. 13. Rubenstein's influence has also been discussed at length by T. R. Payne, with a selected bibliography, in his *S. L. Rubenstejn and the philosophical foundations of Soviet psychology* (1969). The effect of the physical environment upon physiological functions and social behaviour has received much attention during the past two decades. The literature related to these studies has been listed by Francine Butler in two volumes entitled *Biofeedback and self regulation* (1973) and *Biofeedback: a survey of the literature* (1978). These contain over 3000 references, arranged by author and supplemented by a topics index.

We note, however, that there exists as yet no comprehensive literature survey on physiological psychology; given the accumulation of over 150 years of writing on this topic, it may well be too late to expect any one person to produce such a bibliography.

Psychoanalysis

One of the earliest special schools to develop was that of psychoanalysis. It grew out of the medical aspects of psychology and the treatment of quite specific mental and physiological disorders. Its principal founder and chief protagonist was Sigmund Freud (1853–1939), whose personal influence on his students and on European life and culture has been tremendous. The literature spawned by the vigorous members of this movement is very prolific and testifies to the claim made by some that Freud's effect upon the twentieth century has been no less than that of Columbus and Copernicus upon their respective periods of history.

The novice may find Fodor & Gaynor's *Freud: dictionary of psychoanalysis,* 1950, or Rycroft's *A critical dictionary of psychoanalysis* a useful adjunct when reading the often jargon-riddled literature of psychoanalysis, particularly as the authors have included original definitions and their sources as well as the modifications of their current terms by Freud and his followers. Though the former was published over 30 years ago it is still of considerable value. A multilingual dictionary has been compiled by Laplanche and Pontalis; its English edition was issued in 1973 under the title *The language of psychoanalysis*. The major concepts are listed in alphabetical sequence, with French, German, Italian, Portuguese and Spanish equivalents for each entry. The early literature of psychoanalysis is listed in John Rickman's *Index psychoanalyticus, 1893–1926*. This basic bibliography of psychoanalysis first appeared in 1928 in the well-known series of the "International psychoanalytical library". It is arranged according to authors, but under each author books and periodical articles are arranged in chronological order of publication. Users should note carefully that the *Index* does not claim to be exhaustive. Its 4739 entries are drawn from the six leading psychoanalytical journals of the period and the monographs of the three leading publishers in the field as well. This work has been updated by A. Grinstein in his *Index of psychoanalytic writings* issued in fourteen volumes between 1956 and 1973. Both the works by Rickman and by Grinstein are international in scope and include monographs and periodical articles arranged alphabetically by author. Grinstein also compiled a thorough bibliography of the writings of Sigmund Freud; published in 1977, it contains references to almost every printed document issued over Freud's name. There is a good index.

While there exist a number of journals of psychoanalysis there exists no specific current awareness service for this field of psychology.

Because of the wide effect of psychoanalysis on creative writing and the study of literature, it is not surprising that a body of criticism should have grown up around this relationship. N. Kiell has compiled a bibliography of it in 1963 which was published as *Psychoanalysis, psychology and literature.* It covers the years 1900–16 and contains 4460 items arranged under a broad literary classification. Titles in foreign languages are followed by a translation. An extensive subject index completes this interesting and useful bibliography. In the context of the wide influence of Freud's work, we point to one of many bibliographical studies that have been compiled on psychoanalytic literature in various countries. R. C. S. Trahair & J. G. Marshall's *Australian psychoanalytic and related writings, 1884–1940* is an annotated bibliography which shows not only that the work of this school had some considerable influence, but also how certain world events have helped to spread its teachings.

Alfred Adler, contemporary and student of Freud, gave psychoanalysis a somewhat different twist, laying emphasis on individual differences and on a psychotherapy related to social psychology. His followers were numerous in Europe in the 1920s and 1930s, and after World War II Adlerian psychoanalysis gained much support in the USA. Harold & Birdie Mosak compiled *A bibliography of Adlerian psychology* in 1975, which contains over 10,000 entries arranged alphabetically under authors and is equipped with a good index.

Behaviourism

The literature of this school of psychology is still awaiting its bibliographer. Though this interpretation of human actions and reactions has been strongly criticized by other psychologists, the leading figures—B. F. Skinner, J. B. Watson and E. C. Tolman—have also been recognized and respected as great scholars. Skinner's own summary *About behaviorism,* 1974, contained numerous bibliographic references to this important interpretation of man's relationship to the world around him. A strange compilation of references designed to show the errors of this school of psychology was published by A. A. Roback in 1923 as part of his critical discussion entitled *Behaviourism and psychology*; it is now only of historical interest.

We have already referred to Robert I. Watson's *The history of psychology and the behavioral sciences: a bibliographic guide,* 1978, in our discussion of the general background guides to psychology. It suffices to note, here, that this work, though by one of the leading scholars of the behaviourist school, is not, and does not pretend to be, a bibliography of behaviourism. In some respects the same can be said of C. Heidenreich's *Dictionary of personality: behavior and adjustment terms,* which appeared in 1968. Both these books have been compiled by leading members of this behaviourist school and are unquestionably representative of the views of that school. We have mentioned these works here for that reason, but stress that these are scholarly and unbiased reference works which do not include or misrepresent references to other interpretations of human behaviour.

Gestalt psychology

Among the several schools which were spawned in the fertile period of the 1920s and 1930s, Gestalt psychology became one of the more respected endeavours to explain human behaviour in terms of a holistic approach to life processes. There are a number of fundamental expositions of this theory by K. Kafka, D. Katz, W. Köhler, K. Levin, M. Wertheimer and others, but a comprehensive retrospective bibliography is still awaiting a dedicated compiler. W. Köhler's basic work *Gestalt psychology,* 1929, includes a selective literature survey, and W. D. Ellis's *Gestalt psychology and meaning,* 1930, is another systematic overview of the work of this school with many bibliographic references. More recent guides, though only of limited significance as bibliographies, are W. D. Ellis's *A source book of Gestalt psychology,* 1967, and M. Henle's *Documents of Gestalt psychology,* 1961.

Both behaviourism and Gestalt psychology have received considerable attention in the pages of the *Journal of the history of the behavioral sciences,* 1965– , and in the absence of an exhaustive literature survey readers will find that journal an invaluable source of references on these two important schools of psychology.

Affective psychology, cognition, creativity

These broad fields of psychology have been the prime battleground for conflicting theories and schools, each of which offers a different explanation for our emotions, thought processes, learning and memory performance, our imagery and creativeness. In spite of the seeming breadth of the field, it is sufficiently specific to have caused many scholarly monographs to be written which show the close relationship between the several forms of expression and behaviour and man's reaction to his social environment.

There are not many examples of bibliographies that deal specifically with the literature of affective psychology. However, the one obvious and important type of reaction that has been receiving a lot of attention is hostile behaviour, which is the topic of an extensive bibliography by J. M. Crabtree & K. E. Moyer, whose *Bibliography of aggressive behavior* appeared in 1977 and contains almost 4000 citations arranged under categories and linked by a sophisticated index based on code words.

A very comprehensive *Bibliography of memory* has been compiled by M. N. Young. It is international in scope and reaches back to the middle ages. Both monographs and journal articles are included; there is a list of about 400 journals to which reference has been made. Undoubtedly a mammoth compilation which illustrates the persistence of the compiler. Unfortunately, there are no evaluative notes or commentaries.

Though there exists no specific bibliography of the literature on cognitive processes, the extensive review of Piagetian research by Sohan & Celia Modgil referred to on p. 83 contains a comprehensive bibliography which is of course studded with reference to the literature on this topic.

The psychology of creativity, aesthetics and art in general is closely related to investigations into cognitive processes. The literature on this topic goes back to the discussions of the nature of beauty among the Greek philosophers but modern contributions begin in the middle of the nineteenth century. A comprehensive international bibliography of that literature has been published in 1938 by A. R. Chandler & E. N. Barnhart under the title *A bibliography of psychological and experimental aesthetics, 1864–1937*. Though it lacks annotations the entries are divided under useful headings such as the theory of psychological aesthetics, the psychology of aesthetic responses, color, lines and forms, empathy, language arts, humor, music; each of these headings is further subdivided so that we find a rather detailed organization of the material. N. Kiell, whose bibliography on psychoanalysis and literature has already been noted, compiled also an international bibliography on *Psychiatry and psychology in the visual arts and aesthetics*, 1965. Its 7200 entries are arranged under twenty-two headings but again there are no annotations.

By contrast, A. E. Arasteh issued in 1968 an annotated bibliography,

Creativity in the life-cycle which consists of extensive notes on the nature of creativity and its role in childhood, adolescence and adulthood together with a comprehensive literature survey. Together with Josephine D. Arasteh he revised that work and reissued it in 1976 under the title *Creativity in human development*.

A different approach was taken by A. Rothenberg & B. Greenberg, who compiled a two-volume *Index of scientific writings on creativity*. The first volume is a bibliography of creative men and women, arranged alphabetically first under the name of the artist and then under the name of the author of the investigation. The references include contributions in the major European languages. The second volume is a general international bibliography of scientific contributions to the concept of creativity. The almost 7000 entries cover the earliest citation known (mid-sixteenth century) to 1975; they are arranged under broad subject groups which include an extensive section of developmental studies. These subject groups are explained at length in the introduction. An author and a subject index conclude this well-produced bibliography. The two volumes represent excellent models of literature surveys.

A continuing listing of the literature on creativity and problem-solving is contained, under that title, in the *Journal of creative behaviour* which began in 1967. A retrospective bibliography on this topic appeared in volumes 5 and 7, covering the literature of the years 1950–70.

Measurements and tests

Ever since W. Wundt and other physiological psychologists have concerned themselves with nervous reactions and reflexes, great importance has been attached to tests and measurements. The "grand old man" of this empirical approach is the late O. K. Buros who over the past 50 years has edited or sponsored many psychological tests as well as surveys, criticisms and bibliographies of work in this field. Ready-made tests and testing materials have been designed to assist experimental psychologists in the fields of education, industry and physiological psychology. The availability of such materials not only avoids a waste of time involved in designing them but also ensures that these materials and test programmes have been tested under laboratory conditions. Not only are such mental measurements and psychological tests constantly in need of updating but the development of testing technology has greatly improved the accuracy of the tests and enhanced the possibility of correct interpretation. *Tests in print (TIP)*, which first appeared in 1961, is, so to say, the basic collection of such tests and the work also contains references to and abstracts of test reviews and the literature of specific tests. A completely revised edition appeared in 1974 *(TIP II)* and a new edition envisaged to be a complementary work, and not a substitute for *TIP I* and *TIP II*, is now in preparation.

Special Fields of Psychology

Buros also edited the *Mental measurement yearbook* which, however, does not appear annually but every 3–5 years; the latest issue available is the 8th edition, 1978. This keeps the tests listed in *TIP I* and *TIP II* under review and lists latest reports. An important feature of *Tests in print* is the bibliographic reference to the *Mental measurement yearbooks* which contain current evaluations of tests and testing literature.

Another index from the same stable is entitled *Personality tests and reviews, including an index to the Mental measurement yearbooks*; this appeared in 1970. In addition, there is the APA's *Standards for educational and psychological tests*, which is of great importance in this context. Though it is not a reviewing medium nor, strictly speaking, a source of other testing materials, it is nevertheless a basic reference work and is frequently revised.

Associated with this standard work are some other reference tools which form valuable adjuncts to the main body of data. One such is *Personality tests and reviews*, edited by Buros in 1970. This work also includes the *Mental measurement yearbook index* up to 1970. As the title implies, it focuses specifically on personality assessments and within that circumscription it is equally as comprehensive as the parent work.

Of particular interest to psychologists in non-English-speaking countries is a selection from the foreign language material contained in the first seven yearbooks, 1938–72. *Foreign language tests and reviews*, also edited by Buros, appeared in 1974; it includes many references and a bibliographic index.

Regrettably, Buros died in 1978, but the reference works which he compiled or edited with indefatigable vigour and skill have become the most important reference works in the field of mental testing.

A useful complement to the work by Buros is that of Chun, Cobb & French's *Measures for psychological assessment; a guide to 3000 original sources and their applications*, 1975. The compilers' aim is to cover material omitted from the *Mental measurement yearbook*; that material consists of the less formal kinds of tests and of ad hoc devices discussed mainly in journal articles. The entries are reproduced from computer printouts put together by the Institute for Social Research, Ann Arbor, Michigan. They are in alphabetical order and include the descriptive details taken from the original source. There is an author and description index.

For a briefer overview of some of the better-known tests readers may consult Lake, Miles & Earle's *Measuring human behaviour: tools for the assessment of social function*, 1973. This work contains details of 84 tests including such items as "Rokeach's dogmatism scale", "Witkin's embedded figures test" and the "Rosenzweig picture frustration test". There is a compendium of tests, their use and their availability.

For the essential principles of psychological testing there are many excellent text books, e.g. Cronbach's *Essentials of psychological testing,*

1970, which deals with the basic concepts, tests of ability and the testing of typical performance. Its style is clear and concise. Similarly J. C. Nunnally's *Educational measurement and evaluation* (1972) deals with basic principles and then goes on to the construction and standardization of tests and discusses, at some length, the issue of prediction from tests.

Besides the exhaustive work by the Buros Institute, there is a small number of other titles which contribute a further dimension to this topic of tests and measurements. The essence of this field of psychology is, we must repeat, the construction and use of standardized tests and measurements, A. Anastasi's *Psychological testing,* now in its 4th edition, offers sound advice on these issues and lists a selection of available and professionally recognized tests. Another work which has been well received is Lyerly's *Handbook of psychiatric rating scales,* first published in 1963 and revised in 1973. This evaluative review of about sixty tests includes comments on reliability, applicability and validity.

The attempt at comprehensive coverage by the Buros Institute necessarily delays the completion and publication of the *TIP*. It is useful to remember that the education departments of individual countries, and their mental health authorities, quite often produce tests specially adapted to a particular country. An example of this is the *ACER annotated catalogue of educational tests and materials,* the latest loose-leaf edition of which appeared in 1981. Similar catalogues are published by the education departments or official institutes in many countries.

A state-of-the-art literature survey was compiled by Logan Wright in 1968 under the title *Bibliography on human intelligence.* This work was sponsored by the US Department of Health, Education and Welfare, and though dated, is still useful as an excellent starting point for a literature search on intelligence, abilities, IQ tests and psychological testing in general. The compilation is based mainly on entries culled from *Psychological abstracts,* but other sources have also been used.

A special form of measurement is the assessment of the personality, a process which is dependent either on an objective and trained observer's view of our behaviour or on self-revelation stimulated by special means, or both. Two tests in particular have been applied to this end for several decades. One is the Minnesota Multiphasic Personality Inventory, known as the MMPI test, the other is the Rorschach test often referred to as the inkblot test. A comprehensive and well-organized bibliography is available for each of these important assessment tools. E. S. Taulbee and associates have brought together in one volume all existing references to the MMPI test for the years 1940–65; their bibliography which appeared in 1977 was quite deliberately restricted to those years because from then on *Psychological abstracts* has adequately documented the relevant literature. All references are annotated. Author and subject indexes make access to individual documents easy, while a list of references to scales, special scoring procedures and special scales and sub-scales help to find references to particular personality characteristics. A list of journals cited concludes the bibliography.

A. Lang's *Rorschach-bibliography, 1921–1964* (1966) is a systematic list of monographs and journal articles arranged under seven headings: testbooks, general, method, modifications, interpretations, general applications, clinical applications. There is a total of 3855 references with a somewhat excessively complex index numbering, but the system is explained in English, French and German. While the reason for the cut-off date is self evident, it is of course as true of the Rorschach test as of the MMPI test that *Psychological abstracts* cover the literature since 1965.

The literature on self-assessment, both overt and covert, has been surveyed by C. Moss in 1977, under the title *Bibliographical guide to self-disclosure literature: 1956–1976*. The entries are arranged within classes which relate to the character traits they reveal, and to the methods used to elicit and interpret autobiographical statements, be they oral or written. This literature survey supersedes the work by L. D. Goodstein and V. M. Reinecker, whose *Factors affecting self disclosure; a review of the literature* appeared as volume 7 of the series *Progress in experimental personality research*, 1974. Moss's *Guide* has an author and subject index which, together with the classification system used, provide a variety of access points to this interesting literature.

Last on this topic we mention *Advances in psychological assessment,* which has appeared somewhat irregularly since 1968 and contains articles on "new developments in assessment technology". Though this series does not set out to offer an annual literature survey on testing and measurement, chapters in each volume tend to be accompanied by an exhaustive bibliography covering the various specific topics treated by specialist authors.

Developmental psychology

The psychology of children is another special field which has received much attention for a long time. It is now sometimes referred to as genetic psychology but it is more properly speaking a special field or, as some would have it, a particular aspect of the psychological changes that accompany physiological ageing. For that reason, developmental psychology embraces the study of behaviour from earliest childhood to old age.

The systematic study of children goes back to classical antiquity and has attracted the attention of many philosophers before philosophy and psychology were separated at the end of the nineteenth century. William Kessen provides a good overview of the history in his *The child* (1965).

It is, of course, only natural that every specialist school should have something to say about the psychology of children and interpret the "father to the man" in terms of their particular view of human behaviour and its origins. However, among the real specialists on the psychology of children the following names stand out: A. L. Gesell, F. L. Goodenough, G. S. Hall, K. Kaffka, C. Murchison, J. Piaget. Every one of these has contributed major works on this special field, but the classic outline of this topic was C. Murchison's *Handbook of child psychology* which appeared in 1933 and contains a comprehensive and still useful bibliography of the literature to that date. Some confusion may occur through the use of the same title by Paul H. Mussen for his new edition of L. Carmichael's famous *Manual of child psychology* which first appeared in 1946. Mussen edited the 3rd edition of Carmichael's *Manual* in 1970 but considered it necessary to produce a wholly revised work in 1983 under the title *Handbook of child psychology*, which "attempts to reflect the changes that have occurred since 1970". The four volumes of the fourth and newly titled edition of this authoritative survey contain contributions from top experts in all fields of child psychology and form a massive source of recent data.

Another summing-up of the school of developmental psychology has been edited by Benjamin B. Wolman in the monumental *Handbook of developmental psychology*, 1982. Wolman stresses in his compact introductory note how developmental psychology has been affected by the work of others and to what extent it is essentially an eclectic approach to the psychology of "human change from cradle to grave". The work consists of fifty chapters each written by several specialists and complete with a lengthy bibliography; the chapters are divided in six parts under the headings Research methods and theories; Infancy; Childhood; Adolescence; Adulthood; Aging. The literature references are all in English.

The psychology of development is sometimes included in surveys of educational psychology and students of developmental psychology should not fail to consult the standard bibliographies of education. Especially when one's interests lie in the areas of learning and conditioning, adolescence, vocational guidance, etc., there is scarcely a dividing line between education and child psychology.

There appears to exist, to this day, no English-language guide to basic terms and concepts of developmental psychology, but a useful work, compiled by R. Lafon is the *Vocabulaire de psychopédagogie et de psychiatrie de l'enfant*. Terms are arranged alphabetically, followed by translations into German, English, Spanish and Italian. All notes and articles are signed and the major contributions are followed by a bibliography. The range of entries is considerable and the list of major articles in the beginning of the book reflects the encyclopaedic nature of this *Vocabulaire*.

The most comprehensive literature survey for all these aspects of psychology is the periodical *Child development abstracts and bibliography* which has appeared since 1927. It covers books and articles on physical and psychological aspects of child health and also contains critical reviews of books about and for children.

The close link between the psychology of child development and educational psychology will be obvious to all. Those searching the literature on specific topics would do well to consult also the several indexes and abstracting services relating to education. The most comprehensive of the abstracting and indexing series for the literature on education is *Resources in education (RIE)* which appears monthly under the aegis of the US Department of Education and the National Institute of Education, Washington, DC. *RIE* is the printed version of the computerized data base ERIC which is accessible on line (see also Chapter V). The well-known firm of indexing specialists, The H. W. Wilson Company, New York, has published an *Education index* since 1929 which covers about 400 educational periodicals and yearbooks, and the proceedings of major conferences related to education; most of these are North American publications. It is suitably complemented by the *British education index,* which began in 1954 and is issued by the Library Association (UK), and by the *Australian education index* issued by the Australian Council for Educational Research since 1957. A monthly list of references to research sponsored by the US Office of Education has been published since 1966 under the title *Research in education.* Students of psychology should of course always bear in mind that the psychology of education is a special, and indeed a fairly large, field and that it includes many aspects both of education and of psychology which are approached from a specific point of view.

The outstanding and original contributions by Jean Piaget to the study of children and developmental psychology have prompted Sohen & Celia Modgil to set out in eight volumes his methods and influences, and to sum up and comment on the findings of the research institutes that have followed his teachings. *Piagetian research* appeared in 1976 and contains in each volume extensive bibliographies on child development and research in cognitive psychology.

In addition to the overviews and general bibliographies on the psychology of children, there exist also some very specialized studies of the literature of special diseases or particular aspects of child psychology. Two examples will have to suffice. One is a list of reports and activities issued by the Children's Bureau of the US Department of Health, Education and Welfare, issued in 1968 under the title *Research relating to emotionally disturbed children.* We have cited this as a particularly relevant example of the many useful documents issued by the Department of Health, Education and Welfare illustrating the importance of many government publications for psychologists (see also Chapter III).

The other example is C. A. Winchell's *The hyperkinetic child, a bibliography of medical, educational, and behavioral studies*, 1975. Again the entries are lacking annotations, and users of this list have to rely on the classification under broad subjects to get an idea of what the book or article is about. However, on so specific a topic, there is less need for interpretative notes on each citation.

As has already been pointed out, the problems of ageing are of related interest. We will not examine here the philosophical arguments which suggest that from the moment of birth we enter upon a track which can only lead downhill to the loss of all the functions provided for us by nature or acquired by nurture; instead we point out that gerontology is closely related to the same psychological theories and experiments that underlie the study of children. N. W. Shock compiled in 1951 *A classified bibliography of gerontology and geriatrics*, which is a most important source of references to the literature on this topic. It has been updated in 1957 and 1963 but there is apparently no index to the more recent literature on gerontology.

Social psychology

Though there is no paucity of renowned scholars who have made social psychology into a highly respectable field of psychology, there are remarkably few good guides to its literature; yet it has benefited from the influence of several of the great schools of psychology already mentioned. One of the possible reasons for the lack of bibliographic coverage may well be the fact that social psychology is a very large field, on the borders of which many related fields of study such as sociology and anthropology have exerted considerable influence.

The whole subject of social psychology has been reviewed, discussed and explained in Lindzey & Aronson's *The handbook of social psychology*, the second edition of which appeared in five volumes in 1969. It contains, of course, also a large bibliography after each of the chapters. The series of annual volumes entitled *Advances in experimental social psychology* has provided, between 1964 and 1977, a survey of research and scholarship in this field, together with copious references to the literature.

The literature of narrow aspects of social psychology has been surveyed in more detail, such as the structure and operation of small groups on which topic we find A. P. Hare's *Handbook of small group research*; the 2nd edition, 1976, includes the author's earlier bibliographic works on the same subject.

On group behaviour in general, H. Voos has compiled a selective list of references for the years 1956–1966: *Organizational communication: a bibliography*, 1967. More up to date are R. M. Carter's *Communication in organizations*, 1972 and D. E. Morrison & K. E. Hornback's *Collective behavior: a bibliography*, 1976. The last mentioned has a noticeable political emphasis—it tries to illustrate the attempts by the powerless to acquire power—but most of the citations refer to scientific works; there are no annotations.

On the topic of leadership, R. M. Stodgill has compiled both a handbook and a literature survey entitled *Leadership: abstracts and bibliography*. The work covers the period 1904–74; most citations are accompanied by an abstract.

Though there exist a number of older bibliographies, notably from the 1950s, we have omitted reference to them because the later works cited above have wholly superseded them.

As for works on group therapy, we have included them under the section of psychiatry and mental health.

Psychiatry and mental health

Psychiatry is the realm in which medical science and psychology join to provide help for persons whose mind (as one says) is disturbed and whose behaviour does not conform to accepted social patterns. Psychopathology and clinical psychology are integral sub-fields of this branch of medical psychology which, of necessity, also includes neurology, mental deficiency or retardation, forensic psychology, certain aspects of abnormal psychology, social psychology and psychotherapy.

Mental illness has been recognized as such since the days of Aristotle and Hippocrates, and its long modern history has been ably described by Hunter & Macalpine in *Three hundred years of psychiatry, 1535–1860*, and by Alexander & Selesnick in *The history of psychiatry*.

A guide to the terminology of psychiatry has been compiled by Hinsie & Campbell in their *Psychiatric dictionary*, which has been last revised in 1970. Theirs is an encyclopaedic treatment and though now over ten years old, is still a basic and useful aid for students. A helpful companion volume to this book is Bette Greenberg's *How to find out in psychiatry: a guide to sources of mental health information* which appeared in 1978. Structured on similar lines it presents in essay form the important general references to this special field. By contrast, H. Leland & M. W. Deutsch's *Abnormal behavior, a guide to information sources*, 1980, is an annotated bibliography which, though centred on general abnormal psychology, contains many references to works of interest to psychiatrists and mental health workers.

A historical survey of the literature on mental illness has been compiled by M. D. Altschule in 1976 under the title *The development of traditional psychopathology, a sourcebook*. There are bibliographic footnotes, but the book is primarily a collection of excerpts from leading psychiatrists from Hippocrates to the twentieth century.

The monograph literature of this field of psychology is well served bibliographically by the *Mental health book review index* which began in 1956 and has been continued in 1975 under the title of *Chicorel index to mental health book reviews*. The index appears annually and "lists references to signed book reviews appearing in three or more . . . journals". The list of journals has been greatly extended since Merietta Chicorel assumed the editorship in 1976. The *Chicorel index* includes mental health, psychiatry and psychoanalysis.

K. Menninger's *A guide to psychiatric books in English* has for a long time enjoyed a high reputation as a comprehensive and well-ordered bibliography of that subject. The 3rd edition appeared in 1972 but like so many works of this kind it needs constant updating. Entries are arranged under broad headings, but there are no annotations. Better in that respect at least is the *Guide to the literature in psychiatry* by B. Ennis. Issued in 1971, it is rather selective, emphasizing the more important titles, and offering useful notes on the characteristics of the literature types discussed: journal literature, information sources (dictionaries, encyclopaedias, directories, surveys, etc.) textbooks, non-book materials, government documents, etc.

There exist several current awareness services for psychiatrists and medical practitioners interested in mental health. The most important ones are the *Cumulated index medicus* (see also p. 49) and *Excerpta medica*, both of which contain a special section on neurology and psychiatry. The special sections in *Excerpta medica* may be subscribed to separately. Strangely, there is no specialist English indexing service for psychiatry but the traditionally strong German interest in this field has ensured the continuation of the famous *Zentralblatt für die gesamte Neurologie und Psychiatrie*—albeit through mergers and with some minor title changes— which has provided abstracts of the current literature on psychiatry, neurology and psychopathology since 1878. This famous German journal covers the European contribution particularly well, and for the literature in English there is of course always *Psychological abstracts* which certainly cites the major articles in this field.

Two bibliographies on psychotherapy cover an overlapping period of writing but are based on totally different approaches to the topic. One is W. R. Morrow's *Behavior therapy bibliography, 1950–1969* which is arranged alphabetically by author but contains eight indexes which allow retrieval under experimental design, therapy, setting variables, subject's diagnosis and age, target behaviour, modification procedure, use of positive reinforcement by type of reinforcer, use of aversive conditioning, and use of systematic desensitization by manner of presentation of fear stimuli. Each entry is annotated by means of abbreviated code numbers. I. D. Glick and J. Haley's *Family therapy and research* is an annotated bibliography of articles and books published between 1950 and 1970. Entries are arranged in broad categories related to various ways in which families are wholly or in part involved in psychotherapy.

The treatment of mental diseases through group psychotherapy has a long history but the literature on this subject is not nearly as old. R. J. Corsini & L. J. Putzey have provided an overview of it for the first half of this century: *Bibliography of group psychotherapy* (1957), which comprises 1747 entries for books, journal articles and theses. There are also many references to research reports, most of which, however, belong to the 1950s. A sequel was produced by B. & A. W. Lubin: *Group therapy: a bibliography of the literature from 1956 through 1964*. D. G. Zimpfer brought the survey up to 1976 in his *Group work in the helping professions*.

The growth in the literature on community mental health has of course been commensurate with the incidence of mental illness as it is seen to affect the social environment. E. D. Driver's *The sociology and anthropology of mental illness* is a guide to that literature with a special view towards the needs of social scientists and the health professions. The work is international in scope and the 2nd edition lists almost 6000 entries. Though the arrangement is classified under broad headings there are no annotations.

The current literature on abnormal, clinical and pathological psychology has not been covered well by bibliographic surveys. F. G. Alexander and S. T. Selesnick's *History of psychiatry* (1966) contains a selective bibliography only in an otherwise helpful presentation of the development of this branch of medical psychology. *A bibliography of world literature on mental retardation: January 1940–[December 1964]* appeared in 1963 and 1966, and though it covers contributions to this topic from many countries, it now needs updating because of the progress made in the treatment of the mentally retarded. J. Hankin & J. S. Oktay's *Mental disorder and primary medical care*, 1979, covers the recent literature from 1959 to 1975. The 354 entries are classified into three major groups: identification of morbidity, utilization of health services, management of patients. There are annotations and indexes. This is a useful listing which, furthermore, draws attention to the differences in health services in the USA, the UK and several other European systems of providing care for the mentally ill.

Concerned with the styles and strategies humans use to cope with their emotional and nervous stress situations, G. V. Coelho & R. I. Irving have edited under the title *Coping and adaptation* almost 1000 references to the literature on these topics, and have paid particular attention to those contributions which lead to the relief of pain and anxiety. The references are arranged according to the compilers' own classification scheme ranging from theoretical contributions to developmental issues; biological, social and psychological determinants; real-life situations; treatment; and techniques of research. Each entry is bibliographically defined and accompanied by an abstract.

Those wishing to conduct a literature search in the field of psychiatry and mental health will therefore have to rely on *Index medicus*, *Excerpta medica*, *Psychological abstracts* or the very specialized *Psychopharmacol-*

ogy abstracts, either in their book form or through a computer-based retrieval service.

The literature on the problems of refitting damaged human beings into society has been covered, in part, by Riviere's *Rehabilitation of the handicapped: a bibliography, 1940–1946*, which lists 5000 references to this related field of abnormal psychology and forms a good starting-point for investigations on this subject. Graham & Mullen's *Rehabilitation literature 1950–1955*, issued in 1956, brings the bibliography more up to date, but unfortunately there has been no further listing of references in this area.

Suicide can perhaps be considered the psychotherapy that failed, and its incidence is growing in numbers. Somewhat out of date by now is A. E. Prentice's *Suicide: a selective bibliography of over 2,200 items*, 1974, which covers the literature from 1960 to 1973. There is an index to subjects (e.g. absconding, accidental death, Africa, aged, alcohol) but there are no annotations in this rather limited exercise. A better retrospective survey of the literature on suicide is N. L. Farberow's *Bibliography on suicide and suicide prevention 1897–1957, 1958–1967*. It includes references to monographs and journal articles in several languages and covers biological, medical, psychological and social features of suicide.

Death has, of course, always had a great fascination for man. The final demarcation line between an active body and an inactive body has since the beginning of time puzzled those who were able to observe the sudden change. Its incomprehensibility as a natural phenomenon has prompted man to vest it with taboos; it is claimed by some that all religions sprang from the awareness of that change. Besides the extensive volume of literature concerned with the philosophical and religious significance of death, psychologists, physicians and nurses have contributed to the literature on thanatology (the study of the dying) and the best means of helping those who are about to have to face that ultimate moment. There exist two very respectable bibliographies of that literature. One is by M. A. Simpson, whose *Dying death and grief,* in its 4th edition in 1979, lists over 700 books and 200 films, each very sensibly and sensitively annotated. This is the type of annotated bibliography we all admire: simple evaluations, clear and decisive.

A. J. Miller and M. J. Acri compiled a similar work in 1977: *Death: a bibliographical guide* with 3848 references to books, journal articles and audiovisual materials. The compilers claim that theirs is a comprehensive listing of the literature on death from ancient beginnings to 1974, and that claim is probably correct, though to check it one would have to examine every reference since the index leaves much to be desired. Many entries are annotated but, compared with the more modest and relevant compilation by Simpson, Miller & Acri's effort is, sadly, a kind of overkill. The inclusion of the following short note from the well-known journal *Science* leads one to believe that comprehensiveness may have been achieved at the expense of judicious selectivity; the article in question is entitled: "Fighting and death from stress in a cockroach". We must hope that it has some significance for someone.

Forensic psychology and criminology

The study of abnormal behaviour often leads to special investigations into the origins or causes of crime. This in turn will lead to the psychological study of criminals and also of the victims of crime. The literature on this topic is growing and there exist now a number of useful indexing services to help with the retrieval of particular contributions from many countries. While most of these indexes and abstracts are orientated towards the work of, and happenings in, the courts, all of them contain references to the behaviour of criminals or social deviants.

Criminology and penology abstracts has been in existence since 1960; its abstracts are arranged under broad subject headings which include psychology, psychopathology, psychiatry, social behaviour of groups—all of which are of course of interest to users of this book. *Criminology and penology abstracts* is published six times a year in the Netherlands and has an international coverage. All abstracts are in English.

The National Council on Crime and Delinquency (USA) issues a quarterly literature survey *Criminal justice abstracts* which absorbed the *Crime and delinquency abstracts* issued from 1964 to 1972 by the National Clearing House for Mental Health Information. Each issue contains an in-depth analysis of the current literature on a certain topic, with worldwide coverage and an analysis and synthesis of findings. A large number of topics include an assessment of the psychological aspects of the delinquents involved in the particular asocial situations discussed.

To date the *Annual review of psychology* has reviewed the topic twice, in 1977 and in 1982. Both surveys are replete with bibliographical references.

The Australian Institute of Criminology, Canberra, has produced since 1974 an *Information bulletin of Australian criminology* which indexes the Australian literature on crime, penology and selected subjects. The bulletin includes abstracts of current research projects and of recently completed research. There is a subject index which strongly reflects the legal preoccupations of the Institute as distinct from the more societal-related abstracting services noted above.

Psychology, religion and phenomenology

The long traditional links between religion and psychology go back to classical antiquity. They received much impetus in the middle ages and again during the many periods of religious and political fervour that stirred Europe during the past six centuries, reaching various climactic peaks through seers, visionaries and martyrs. Every one of these advocated social reforms on earth to attain a new heaven, or threatened new hells should the reforms not be adopted. All were persecuted by the established religious or political power, or both; then as now, the defenders of the status quo almost invariably accused the challengers of being madmen or psychopaths. It is all a matter of firmly held beliefs uttered from pulpits, chancery balconies and soap boxes as well as printed in broadsides, pamphlets, or large books, or smeared on the walls of houses with a wide brush. Of particular interest to us is a bibliography of the more recent contributions, about 300 of them during the last hundred years, compiled by W. W. Meissner in 1961: *Annotated bibliography in religion and psychology*.

Phenomenology, by contrast, cannot be said to have "links" with psychology and psychiatry but, as Herbert Spiegelberg has phrased it, phenomenology has infiltrated all fields of psychology (and much else) because it asks fundamental questions about relationships. It does so by means of a systematic process, a phenomenological methodology. Its most influential figure was the German philosopher E. Husserl. There exists no separately published bibliography of phenomenology, but Spiegelberg's *The phenomenological movement* (1965) and in particular his *Phenomenology in psychology and psychiatry,* 1972, contain very extensive literature surveys embodied in the text and as appendices. G. Thinès also added a fourteen-page bibliography to his historical survey published in 1977: *Phenomenology and the science of behaviour.*

Applied psychology

For some strange reason the term "applied psychology" has crept into the professional terminology in the twenties and thirties. It was to signify, presumably, that those who practised it were getting away from, or were unconcerned with, the theoretical aspects of this discipline though Hugo Muensterberg used the current term as early as 1913 in his book *Psychology and industrial efficiency.* After World War II it has been used less and less, and has now been largely replaced by "industrial psychology", "vocational psychology" and "organizational psychology" which certainly describe more adequately what this branch of the discipline is about. M. D. Dunnette's *Handbook of industrial and organizational psychology,* 1976, contains many bibliographic references in an attempt to present a solid overview of the substance of this domain where experimental, behavioural and social psychology meet.

Those working in this field will find the older literature also partly covered in D. H. Fryer & E. R. Henry's *Handbook of applied psychology,* 1950. J. G. Marshall & R. C. S. Trahair listed the older Australian contributions to this topic in their annotated bibliography of almost 1600 items, *Industrial psychology in Australia to 1950,* which appeared in 1981.

Those specially interested in military psychology—which is of course one particular aspect of applied psychology—should search through the

Monthly catalog of United States government publications (see p. 35, because the US Army and other services, and the Department of Health, Education and Welfare, have promoted the publication of several bibliographies on this aspect of industrial psychology. To cite but one example, there exists a *Bibliography of military psychiatry, 1952–1958* compiled by C. Roos & J. Barry in 1959 which continues an earlier survey for the years 1947–52.

Parapsychology

This subject is not part of the run-of-the-mill university courses in psychology, but some institutions have taken it seriously and there are genuine scholars involved in examining phenomena which cannot be readily classified as falling within the realms of physics or of experimental psychology. Excessive claims and proven hoaxes have not helped to establish research into psychic phenomena as a genuine scientific activity. R. A. White & L. A. Dale compiled a survey of the literature on this topic under the auspices of the American Society for Psychical Research. Their *Parapsychology: sources of information* is a well-organized list of relevant books and periodicals. (It is not an index to the contents of these periodicals.) There is also a chapter entitled "Scientific recognition of parapsychology", a glossary of terms and several indexes.

At a more fundamental level, the beliefs of early men form part of this same subject, even though anthropologists will claim to have a pre-emptive right to the study of primitive religions. It would lead too far to open up here the close and fertile link between psychology and anthropology. We therefore cite merely as an example. I. I. Zaretsky & C. Shambaugh's literature survey of this allied field: *Spirit possession and spirit mediumship in Africa and Afro-America,* 1978. The compilers have listed over 2000 references, very many of which belong quite obviously to the realm of psychology. Several indexes allow access to the alphabetically arranged author entries under location, religion, language and other important criteria.

CHAPTER 7

Preparations for Research

1. Framing the question

The purpose of this chapter is to identify two fundamental steps which must be fully understood before any research strategy can be developed. The mastery of the techniques involved is in fact a common prerequisite for research in any discipline, but in dealing with the topic here, we have of course drawn examples from the fields of psychology.

It is very plain that no research venture will succeed until a great deal of trouble is taken in framing the question. It is improbable in the extreme that a satisfactory answer will result from a question that has not been carefully thought out. It may help when framing the question to imagine a target reader to be the kind of person that one might encounter as an examiner, and the kind of questions that they would ask: what exactly do you want to know? For what purpose do you want to know it? Is the question a multiple or complex one? What is the most economical way of going about finding out about the question. Who or what may help? To what particular ends? It is assumed that behind each question there is some point that needs to be answered because it satisfies a need of either practical or theoretical importance.

A great deal has been written about the origins of questions, and some of the more circumscribed views entertained among scientists hold that questions are derived from already formulated and demonstrated hypotheses, a technique known as the hypothetico-deductive method; they may also be derived by the generalization of propositions derived from particular cases. We entertain the heretical view that the origin of questions is of no importance. They may be derived by the hypothetico-deductive method, they may result from an alcohol-lubricated conversation at a nearby hostelry, or may be a divine communication from the Archangel Gabriel. What does matter, and is indeed crucial, is that these questions should be testable, the hypothetical form of it potentially falsifiable, and framed for some identifiable reason.

A good deal depends, of course, on the student's or investigator's frame of reference. Wide experience in human relationships will help to see issues which may be worthy of investigation and the researcher's degree of maturity will determine the choice of topic that might lead to the identification of testable questions. It is of course not suggested that hoary old age is a prerequisite for that desirable degree of maturity. Much can be learned from the experience of others and the role of literary works is of special significance in this context. D. Rose & J. Radford make this point very well in their note on the value of the "conveniently packaged 'social world' " that exists in many novels.* The same point was made a century ago by Sir William Osler when pointing out to his students that since they cannot live long enough to get acquainted with all social types, they would do well to take a short cut by reading all of Dickens's novels.

In some instances the kind of question that is being asked, and the kind of answer that is being sought, may be in breach of codes of ethics or codes of professional conduct, and investigators should be aware that ethical considerations may be an intrinsic feature of some questions.

If the question that is being framed is an empirical research question, one also needs to plan strategic considerations such as whether one will use the cross-sectional or longitudinal approach. Cross-sectional strategies depend on variable data being observed at one point in time; longitudinal approaches require one set of data being observed over a period of time. The advantages of cross-sectional studies are that experiments are readily repeatable, that they help to avoid the subjects regarding themselves as being special or select cases and thus producing practice-effects through constant retesting, that the "drop-out" rate is minimized, and that social changes and events are less likely to intervene and make the experimental conclusions ambiguous. In fact cross-sectional studies are cheaper than longitudinal studies. Longitudinal studies, by contrast, consist of repeated examinations of identical subjects or subject groups over a carefully designed time scale. This approach offers quite specific advantages over cross-sectional studies.

Other considerations which will affect the formulation of an empirical research question are whether one wants to use *ex post facto* designs or prospective studies. *Ex post facto* designs or strategies hinge on the notion that certain matters can be, or ought to be, taken for granted or as having been examined previously, and *ex post facto* designs may well be conceived as longitudinal studies, since they are capable of being resolved within a short space of time because the previous data are already available on record. Other design features may include whether the study uses the case method; whether subjects within the study act as their own "controls"; whether a counterbalanced order is used to control serial effects; and what sample size is sought, bearing in mind statistical and logistic considerations.

A carefully framed question will, in the empirical realm, be designed to test a hypothesis. Since a scientific hypothesis is a statement of the relationship between two variables, the design of the experiment should be

---

*Rose, D. & Radford, J. (1981). "The use of literature in teaching psychology", *Bulletin of the British Psychological Society*, **34**, 453–455.

an attempt to illustrate and prove the firmness of that relationship. Some of the neatest designs are critically evaluative of hypotheses and are therefore often referred to as *experimentum crucis*. In other words these experiments are critical for the purpose of choosing between rival hypotheses. The concept of an *experimentum crucis* may be illustrated by the popular notion of "birth signs". Let us suppose that there is an apparent relationship between "birth sign" and being "distinguished" in a particular career or calling. One could imagine that a simple explanation is that it has something to do with the season of birth but of course, if the birth sign hypothesis were tenable, then one would expect disjunctions within the season so that, for example, the months of May and June are adjacent in season but have different birth signs. The *experimentum crucis* would be to use a design which tests distinguished people chosen, say, from *Who's who* but compares them on country basis by selecting some from the northern hemisphere and others from the southern hemisphere, say, Canada and Australia. It would become obvious that the birth sign has not changed but that the seasons are inverted and therefore the design permits one to draw conclusions as to the relative explanatory powers of season versus "birth sign". Once the question has been adequately and appropriately defined, the next step in any research method is to ascertain what work in general, and what experiments in particular, have already been written up on the same topic. In order to execute that aspect of the research programme we must make sure that the terms used in our questions conforms as much as possible with the thesaurus of the discipline to which we referred at some length in chapter 5.

For the purpose of this book we distinguish between questions which are given (be it by an instructor or by a client) and those which are self-generated. If the question is framed by someone with expertise then there is a presumption that the question is of a level appropriate to the student and that it is solvable; if the question has arisen out of a broader framework, e.g. a consultancy, the earlier comments will be relevant about reducing it to manageable proportions (e.g. by splitting it up into component parts) and expressing it in an appropriate terminology. If the question is self-generated a wider judgement, and possibly advice from experienced practitioners, may be called for.

For those with a need to choose a topic for themselves there are a number of sources, which will offer a wide range of suggestions; these include first of all the professional journals such as the *Annual review of psychology* and *Psychology today*. Next, students are advised to keep notebooks to record problems, ideas, comments from teachers; to talk to fellow-students, or maybe to sit still and watch the world around them with an alert eye seeking explanations and interpretations. Should there be a number of options and the problem is one of choice, then it is appropriate to consider whether the topic is sufficiently interesting, whether it is of the appropriate size, and whether one can have a non-partisan view of it.

In summary then, the issue of the question is one where consideration is given to the purpose one is trying to achieve. If one is not clear about the question then it is highly improbable that a suitable search can be conducted.

Lastly it is worth distinguishing between two general categories of questions. The first is known as the convergent type which seeks an answer to some specific detail. A convergent question allows us or presumes that we proceed from the general to the particular, e.g. in perception, what does the Purkinje phenomenon refer to?

The second kind of question is known as the divergent type and is concerned with the expansion of a concept or an idea, with the need to diverge. An example would be the quests for an estimate of some effects on psychopathology if personality characteristics were to be more homogeneous within the community.

Having carefully prepared our question, the next step in any research programme is to find out whether the same question has not already been answered in some research report or journal article, or even in a text book, or whether a closely related topic has been treated by some other investigator and reported in the literature. This aspect of the research methodology is known as the literature search. It is conducted in libraries and the next section of this chapter explains the procedures involved.

2. Literature Searches

While it is useful and economical to be aware of the principles underlying the execution of a thorough literature search, the actual performance is an art rather than a science.

One might draw a parallel with painting. In that art form it is important to know something about perception, about the qualities of canvas and of pigments; what cannot be conveyed scientifically is an instruction on how to produce a masterpiece. So it is with information searching. One may know how to use catalogues, what the principles of the Dewey Decimal Classification are, and have a general idea of information sources. That, however, will not necessarily result in a splendid outcome. Like art, one must know the basics and then practise. With such practice the results will range from the recognizable to the superb; without such practice the results will most likely be lamentable.

In this section the main aim is to present, as a point of departure, some of the principles underlying a library search. From this base students can move on to develop their own insights into information research, which grandiose term is mostly a synonym for an intensive literature search in a specific discipline.

We have already intimated that literature searches are normally conducted in libraries—and the larger the library the greater the chance of such a search being successfully exhaustive. By "large" we mean of course richer in bibliographic resources, i.e. the more volumes and serials there are in our own discipline the better it is. A large library collection in the fields of psychology would contain thousands of monographs (the technical term for books) and at least a hundred or more of the most used journals (see chapter 3). Quite obviously, a large collection must be organized in some way and librarians have devised a variety of classification systems to arrange books and journals in such an order on the shelves that library users find books on the same topic filed side by side. In most libraries journals form a separate sequence. Since most research libraries contain books on many disciplines, it behoves us to examine very briefly where books and periodicals on psychology fit into the general scheme of the order of knowledge as perceived by librarians.

The most widely used systems of library classification are Dewey Decimal Classification (DDC) and the Library of Congress Classification (LC). Both are well over a hundred years old and reflect an approach to the categorization and organization of knowledge which is no longer altogether appropriate to the end of the twentieth century. The development of the pure and applied sciences, the impact of social theories and the demotion of religion as a prime motivating force among western societies have greatly changed the relationship between many disciplines. Nevertheless, the two systems continue to be used in libraries, perhaps mainly because to change to some other system is a very costly proposition.

The DDC is not without a philosophical infrastructure; we have attempted to show this in a diagram (Fig. 11) which offers a schematic view of Melvil Dewey's taxonomy of human knowledge. The diagram shows how disciplines are classified, and the numbers that are used to identify broad areas of knowledge. It will be noted that psychology is classified as an extension of philosophy; a feature that reflects both its origin and its recency as an independent discipline. Readers will appreciate that no value judgement should attach to the Dewey number that is assigned. Convention has decreed where a reference is located and the important thing is to know *where* to find the references that one is seeking.

The one caveat that should be entered is that some works seek to link areas of knowledge or disciplines. In that event library cataloguers will assign the work to the area that they see as most appropriate. Searchers should simply be aware that works which link psychology and something else may be assigned to the something else category rather than to the psychology class.

A synopsis of the DDC is shown in Figs 12a and 12b. The three summaries reflect the decimal character of the system; artificial as it is, it is simple and the structure of relationships is clearly evident. The first of the three digits has been used to mark off from each other large classes of disciplines (the first summary). The second digit of each three-digit class

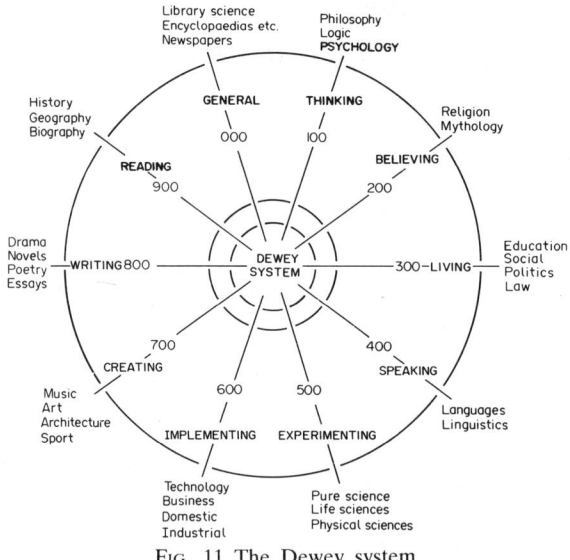

FIG. 11 The Dewey system

First Summary
The 10 Main Classes

000 Generalities

100 Philosophy & related disciplines

200 Religion

300 Social sciences

400 Language

500 Pure sciences

600 Technology (Applied sciences)

700 The arts

800 Literature (Belles-lettres)

900 General geography & history

FIG. 12a. The DDC system: first summary

Preparations for Research

Third Summary *
The 1000 Sections

Generalities

000	**Generalities**	050	**General serial publications**
001	Knowledge	051	American
002	The book	052	Others in English
003	Systems	053	In other Germanic languages
004		054	In French, Provençal, Catalan
005		055	In Italian, Romanian, Rhaeto-Romanic
006		056	In Spanish & Portuguese
007		057	In Slavic languages
008		058	In Scandinavian languages
009		059	In other languages
010	**Bibliography**	060	**General organizations & museology**
011	Bibliographies	061	In North America
012	Of individuals	062	In British Isles
013	Of works by specific classes of writers	063	In central Europe
014	Of anonymous & pseudonymous works	064	In France & Monaco
015	Of works from specific places	065	In Italy & adjacent territories
016	Subject bibliographies & catalogs	066	In Iberian Peninsula & adjacent islands
017	General subject catalogs	067	In eastern Europe
018	Author & date catalogs	068	In other areas
019	Dictionary catalogs	069	Museology (Museum science)
020	**Library & information sciences**	070	**Journalism, publishing, newspapers**
021	Library relationships	071	In North America
022	Physical plant	072	In British Isles
023	Personnel & positions	073	In central Europe
024		074	In France & Monaco
025	Library operations	075	In Italy & adjacent territories
026	Libraries for specific subjects	076	In Iberian Peninsula & adjacent islands
027	General libraries	077	In eastern Europe
028	Reading & use of information media	078	In Scandinavia
029		079	In other areas
030	**General encyclopedic works**	080	**General collections**
031	American	081	American
032	Others in English	082	Others in English
033	In other Germanic languages	083	In other Germanic languages
034	In French, Provençal, Catalan	084	In French, Provençal, Catalan
035	In Italian, Romanian, Rhaeto-Romanic	085	In Italian, Romanian, Rhaeto-Romanic
036	In Spanish & Portuguese	086	In Spanish & Portuguese
037	In Slavic languages	087	In Slavic languages
038	In Scandinavian languages	088	In Scandinavian languages
039	In other languages	089	In other languages
040		090	**Manuscripts & book rarities**
041		091	Manuscripts
042		092	Block books
043		093	Incunabula
044		094	Printed books
045		095	Books notable for bindings
046		096	Notable illustrations & materials
047		097	Notable ownership or origin
048		098	Works notable for content
049		099	Books notable for format

* Consult schedules for complete and exact headings

473

FIG. 12b. The DDC system: third summary

Dewey Decimal Classification

Philosophy and related disciplines

100	**Philosophy & related disciplines**	150	**Psychology**
101	Theory of philosophy	151	
102	Miscellany of philosophy	152	Physiological psychology
103	Dictionaries of philosophy	153	Intelligence & intellect
104		154	Subconscious states & processes
105	Serials on philosophy	155	Differential & genetic psychology
106	Organizations of philosophy	156	Comparative psychology
107	Study & teaching of philosophy	157	Abnormal & clinical psychologies
108	Treatment among groups of persons	158	Applied psychology
109	Historical treatment of philosophy	159	Other aspects
110	**Metaphysics**	160	**Logic**
111	Ontology	161	Induction
112		162	Deduction
113	Cosmology	163	
114	Space	164	
115	Time	165	Fallacies & sources of error
116	Evolution	166	Syllogisms
117	Structure	167	Hypotheses
118	Force & energy	168	Argument & persuasion
119	Number & quantity	169	Analogy
120	**Epistemology, causation, humankind**	170	**Ethics (Moral philosophy)**
121	Epistemology	171	Systems & doctrines
122	Causation	172	Political ethics
123	Determinism & indeterminism	173	Ethics of family relationships
124	Teleology	174	Professional & occupational ethics
125		175	Ethics of recreation & leisure
126	The self	176	Ethics of sex & reproduction
127	The unconscious & the subconscious	177	Ethics of social relations
128	Humankind	178	Ethics of consumption
129	Origin & destiny of individual souls	179	Other ethical norms
130	**Paranormal phenomena & arts**	180	**Ancient, medieval, Oriental philosophy**
131	Well-being, happiness, success	181	Oriental
132		182	Pre-Socratic Greek
133	Parapsychology & occultism	183	Sophistic, Socratic & related Greek
134		184	Platonic
135	Dreams & mysteries	185	Aristotelian
136		186	Skeptic & Neoplatonic
137	Analytic & divinatory graphology	187	Epicurean
138	Physiognomy	188	Stoic
139	Phrenology	189	Medieval Western
140	**Specific philosophical viewpoints**	190	**Modern Western philosophy**
141	Idealism & related systems & doctrines	191	United States & Canada
142	Critical philosophy	192	British Isles
143	Intuitionism & Bergsonism	193	Germany & Austria
144	Humanism & related systems	194	France
145	Sensationalism & ideology	195	Italy
146	Naturalism & related systems	196	Spain & Portugal
147	Pantheism & related systems	197	Russia & Finland
148	Liberalism & other systems	198	Scandinavia
149	Other systems & doctrines	199	Other geographical areas

474

FIG. 12b (Cont.). The DDC system: third summary

shows a division of the large classes of disciplines into narrower, more precise fields: 150—psychology; 370—education; 820—English literature. The third summary shows how the third digit in the three-digit system separates more carefully and in detail one relatively narrow area of knowledge from another. To avoid too much detail we have restricted the illustration to the fields of Generalities, which includes reference works and encyclopaedias (010 and 030) divided according to their scope or language, and to the class 100—Philosophy and its subdivisions related to psychology. If this collocation of subjects arouses curiosity, readers should note that the DDC was first published in 1876, at a time when philosophy and psychology were still treated as one discipline—albeit with two heads—in most universities (see Chapter 1). Since then, many refinements and adjustments have been made to the DDC schedules, but the first and second summaries have never been substantially altered.

It is a particular characteristic of the DDC that almost every three-digit class can be further subdivided by the addition of a point and further digits, e.g. 150.1 or 150.0994 which, though it has to conform to rules and conventions, allows for a very fine classification system. Three examples shown in Fig. 12c will suffice to illustrate this point.

(1) 152 — Physiological Psychology
152.16 — Chemical Sensory Perception
152.167 — Gustatory Perception

    152.167   KARE, M. R. ed.
Physiological and behavioral aspects of taste, edited by Morley R. Kare and Bruce P. Halpern. Contributors: Robert B. MacLeod and others. Chicago, University of Chicago Press, 1961

(2) 153 — Intelligence, Intellectual and Conscious Mental Processes
153.94 — Aptitude Tests
153.9478 — Tests for Musical Ability (NB: 780 — Music)

    153.9478   BENTLEY, A
Musical ability in children and its measurement. London, Harrap, 1966

(3) 155 — Differential and Genetic Psychology
155.4 — Child Psychology
155.40994 — Child psychology in Australia
(NB: 994 — Australia)

    155.40994   CAMPBELL, W. J.
Growing up in Karribee; a study of child growth and development in an Australian rural community, by W. J. Campbell assisted by Jan Davies. Melbourne, Australian Council for Educational Research, 1963

FIG. 12c. Expansion of DDC classification numbers: three examples

LIBRARY OF CONGRESS CLASSIFICATION SCHEDULES

A	General Works
B–BJ	Philosophy. Psychology
BL–BX	Religion
C	Auxiliary Sciences of History
D	History: General and Old World (Eastern Hemisphere)
E–F	History: America (Western Hemisphere)
G	Geography. Maps. Anthropology. Recreation
H	Social Sciences
J	Political Science
K	Law (General)
KD	Law of the United Kingdom and Ireland
KE	Law of Canada
KF	Law of the United States
L	Education
M	Music
N	Fine Arts
P–PA	General Philology and Linguistics. Classical Languages and Literatures
PA Supplement	Byzantine and Modern Greek Literature. Medieval and Modern Latin Literature
PB–PH	Modern European Languages
PG	Russian Literature
PJ–PM	Languages and Literatures of Asia, Africa, Oceania, American Indian Languages. Artificial Languages
P–PM Supplement	Index to Languages and Dialects
PN, PR, PS, PZ	General Literature. English and American Literature. Fiction in English. Juvenile belles lettres
PQ, Part 1	French Literature
PQ, Part 2	Italian, Spanish, and Portuguese Literatures
PT, Part 1	German Literature
PT, Part 2	Dutch and Scandinavian Literatures
Q	Science
R	Medicine
S	Agriculture
T	Technology
U	Military Science
V	Naval Science
Z	Bibliography. Library Science

FIG. 13a. Library of Congress classification schedules

B
PHILOSOPHY—RELIGION

	Philosophy
B	Collections. History. Systems
BC	Logic
BD	Metaphysics

      10– 41   Introductions to philosophy
      100–131   General works
      150–241   Epistemology. Theory of knowledge
      300–444   Ontology
      493–708   Cosmology. Teleology

BF	Psychology

      1001–1999 Metapsychology. Psychic research. Occult sciences

BH	Esthetics
BJ	Ethics

      1–1531   General works, history, systems, etc.
      1545–1725 Practical and applied ethics. Conduct of life, etc.
      1801–2193 Manners. Etiquette. Social usages

	Religion. Theology
BL	Religions. Mythology. Free thought
BM	Judaism
BP	Mohammedanism. Bahaism. Theosophy
	Christianity
BR	Generalities. Church history
BS	Bible and Exegesis
BT	Doctrinal theology. Apologetics
BV	Practical theology

        5– 525   Worship (public and private)
        590–3799 Ecclesiastical theology. The church
        1460–1615   Religious education
        2000–3705   Missions
        4000–4470   Pastoral theology
        4490–5099   Practical religion. The Christian life

BX	Special sects

      1–9   Church unity. Interdenominational cooperation

FIG. 13b. Library of Congress classification schedules

BF		PSYCHOLOGY	BF
		Early works through 1850	
110		Latin	
111-118		Other 1/	
		1851-	
121-128		General works, treatises, and advanced textbooks 1/	
131-138		Handbooks, manuals, etc. 1/	
139		Elementary textbooks	
141		Outlines, syllabi, etc.	
145		Popular works	
		Cf. BF638+, New thought	
149		Addresses, essays, lectures	
	.5	Juvenile works	
	.8	Facetiae, satire, etc.	
		Mind and body	
		General works	
150-158		Early works through 1850 1/	
161-168		1851- 1/	
171		Addresses, essays, lectures	
172		Alexander technique	
		Psychoanalysis	
		Class psychoanalytical studies of individual persons with biography of person concerned	
		Cf. BF315, Subconsciousness	
		RC500+, Psychiatry	
		RJ504.2, Child analysis	
		For psychoanalysis applied to childhood, see BF721+	
173.A2A-Z		Periodicals. Societies. Serials	
.A3-Z		General works	
175		General special	
176		Psychological tests and testing	
		Cf. BF431+, Intelligence testing	
		BF698.5+, Personality testing	
		LB1131, Education	
		For works on testing a particular aspect of behavior, or group of people, see the aspect or group in classes A - Z	
		Experimental psychology	
		Cf. QP351+, Physiology	
180		Periodicals. Societies. Serials	
181-188		General works	
191-198		Elementary textbooks. Outlines, syllabi, etc. 1/	
		Laboratory manuals, see BF79	
199		Behaviorism	
200		Psychological experiments, etc.	
202		Whole and parts (Psychology). "Ganzheit"	
		Cf. BD396, Philosophy	

1/
For subarrangement by language, see Table 6, p. 185

FIG. 13c. Library of Congress classification. Extract of schedules, BF: Psychology

BF   PSYCHOLOGY   BF

	Experimental psychology - Continued
203	Gestalt psychology
	Cf. BF698.8, Personality tests
204	Humanistic psychology
.5	Phenomenological psychology. Existential psychology
205	Special topics, A-Z
	.F3 Fasting
	.F5 Fire walking
	.H3 Hand
	Cf. BF698.8.H3, Hand test
	.M6 Motor abilities
	.N6 Noises (Effect)
	.R4 Rest pauses
	.T6 Tobacco smoking
	Cf. HV5725+, Tobacco habit
	QP981.T6, Experimental pharmacology
	.T8 Typewriting
	Psychotropic drugs
	Cf. QP901+, Physiological effects
	RC483+, Psychiatric psychopharmacology
	RC566+, Narcotic habit. Drug abuse
	RM315+, Medical psychopharmacology
207	General works
209	Special drugs, A-Z
	.C3 Cannabis. Marihuana. Hashish
	Hashish, see .C3
	.L9 Lysergic acid diethylamide
	Marihuana, see .C3
	.M4 Mescaline
	.T5 Thiazinamium methyl sulphate
210	Electronic behavior control
	Anatomy and physiology of the nervous system, see QP361+; RC360+
	Sensation. Aesthesiology
	For physiological discussions, see QP431+
	General works
231	Early works through 1800
233	1801-
237	Psychophysics
	Including Weber's and Fechner's law, etc.
	Cf. QP360, Physiology

FIG. 13c (Cont.). Library of Congress classification. Extract of schedules, BF: Psychology

The LC classification is quite differently constructed and based on a different premise. Though widely used in North America, Australia, New Zealand and South Africa (and indeed also in some non-English-speaking countries) it is a system based on the shelving practice in one very large library which, however, has never been designed for open access to the public at large. The main divisions reflect subject groupings and have, over the years, been adjusted to meet the needs of open-access libraries, so that the collocation of books on the shelves also brings together the printed books and documents related to one narrow discipline or aspect of a discipline. The LC classification is now as rigid a procrustean bed of the organization of knowledge as the DDC—the most severe criticism of both systems, but because it is an alphanumerical classification (i.e. letters plus numbers) it has a large digital base for the main divisions. An outline of the LC classification and of the Division B: Philosophy—Religion which, it will be noted, includes Psychology at BF, are shown in Fig. 13a, and two extracts of the sub-division of class BF: Psychology are shown in Fig. 13b.

Many unkind words could be said about these antediluvian classification schemes which reflect the state of knowledge and of academic research of the nineteenth century rather than the late twentieth. The treatment of psychology is of course not the only instance in which the expansion of knowledge and the shift of interest during the past hundred years is inadequately reflected in the classification systems most commonly used in libraries. This is, however, not the place to examine that problem in detail and students are advised to accept the fact that at best classification schemes will help bring books on like topics together in one set of shelves, more or less. Nevertheless, a study of library classification schemes will well repay the effort; conceived as systems for the classification of knowledge, however imperfect, they provide food for thought and a wider insight into the relationship between disciplines.

Of course, every library has a catalogue of its own monograph and serial holdings. These catalogues, whether in card form or microfiche or, as is no longer uncommon, on-line and to be consulted by means of a visual display unit (v.d.u.), provide access to the library's or the library system's bibliographic resources via three approaches: the author or authors of a book, the title of the book and periodical, and a subject entry for books and for periodicals. Some libraries have listed these approaches in separate files, others have an author and title catalogue with a separate subject catalogue, and some have a separate periodicals catalogue. Occasionally one finds additional separate catalogues for special collections within the whole system, e.g. a separate government documents catalogue. When visiting a library for the first time it is important to find out which of these various combinations have been employed to list the library's holdings. It should be borne in mind that except in some highly specialized libraries, usually small, the contents of library periodicals are not shown in the public catalogues (see also chapter 4). How to use these catalogues, and how to interpret the location marks shown on each entry, is usually explained in some form of guide to the library.

Most academic libraries offer orientation courses for new and advanced students. These courses are usually subject-oriented, and those for third-year and graduate students are designed to help in the retrieval of references to research-related literature surveys. The following notes on systematic literature searches are intended to be complementary to such courses.

Chapter 3 outlines the major sources of reference to the literature on psychology. Here we stress that these works offer answers to the search for the existing literature on the questions formulated in accordance with the precepts outlined at the beginning of this particular chapter. If the question has been appropriately formulated, using the terms recommended in the thesaurus, the search for previous treatments of the same topic will be relatively easy. Appendix A shows four types of inquiries which can be satisfied by using the reference works cited or similar ones referred to in chapter 3.

Students should note, however, that we merely cited one or two reference works for each question as an example. It is not suggested that the reference work cited is the only such work likely to provide the right answer.

Generally speaking the quest for the right word to use in a written paper should not present great difficulties to a university student or anyone who has had a sound secondary education. Acquaintance with the standard dictionaries, e.g. the *OED* in its various sizes, *Webster's universal dictionary* and *Roget's thesaurus* is surely a prerequisite for admission to any course of academic studies. As for foreign-language dictionaries there are many, and students are urged either to test them out themselves, or to seek advice from appropriate scholars. It might be usefully added, however, that specialist foreign dictionaries are all too often weak in their presentation of basic syntactic problems; instead they tend to contain obviously equivalent terms.

People, events and general statistical data are topics which make up a large group of inquiries. We have pointed out some specialist reference works containing answers to such questions in the field of psychology and related disciplines. Academic and research libraries tend to gather in one section, the so-called Reference Area, hundreds of general reference works with which, again, every serious library user should spend some time on becoming acquainted.

CHAPTER 8

Citations and The Card File

1. Reference and citations

We have discussed at some length where to identify the literature relevant to the areas of psychology and how to find it in the academic and research libraries. Having found it, what do we do with it? It is a good rule, for any researcher in any field, to make a note of everything, including the books, journal articles and other sources of data, encountered in one's search. Such notes should of course be set down in such a way that the reference can be found again without having to go through the lengthy process of identification which first brought it to one's notice. There are many ways of doing that but it is strongly recommended, especially for beginners, to adopt a uniform and consistent system of bibliographic description. Furthermore, it is more economic in time and effort if a standard and national or international system is adopted. The argument in favour of such a system is that when the essay, paper or thesis, the report of an investigation and even a book has to be prepared for publication, the references gathered for citation will already be in a form acceptable to the publisher. It is merely a matter of habit to use one system only and conform with it at every step.

There exist a good many acceptable systems, such as the Chicago University Press style manual for citation, or the Modern Languages Association style guide. Because this book addresses itself to psychologists, it is recommended that students of psychology use the style of citation laid down by the APA in their *Publication manual,* the second edition of which appeared in 1974. This APA *Publication manual* sets out in some detail the citation rules accepted by all the learned journals produced by, or affiliated with, the APA. In effect, it does not differ substantially from most other properly developed standards of citation, but it has some idiosyncrasies. Once one has got used to it, it is easy enough to apply, but it is likely that authors may be obliged to refer to types of documents which do not obviously match with the samples shown in the *Publication manual.* If in real difficulties, consult with a reference librarian whose wide expertise in bibliographic citation will help to cope with the really difficult cases. Note also that the *Manual* is updated every few years.

It would be pointless to reprint here the whole APA *Publication manual,* but we draw attention to certain basic practices and urge potential authors to acquire a copy of the manual as a desk copy so that they may refer to it whenever there is any doubt as how to set out a citation or reference.

Let us begin by stating that a citation is a pointer to a work by another author within the text of the essay, paper, book, etc. For instance

In a study of national differences Milgram (1968) showed that . . .

This tells the reader that the writer is quoting the opinion of another, i.e. Milgram, and that the author does not claim responsibility for the view about to be cited. The writer may agree with Milgram or he may not—that is to be deduced from the rest of the sentence or the paragraph.

This example represents a very simple case. If there are two authors responsible for a text, it is common practice to name them both, e.g.

It was demonstrated by Amidon and Carey (1972) . . .

Alternatively one might write:

In a recent study (Amidon & Carey, 1972) it was demonstrated that . . .

When there are more than two authors, or editors, or when there is no clearly identifiable author or editor, practices vary but it might make the citation much less complex if the title of the work and its date are shown instead. It would be too taxing to try and illustrate the scores of combinations and variations that can occur in the authorship of any work; suffice it to stress that besides personal authors, singly or severally and jointly, there exist corporate bodies as authors and there exist anonymous works. Students and novices in the art of writing for publication in a journal are urged to examine copies of the journal to which they intend to submit their paper and to acquaint themselves with its layout and general typographical practice.

References, by contrast, show the full details of where the citation may be found. These details must include, in the order set down in the APA *Publication manual,* the place of publication, the publisher and the year of publication in the case of books (these three data are known as the "imprint") or the name of the journal, volume, pages and year of publication. Two simple examples will show the essence of this prescription:

Author	Date	Title	Place	Publisher
FREUD, S.	(1937)	The ego and the id	London	Hogarth Press

Author	Date	Title		Place/Publisher[*]
JONES, E.	(1938)	"The impact of psychoanalysis"		in *The Journal of theoretical psychology* vol. 5: 10–15.

[*]In the case of reference to journals, the place of publication and the name of the publisher are not set out in detail because they are often too complex and there exist special lists where these details can be found.

There exist numerous rules for the sequence of the components that make up a standard bibliographic citation and we stress that we have here chosen to follow the APA *Publication manual,* for the obvious reason that we are addressing ourselves to students of psychology. It is also emphasized that the adoption of this model, or of any other, is largely a matter of habit. Consistency in the practice of bibliographic citation should be looked upon as a fundamental principle and it matters less what pattern is adopted; however, since one pattern and one only may be adopted, it does make sense to choose one which is recommended by those who have long practised it in their writings in a particular discipline.

It is quite beyond the scope of this book to offer a detailed paraphrase of the APA *Publication manual,* nor is there virtue in swelling the pages of this book by reprinting the whole *Manual* here. Students are recommended to acquire a copy of the latest edition and keep it at hand and refer to it systematically until the recommended practice of citation has become second nature to them.

Attention is drawn to the fact that the bibliographic description of a document must comply with certain international rules. Not only is this a common-sense prescription for a discipline which claims to know no national boundaries, but it is becoming an absolute necessity because of the widespread use of computer-based data banks of bibliographic references. The more man relies on machine-readable reference retrieval methods, the greater the need to have uniform bibliographic entries. To construct the requisite software to translate one system of citation into another is uneconomic in every respect.

Skills in constructing a reference should be developed as thoroughly as skills in manipulating statistical data. The difference between the reference to a monograph or to a journal article should be registered automatically; the use of capital letters should be avoided except where it conforms with general practice in the English language; the significance of the use of italics (or of underlining where an italics typeface is not available) should be fully understood; the transliteration of non-Roman alphabets should follow accepted international practice (where it exists).

All these things pertaining to presentation are important; they seem difficult because the rules are full of minutiae. But they may make the difference between ambiguity and precision. Hence, conformity matters even on these small issues.

2. The card file

Nothing is more irritating than to have lost or forgotten the source and the correct words of a piece of vital information. This is as true for the mature scholar as for the raw student—but it happens more rarely to the experienced scholar because either he has developed a perfect memory for books and papers read or, more likely, he has developed a record system which enables him to retrieve with ease references to his accumulated reading, his notes, his whole apparatus on which his work is based. And we emphasize immediately that such a record system need not be based on a computer costing millions, or even thousands, of dollars but may consist of nothing more than a set of edge-punched cards.

Some of the particular problems that many students face when writing essays and research papers are:

> Difficulties in handling the material contained in the literature references; inability to recall a reference which may be relevant to the project; loss of time and waste of effort in writing out references on the completion of the project; poor referencing which may result in misleading the reader.

But even the advanced researcher will come up against some of these problems and he will at any rate want to save time and effort when engaged in the final drafting of his report or paper without having to go through the motions of writing out his references or finding the correct working of a quotation.

These and other related problems can be overcome with the use of a retrieval system based on simple edge-punch cards. References can be symbolized by notching out the appropriate hole on the edge of the card, and then lifting the file so that notched cards stay behind. This permits quick access to references and easy sorting of them.

The following are some suggestions for a system which will bring the twin benefit of economy and efficiency. The suggestions contained here are appropriate both for undergraduate study and for postgraduate and professional work, and the examples have of course been chosen with special relevance to psychology.

This card record system here recommended is simple in design, convenient to use and compact in size, all of which means that it can be easily carried and used anywhere. The cards may be obtained in various sizes at stationery stores for a modest cost; a very commonly used one measures approximately 165 × 100 mm. Other items of equipment needed are a needle sorter, an edge clipper and a box for storing the cards. A shoe box will do the job very well and it is suggested that a piece of sandpaper glued into the bottom of the box with the rough side up will stop the cards from sliding about.

Most cards are sold already lined, but anyone requiring a special design or layout of lines may commission such cards from a printer.

To code edge-punched cards the appropriate classified hole is punched so that it becomes an open notch. To select the required reference card the needle sorter is inserted in the hole at the desired location of a batch of reference cards. Those cards which have this notched hole will fall from the pack whilst the remainder will be suspended on the needle sorter.

Obviously, more than one hole may be used to identify a reference or set of references; by inserting two needle sorters at once or seriatim and lifting the pack, two categories of references will be dropped from the pack. Figure 14 is an example of a standard card.

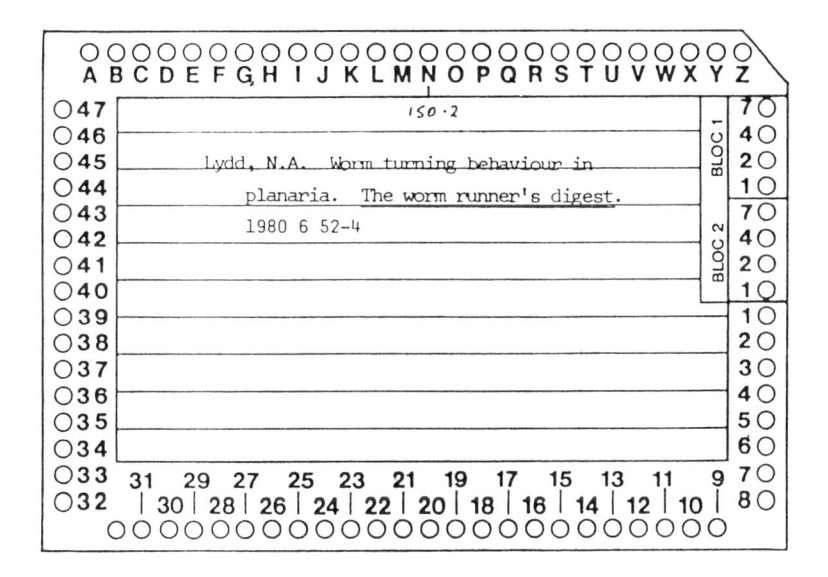

```
○○○○○○○○○○○○○○○○○○○○○○○○○○
A B C D E F G H I J K L M N O P Q R S T U V W X Y Z
○47                          150·2                      7○
○46                                                     4○  BLOC 1
○45        Lydd, N.A.  Worm turning behaviour in        2○
○44        planaria.  The worm runner's digest.         1○
○43                                                     7○
○42                  1980 6 52-4                        4○  BLOC 2
○41                                                     2○
○40                                                     1○
○39                                                     1○
○38                                                     2○
○37                                                     3○
○36                                                     4○
○35                                                     5○
○34                                                     6○
○33   31  29  27  25  23  21  19  17  15  13  11    9  7○
○32    |30|28|26|24|22|20|18|16|14|12|10|             8○
     ○○○○○○○○○○○○○○○○○○○○○○○○○
```

FIG. 14. Standard edge-punched reference card

It will be noted that besides containing forty-seven numbered holes, there are also twenty-six holes marked with the letters of the Roman alphabet, thus offering a total of seventy-three identifiers to categories of records. This is quite a large number in relation to such topics as are normally contained in a journal article, a thesis or a term paper. There are also two blocks containing four holes each, marked 1, 2, 4 and 7. Of these more below.

It is customary to note on the front of the card the name of the author of the reference to be retrieved, taking good care to ensure that the reference is set out in conformity with the APA *Publication manual*. It may be useful to add an abstract of the article or book referred to on the back of the card, but most important is the addition, on the front, of the subject terms under which the reference is to be found by means of the search needle. It may indeed be helpful to add a short note summarizing the point that the particular reference is to prove or illustrate. When that has been done notch the hole which has been allocated to the subject matter of that reference card.

Let us suppose, for instance, that the record system is to "underpin" an essay on "A psychological approach to abnormal behaviour". During our preparatory reading we have made references to some 175 articles in journals, each carefully noted on an edge-punched card. The essay is to deal with the following aspects of "abnormal behaviour":

> Abnormal behaviour defined. (1)
> History of abnormal psychology (14)
> Criteria of abnormality and diagnostic practices (10)
> Psychophysiological disorders (20)
> Personality disorders (17)
> Schizophrenia (21)
> Sexual behaviour (22)
> Addictive behaviour (2)
> Brain disorders (5)

The author of the essay has assigned to every aspect a number within the range 1–47; it matters little in which sequence these numbers are assigned, but it seems reasonable to assume that initially the literature search begins with expositions of a definition of the topic. That aspect of the essay is therefore assigned notch no. 1, but if the historical approach had been chosen first, the aspect "history of abnormal psychology" would probably have been assigned no. 1 notch. During the literature search the author has become aware, if he did not know before, that several sub-topics are assuming major proportions, and he therefore lists them and assigns notches to them, ending up with the following list:

1. Abnormality defined
2. Addictive behaviour
3. Adjustment
4. Behaviour modification
5. Brain disorders
6. Deviance
7. Cognition
8. Conditioning
9. Cultural studies
10. Diagnostics
11. Genetics
12. Hereditary factors
13. Environmental factors
14. History of abnormal psych.
15. Psychotherapy
16. Morality
17. Personality disorders
18. Personality theories
19. Psychoanalysis
20. Psychophysiology
21. Schizophrenia
22. Sexual behaviour
23. Social behaviour
24. Statistics

For every article or book consulted, a reference card is filled in, annotated to show briefly but unambiguously its relevance to the topic or such topic, and then notched at one or other of the numbers.

It will be noted that this list of topics is alphabetical: for ease of finding this is desirable but some deviations will occur. A common reason is that one will add to the list as new topics occur. In such an event one would not re-order the topics list since that action would require all previously punched cards to be re-done. With the needle sorter the strict alphabetical list is not obligatory.

In this particular example the author is at a stage where he needs literature back-up for a chapter or section of his essay on psychoanalysis. He passes the needle through notch no. 19 and then extracts the references he has collected on that aspect of abnormal behaviour. If he wants to relate psychoanalysis to psychotherapy he will have to pass the needle through notch no. 15. There may be some cards that contain both subject references and these will fall out on both occasions; if not, the references will have to be correlated and some constructive thinking and writing will then have to be undertaken.

It may be desirable, when working on a large body of literature, to add such identifiers as "country of origin" of the references, or to indicate in which library the reference has been located. The following examples of notches assigned illustrate the point:

32. Australia   A. Library of Congress
33. Canada   B. Bodleian
34. New Zealand   C. National Library
35. United Kingdom   D. State library
36. United States   E. Local university library
37. Other   F. Self holds copy

Provided there are enough notches, there may be other data which a researcher wants to recapture, e.g. the physical characteristics of a reference (off-print, computer print-out, statistical tables). We suggest, however, that library location marks (i.e. what librarians refer to as call numbers) be added to the reference transcript on the card. It would greatly overtax the edge-notched system if this datum were to be retrieved through notch clipping.

In the example card given it will be noted that the letter "N" has the number 150.2 written beneath it. This indicates (for example) that the publication is held in the National Library (hence "N") and the call number is 150.2.

If one wished to extend the card system, this is really a simple matter. The numbers 7, 4, 2 and 1, singularly or in combination, give any number between 1 and 9. They are set as an addition in two blocs and can be used in the same manner as a prefix or as the whole numbers of a decimal system. Thus, by having two groups of these numbers one can have a numeric system which gives 88 more place references (nos. 11-99), one group for tens and the other for units.

Suppose one wished to select reference point 38 from the extension system one would needle sort the 3 (nos. 2 and 1 from Bloc 2 and *then* 8 (nos. 7 and 1) from Bloc 1. By such a needle sort the extension number would fall free from the pack. The addition of a Bloc 3 would extend the system to 888 reference points and the provision of Bloc 4 to 8888 points.

Blocs 1 and 2 in combination start at 11 and go to 99. The numbers 11 to 99 minus the decade numbers of 20, 30, 40–90 are missing since there is no zero. The possible number of locations for Blocs 1 and 2 is, then, 99−11 = 88, minus the decade numbers 20–90, of which there are eight.

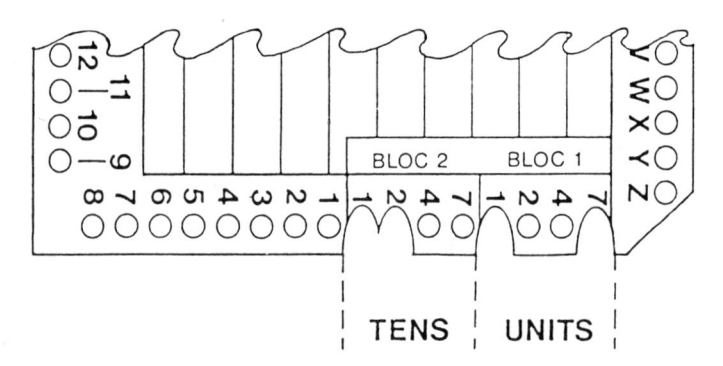

Fig. 15. Expansion of locatable categories

There are, therefore, 80 topic locations possible on Blocs 1 and 2 when used in combination. If one wishes to use zeros then the rule is that if any number is clipped in Blocs 1 or 2 and the other bloc is not clipped, a zero is implied. This technique gives another 19 locations. (see Fig. 15).

Those writing a book or dissertation may wish to select numbers as chapter identifiers. This may be done by selecting some number run (e.g. 31 = chapter 1, 32 = chapter 2).

If the number of cards gets very extensive (say over 500) a simple solution would be to handle them as two sets with exactly the same codes but using for each a different colour. This colour coding for sets may also commend itself to those operating parallel systems.

When the time for producing the final essay or report arrives the cards can be ordered according to the desired form the article will take. The advantage of this system is that the information contained in the reference material is thoroughly distilled since it has to get onto the space provided by the card, and once the article is written the references can be simply rearranged into alphabetical order ready for listing under "references". In addition one's own work and ideas can be readily interspersed among the other material by placing them also onto cards and assigning to them appropriate numbers and notching the holes accordingly.

It cannot be denied that the use of a suitable computer to handle a reference retrieval system would offer many advantages which are denied to an edge-notched card system. Strangely, the design of the software for such a computer will be greatly aided by a full understanding of the card-based system. However, the availability of computers is often restricted, and the cost is inevitably much greater. Those who are fortunate in having access to a computer should acquaint themselves with the personal documentation logistics outline by Stibic in his *Personal documentation for professionals*. In many respects this is an admirable work. It is a counsel of perfection and, as such, more suited to the beginning professional than to the established one. Its greatest merit is that it shows a large array of possible systems, though the descriptions of some of them are often too brief (the edge-notched card system on p. 111 for example).

There is also a detailed descriptive account of data handling for science and technology in Rossmassler & Watson's book of that name. It deals, inter alia, with the generation, treatment, analysis and evaluation of data. While its relevance to psychology is not total, it does contain useful guides to standards, both national and international; it is an overview and a sourcebook. For those with an interest in the theory and principles of information retrieval (from a mathematical point of view) there is Kochen's *Principles of information retrieval*. Its value is for the theoretician and teacher rather than for those with a need for a "hands-on" account.

CHAPTER 9

Quantitative Psychology and its Methodology

1. Statistics

PSYCHOLOGY's aspiration to be a science must, as is the case with other sciences, rest not so much upon its achievements as upon the way it goes about its task. Whether it is the discovery of new principles or the application of known ones, precise usage is imperative in the construction and description of all experiments.

This precision is expressed or implied in various ways: one is carefully to frame the problem; another is to ensure that one's inferences are logically valid, and a third to arrive at and use numerical precision.

Although psychology still shares a number of notional concepts with philosophy and theology, there is a difference of approach. Psychology is distinguished from its parental disciplines above all by its empirical base and its use of quantitative methods.

It is not uncommon to find that quantitative psychology causes many students serious concern. Since it is not possible to become a psychologist without at least some statistical training, numerophobia can be a real problem for some. The cause of this "disease" may have its origin in the earlier teaching of numerical skills in primary school. Mathematical processes may be presented as arcane exercises of minimal relevance to the practical world. In the absence of insight into the reason for numerical processes an exercise may turn into an experience wherein ill-understood rules are applied to achieve a result no less mysterious. The obvious solution is to desensitize phobic students by having them master the principles and reasoning behind the numerical process and then to work through numerous examples of the less complicated kind. For instructors wishing to mount a statistics desensitization course for students there is a recently published report by W. R. Bartz *et al.* (1981) entitled "Effects of reducing student anxiety in a statistics course". The report is based on research conducted in Australia, and shows how students can be made to overcome their fear of statistics and can become used to handling statistical material.

Different casts of mind may approach the problem from different directions. For this reason there is something to commend the notion of searching for a statistics text which is intellectually congenial. A first edition of a now standard text by A. L. Edwards, *Statistical analysis* (1946) was one such work (although later editions dispensed with some of its sympathetic charm). This early work by Edwards had the singular merit of assuming that the reader knew no more than the basic arithmetical processes such as addition and subtraction. From such an elementary base the reader was led to the moderately complex forms of statistical reasoning.

As statistics is a well-served field in the number and range of textbooks available, the concerned student has a wide range from which to choose. Perhaps one of the best-known general introductions is the brief, and often amusing, book by D. Huff, *How to lie with statistics,* first issued in 1954 and now available as a paperback. For those who have overcome the deeper apprehensions of mathematical reasoning there is a clear statement of the relationship between mathematics and psychology in the chapter entitled "Mathematics measurement and psychophysics" which appeared in S. S. Stevens's *Handbook of experimental psychology* (1951). This reference, now 30 years old, is still a classic statement in the field.

More conventional texts on statistical analysis abound. One of the best-known and highly regarded books is J. P. Guilford & B. Fruchter's *Fundamental statistics in psychology and education,* which has appeared in several editions. For those able to follow the higher flights there is the seminal three-volume work by Kendall & Stuart, *The advanced theory of statistics.* This work is more likely to appeal to those with special interests or the need to solve special problems.

The main purpose of statistics is to serve as an aid to both precision and quantification. Within this framework there are two basic modes of approach. One is called descriptive and the other called "inferential". Descriptive statistics are statements of the salient numerical features of an array of data. Inferential statistics, on the other hand, are ones in which conclusions are drawn from an analysis of quantitative data. These conclusions are often an assessment of differences between sets of data, and usually applied as tests of significance values and levels. The more commonly used tables of significance are to be found in most textbooks on statistical analysis. Two of the more comprehensive sets of tables published separately are those by Fisher & Yates, *Statistical tables for biological, agriculture and medical research* (1963) and by T. L. Kelley, which are known as *The Kelley statistical tables* (1948).

There is a view that much of the statistical analysis of psychological data is best carried out through non-parametric tests. Such tests are also referred to as "distribution-free" tests. One of the major advantages of this approach is that "distribution-free" tests make no assumptions about the data under analysis, having been drawn from a population in a particular way, e.g. from a normally distributed population. Operations using non-parametric tests may be conducted on numerical data that are "weaker" than the conventional ratio scales (a ratio scale has equal intervals between all points on the scale and has an absolute zero—a measurement in millimetres, for example).

If one's data are of, say, rank order values or if the numbers in the sample are small (as they might be in the case of survivors of a tragedy) then non-parametric tests may be the most appropriate analytical tools to use. One of the best standard references on those techniques is Siegel's *Nonparametric statistics for the behavioral sciences,* 1956. Although the book was written some time ago it is still, deservedly, in print. It contains excellent explanations of the basic concepts, including a clear, concise statement on hypothesis testing and Type I and Type II errors. There are numerous worked examples and an extensive appendix of tables of significance.

More recently Singer's *Distribution-free methods for non-parametric problems* appeared as a monograph of the *British journal of mathematical and statistical psychology* (1979). This work is a classified and selected bibliography which lists contributions up to April 1978. It is a useful complement to Siegel's book.

For those with an interest in statistical theory and method there is a very good periodical overview in the *International journal of abstracts* which began in 1959. This journal contains abstracts of articles from various sources on statistical theory and method. It also includes reports, conference papers, etc.

Apart from journals dedicated specifically to statistical material, other general journals sometimes canvass issues of a fundamental statistical nature. These issues may arise from a methodological investigation of an experiment or be the result of theoretical investigations. We cite, as a typical example, C. A. Boneau's classic article "The effects of violations of assumptions underlying the 't' test" (1960). It is a systematic examination of the consequences of violating certain assumptions which underlie a parametric text (such as skew and kurtosis). Although this work may seem dated, it has remained an important source and is often quoted.

The felt need for statistical methods and approaches stems from the basic tenets of a scientific approach. This need would have generated a great deal of dull computational work had it not been for a recent technological advance—that of the electronic calculator. For a very small sum one may purchase a simple machine and for still small sums a machine capable of the mathematical functions normally required in psychology. These include such functions as squares, square roots, sums of squares, cross-products and reciprocals.

More recently, programmable calculators have appeared on the market, and some have even been developed to the level of sophistication where a set of data may be entered and recorded in magnetic form so that it does not vanish when the machine is switched off.

With the relatively easy access to computers it is improbable that such devices will become common, as has been the case with the simpler machine.

Where one is performing the conventional psychological–statistical exercises on a computer, one need not write the program because such programs are already available. Of these the best known is the Statistical Package for the Social Sciences (SPSS), which has been described and explained by N. H. Nie *et al.* in a book with that very title (1975).

It will be apparent that quantitative psychology is a burgeoning field. This is not only due to a substantial inherent interest but rather because it is a direct consequence of the growth of psychology.

2. Experimental design

We have drawn attention, in the preceding section of this chapter, to the importance of statistical analysis, but it is quite obvious, we hope, that statistical or quantitative analysis is intimately linked with the methodology of research. In this section we are going to comment on the sources of methodology itself; but we stress right away that we are referring to the methodology of empirical investigations, and not to methods of psychotherapy nor to the superordinate methods used in discussing how to understand a science. The focus here is clearly on the application of conventional scientific modes of inquiry applied in psychology. It will also be appreciated that we are not offering an account of methodology but, rather, a guide to key issues and where they may be pursued.

A relatively common misunderstanding is the distinction between experimental and empirical psychology. Empirical means derived from experience and experimental is a sub-category of that concept. An approximation to the difference between the two is that in empirical work one collects data in a systematic manner toward the support or proof of a hypothesis; in experimental work one does just that, but from a contrived set of conditions under the experimenter's control—usually, though not always, in the laboratory.

Some textbooks on experimental design and methods are structured on the assumption that not all students are seriously interested in this aspect of psychology. That assumption appears to be justified since, in spite of the inclusion of courses on experimental psychology in most academic courses on this discipline, the majority of psychology students enter, after graduation, into non-experimental work areas. It is particularly useful to have at least one textbook which recognizes these limitations among student interest and uses the approach of emphasizing wider aspects of experimentation; the book is by M. W. Matlin and appeared in 1979 under the title *Human experimental psychology*. It is a very helpful pointer to the scope of experimental psychology.

It is appropriate that we should start by referring readers to a recent publication that presents a simultaneous treatment of both the design and the analysis of experiments in psychological research. *The numbers game; statistics in psychology* by J. G. Snodgrass (1977) makes it quite clear that experimental design and statistical analysis depend upon each other and must be considered together from the starting pointing of every piece of psychological research.

Methodological considerations will be seen to be either of the statistical (academically proper) kind or of the practical (strategic) kind. Ideal designs of empirical investigations are not always capable of being translated into logistically possible enterprises in a sometimes difficult world. Yet we assume their existence, if for no other reason than to ensure proper standards in those designs that can be executed, and that our strategy and logical processes are appropriate to the purpose. Not surprisingly, there are very many works on "ideal designs". Some, although not of recent date, have a timeless quality and are deservedly still consulted, e.g. B. J. Underwood's *Experimental psychology*, the 2nd edition of which appeared in 1949, was re-issued in 1966 and is still in print. This work affords an excellent outline of the methods of psychology, especially on psychophysical methods.

Of particular interest is a more recent publication on design and method, *An introduction to experimental design in psychology; a case approach,* by Johnson & Solso, the 2nd edition of which appeared in 1978. This workbook is designed to teach the principles of experimental design, using actual experiments the analysis of which teaches the principles. Because of its excellent didactic quality, it should commend itself to those who wish to take part in a course aimed at fostering understanding of experimental principles but do not wish to start off with the abstract principles of design and analysis.

It is not always possible to distinguish clearly between principal and subordinate strategies in a research design, a point which has been addressed successfully by Campbell and Stanley in their *Experimental and quasi-experimental designs for research* (1963). Though about 20 years old, this work stands alone in offering useful approaches to quasi-experimental designs. It is concisely written and has not been superseded in quality by any more recent publication.

It is not always necessary—and indeed at times it is quite difficult—for psychological researchers to collect their own raw data. This is often particularly cumbersome in the fields of social psychology and in certain aspects of educational psychology. However, data may be already available either in some statistical form published by government departments, or as data on file, such as educational records or the tapes and files of ICSPRI. The bureaux of statistics of most countries issue all sorts of data in their many regular reports on the economic and social conditions of their country, and a useful general guide to their use has been compiled by Shonfield & Shaw under the title *Social indicators and social policy* (1972).

The studies just referred to are about real-life variables. Another way of studying real-life situations is the observation of behaviour in natural settings, as described in P. G. Swingle's *Social psychology in natural settings* (1973). The studies discussed in this work have come to be called "unobtrusive measures", because their aim is to obviate the difficulty, found in some experimental settings, that the subjects, aware of the study being done, become self-conscious and thereby offset the outcome, e.g. acting on candid camera. Closely related to this difficulty is the work by E. J. Webb and others, *Unobtrusive measures: non-reactive research in the social sciences* (1966). This is a comprehensive survey of the problems of "objective" experimentation; its versatile approach makes it particularly valuable.

In setting up any experiment, either within the laboratory or without, it is essential that the design of the study be thoroughly understood. If the design is not appropriate or if it is not properly controlled no valid inferences can be drawn from the data obtained. It is obviously particularly difficult to keep tight control in social psychological studies—much more so than, say, in the field of perception. A number of experienced researchers have concerned themselves with just that problem and as long as 25 years ago a seminal article by D. T. Campbell, "Factors relevant to the validity of experiments in social settings", examined the validity of certain types of social experiments.

The purpose of methodology is primarily to help establish a relationship between the independent variable (the manipulanda) and the dependent variable (the response measure). With that ideal situation in mind, it was the original intention of scientific behaviourism to hold everything constant in an investigation and then manipulate one variable at a time. For instance, in a study of perception it might be arranged to manipulate exposure time, or the retinal angle subtended by an object, or the degree of illumination. However, it is sometimes possible to evaluate several variables taken in combination and for this field of "manipulative data analysis", as it is called, there is a standard reference work edited by R. B. Cattell, *Handbook of multivariate experimental psychology* (1966). This work is intended for the experimenter with a strong mathematical bent. It is divided into two parts; the first deals with the abstract method, and the second with substantive psychological concepts. Although this work is not of recent vintage it is still a useful resource. Cognate books on multivariate approaches are relatively common and we note here as an example the more broadly conceived work by Lawlis & Chatfield, *Multivariate approaches for the behavioural sciences* (1974), which contains many references to related material.

The psychologist's search for relationships is sometimes extended to a search for causal relationships. There are very difficult problems associated with the drawing of causal inferences and the problem is particularly acute in non-experimental research. One work that attempts to pull together the scattered material on that topic is H. M. Blalock's *Causal inferences in nonexperimental research* (1964).

It should be plain to the reader that there are no "higher-order" methods in psychology by which other methods may be judged. There is no substitute for plain logical judgement and all we can show are mistakes of inference in causality due to the uniquely reactive nature of behavioural sciences research. A clear exposition of this problem—with evidential studies—is to be found in Rosenthal's works: *Experimenter effects in behaviour research* (1966) and *The volunteer subject* which he wrote together with L. Rosnow in 1975.

Though the findings of psychological research are often of primary importance for the enhancement of our basic scientific knowledge, this need not always be so. There are numerous works which aim at showing how basic research findings may be applied to everyday problems. One of the distinctly better ones is J. A. Varela's *Psychological solutions to social problems* (1971), which is a felicitous account of the way that scholarly findings may be applied to everyday life.

Certain experimental designs carry implications that certain instrumentation will be used. Reaction time experiments, for example, require some form of chronoscope or timer. The tie between experimental designs and instrumentation needs no emphasis, and for those who wish to find out about the special equipment used in psychology there are two excellent accounts in J. B. Sidowski's *Experimental methods and instrumentation in psychology* (1966) and in A. Cleary's more recent *Instrumentation for psychology* (1977). The first-mentioned work has the additional merit of covering the spectrum of behaviour from the biological to the social.

Psychology is one of the disciplines that are beset by the problems of conducting research on small samples. Although this is not always a problem, it occurs frequently enough to justify special consideration. A recent publication by Robinson & Foster (1979) has paid special regard to the issue. Their *Experimental psychology: a small-N approach* is divided into three parts; the first sets out the historical perspectives of the problem; the second deals with examples from different fields, and the third provides the small–large N comparison.

In the social sciences a variety of techniques are available to complement the experimental approach. This search for alternatives to the experimental method resulted in a British Psychological Society (BPsS) sponsored conference in Oxford in 1975. The results of that discussion appear in a book edited by Ginsburg in 1979 under the title *Emerging strategies in social psychological research*.

One of the purposes of science is to examine relationships between variables: experimentation is one way to examine such relationships; correlational analyses are another. The arrangement in an experiment designed to evaluate a specific relationship is called the research design.

Conclusions that are consistent with a hypothesized relationship should of course not be interpreted as having favoured that hypothesis; the demonstrated relationship may well be explained by other consistent alternative hypotheses. We know, for instance, that the rate of personal violence goes up with rising temperatures in New York City in the summer (the "thermic law of delinquency"), yet the rising of the violence rate with rising temperatures may result not from the temperature affecting body chemistry but from the warmer temperatures encouraging people to go more outside, thereby increasing the opportunities for social tension which could lead to violence. It should be noted that the empirical observation is consistent with both hypotheses—and it may be that both are true!

Experimentation is a carefully contrived arrangement designed to look for significant relationships. Within ordinary scientific endeavours the results are of abstract interest with possible applications yet to be determined. In clinical research, as an instance of applied research, the aim is to optimize the use of the results while minimizing the risks of such an application.

While results may be statistically significant they may be of minimal clinical relevance and there are many different factors that may determine the experimental process. For example a particular therapeutic intervention might be 80 per cent effective for 10 hours of treatment. It could be made 90 per cent effective with a further 150 hours of therapy, but if that cost $12,000 and the condition being treated is not a serious one, the clinician might pause before embarking on it.

Issues on statistical significance versus practical significance are dealt with in Kazdin's book *Research design in clinical psychology* (1980). Although this excellent work is about clinical psychology the insights that he brings to bear are applicable in a wider context.

Another important feature in organizing research is to follow accepted models and to adapt them to one's own needs and situation. Much can be learned in this respect from the examinations of the theories of social psychology by W. Schmalz (1971) and by R. Lynn (1971).

It does need stressing that these precise accounts of methodology should be carefully studied and the practical hints mastered; but that is not everything. There are many examples of divergent thinking producing highly original studies not otherwise possible. Above all, an investigator must use his imagination and not shy away from unorthodox procedures.

CHAPTER 10

Presentation of Results

1. Physical forms

Whether one conducts a research programme to attain an academic qualification, or to meet the demands of a consultancy contract, or perhaps just to explore a hypothesis the proof of which may satisfy one's own intellectual curiosity, the results of one's endeavours are relatively useless unless they are presented in a form in which they can be assimilated by others, and in particular by those for whom they are destined. No amount of information searching, experimentation or thinking can be considered adequate unless it can be seen to have come to fruition. Well conducted research—no matter how elegant—is valueless until it is reported or presented.

To that end we wish to offer some suggestions on how to go about presenting it and as to what sources of information should be consulted in order to achieve quality presentation and readable style. We must state at the beginning of this chapter, however, that we are restricting our comments to presentation in typed or printed form; no pointers are offered here on other forms of communication.

Within the limitations upon the range of suggestions to be offered, it is first of all essential to be clear on the physical form in which the report or the essay is to appear. There is a world of difference between a document prepared by a typist, however able, on an ordinary office typewriter and a printed report set up by a competent printing house. Seventy-five years ago it was by no means uncommon—indeed, it was then still obligatory at many European universities—to present one's doctoral dissertation properly typeset and bound in book form; it is now no longer compulsory to go to that expense. Theses are accepted if properly presented in typed form and modestly bound.

The same goes for most reports presented as the result of consultancy work, unless it be for a government department when the report may be printed by the government printer for presentation to some high authority or for wide distribution.

The question of physical presentation need not concern us too much, but it should be remembered that the techniques of document reproduction have developed remarkably fast, during the last 2–3 decades, and while most depend on a first-class typist, the problem of producing many copies of the same document is really a problem no longer. But we emphasize that it all starts with a neatly typed copy.

There exist numerous guides for the general layout of a typed report, and there are more or less universal conventions. But enough scope is left to the creator of a report, or author of an essay, to use imagination and initiative in order to create a typographically pleasing product.

Consistency is one of the more important criteria by which the physical form of a report will be judged. Paragraphs should not be too long, they should either all start at the left hand margin or all be indented by a certain number of spaces. There is no rule except that of consistency.

There are hundreds of dos and don'ts in the typing up of a report and to list them here is quite impossible. A large number of style manuals include detailed advice on how to cope with the use of inverted commas, punctuation in general, underlining and other means of lending emphasis to a word or a passage with the use of italics, of roman numerals, of ordinal numbers. Since this book is addressed primarily to psychologists, we feel obliged to stress once more the value of the APA *Publication manual* which contains so much good advice even on the question of form and layout for typed presentation.

We hasten to add, however, that the differences in the usage of words and phrases between the UK and North America oblige us to draw attention also to the recommendations prepared by the BPsS on style and presentation. The Society's Standing Committee on Publications produced in 1979 *Suggestions to contributors*, which gives detailed guidance on manuscript preparation from abstracts to references, how to deal with abbreviations, how to set out tables and diagrams, advice on copyright, etc.

Journals which are outside the APA or the BPsS influence may, of course, impose quite different requirements for the preparation of articles and it would be wise to check a current issue of the journal for "Notes to contributors" or with the editorial office of the journal to which one wants to contribute.

As for term essays and theses, psychology students are urged to adopt the APA recommendations and to become so familiar with them that they can follow them automatically.

2. Style of writing

We quoted earlier a statement once made about the brothers Henry and William James who, each in his own way, contributed so much to the culture of the English-speaking world; one as a great novelist, the other as one of the founders of modern psychology. Yet it has been a matter of opinion among many learned people of their time who did what. In effect, both wrote a wonderful style of English and their respective success is unquestionably due to the fact that they knew what they wanted to say, and how to say it.

Nobody is born as a writer; there may be basic gifts, genetically determined even if not, as yet, predictable; but the really high pitch of the art can only be attained by long practice. Guidance will help, above all when it fosters self-criticism. Nor should any writer ever be shy of criticism by others, friends or foes. If one's friends cannot understand the drift of the argument, one's foes are sure to pick it to pieces in no time. And beware of the false friend who will not tell you what is wrong with the essay, the paper, the report.

A first-class dictionary of the English language, Roget's *Thesaurus*, Fowler's *A dictionary of modern English usage* and a good dictionary of psychology are the essential tools that must be always within arm's reach of the writer on psychology.

Besides, there are useful hints in such books as L. F. Shaffer's *Preparing doctoral dissertations in psychology; a guide for students* (1967) and *Thesis and assignment writing* by J. Anderson *et al.* (1970). Strunk & White's *The elements of style* (1972) is another guide book which has much appeal, as is also Sternberg's *Writing the psychology paper* (1977). New textbooks of this kind are appearing frequently and it is important to be aware of changes of the use of expression due to social pressures, e.g. the current taboo on terms which could be interpreted as sexist, racist, etc.

More important by far, in the eyes of the writers, is the proper and meaningful use of the English (or any other) language. To improve one's awareness of the lack of precision from which so many writers suffer in this day and age, we very strongly recommend the study of Sir Ernest Gowers's famous book *Plain words* (1948) which was later enlarged and reissued as *The complete plain words* (1973). Besides being illuminating, we also found it rather good fun to read.

More precisely directed at the presentation of psychological material, and particularly useful because it deals with the problems of physical presentation as well as with those of expression and literary style, is Miller & Swift's *Words and women* (1976).

Words, however well chosen and syntactically arranged, are of course not enough. They must, for the purpose of the exercise, be part of a plan, of a structured presentation.

Among the more common errors of writing style are the absence of a clear framework for the presentation and the non-orderly flow of the exposition. Without an outline, skeleton, or plan, it is highly improbable that a clear argument will emerge. When points are made it should be made plain how they develop, one from the other. The absence of continuity of argument can be quite as much a cause of concern as the disorderly presentation of words in sentences. Where there is no smooth orderly presentation of ideas, and where there is no sequential development of an argument, the suspicion must be present that the writer has not got one or is confused about it.

Some fortunate few are able to construct good orderly prose straight onto a typewriter, or even to dictate it. That rare gift is something to be treasured since most serious writers can only work slowly and carefully with pen in hand.

Poor presentation is frequently due to the lack of clarity as to who is the target reader. The first-year psychology student is often heard to say "I didn't say that because I knew that the examiner knew it". At that level the target reader that the writer should have in mind is the interested intelligent layman. For dissertations one might choose a different target reader—perhaps the interested informed professional in a cognate field of psychology. No matter how high-powered the rifle, it is of no use unless it is properly aimed.

3. Structure of a report

There are great differences between the various types of reports. A report on a piece of academic research should not be organized on the same lines and in the same form as a report for a business or firm on matters of industrial psychology. What has been said above about the target reader is obviously relevant.

A fundamental distinction is the intrinsic difference between case reports and empirical reports. The former are concerned with a specific person or a set of persons having in common some characteristic traits, say deafness, which is the subject of the investigation; case reports are obviously more common in clinical psychology but they are also often required for psychiatric or forensic purposes.

Empirical reports, by contrast, are the results of experimental investigations, be it in an academic setting or in the competitive world of industry and business. They are directed at an audience which desires to see an explanation of a hypothesis or assess a programme; or of the causes for varying performance rates in a process dependent on controlled changes of conditions.

Each of these types of reports demands a different form, but the academic research report has a commonly agreed structure, while all other types have to meet the demands of those who commissioned them. Nevertheless, there are general principles and conventions which the report writer is well advised to observe. In particular, ethical questions may obtrude into empirical reports and should be carefully watched. Examples are the use of deception, breaches of confidentiality, and arguments ad hominem.

Research reports, whether of the case report type or of the empirical variety, should be at once precise and concise. This category of reports for which students frequently prepare in their advanced years of study should aim at communicating an issue and presenting its empirical resolution in an unambiguous and impersonal manner. Personal points of view may, of course, be included but they should not be allowed to be mixed up with statements of verifiable facts. Perhaps writers of reports should bear in mind the well-held precept that a good empirical report contains enough basic information to allow another investigator to duplicate the experiment.

For the conventional psychological report there are standard sets of headings used; their purpose is to serve both as a reminder about which issues ought to be canvassed, and as a reliable framework that allows and helps the busy reader to gain a quick and focused grasp of the contents. In particular, beginners (and some older hands, too) should remember that the report should *develop* an argument rather than just report points, and that there should be a clear line of demarcation indicating where factual accounting ends and speculation begins.

Bearing in mind that report writing is an acquired skill, not an inborn quality, we stress that a substantial component of that learning—especially for beginners—is to use the formal structure until it has been properly mastered. To this end we suggest that it is good sense, in presenting an empirical report, to start with a relatively wide frame of reference, to narrow it to a study of objective and manageable proportions, and then to interpret the results of one's study back into their wider context.

This point is presented diagrammatically in Fig. 16. While the diagram is self-explanatory as regards the sequence of the main sections of a typical report, the following comments may be helpful for beginners:

(1) The *title* should be brief, descriptive and use key terms.
(2) The *introduction* must, as its name suggests, say what the study is about and set it into context. A review of the issues involved takes the views and findings of others into account; from this consideration of major examples and quotes from the relevant literature consensual views may emerge, or there may be disagreement on issues. From the appraisal of the issues, the framework for the current study should emerge, leading to a statement of the aim of the report and why the study is important practically or theoretically, or both.
(3) The *method* section must offer a clear and concise description of the basic issues, including an identification of the independent and dependent variables, together with a description of how they are being manipulated. Logistics and strategy form an important ingredient of this section, together with an account of apparatus and subjects which should be listed here. The subjects are identified by their salient characteristics and the procedure of conducting the experiment expressed in such a way that others may repeat it.
(4) The *results* section is just that. It should not include any interpretation of the results—simply a factual reporting. If tables are included with the results this is where they belong (unless of course, they are extensive tables of basic data rather than analytical data—in which case they may be relegated to an appendix). Graphs and figures are used

only where they are either indispensable because of the type of data used or formed, or because they form an economical method of presenting numerical data; they may also be used to highlight certain aspects of the results.

(5) The *discussion* is there to summarize and interpret the salient findings; it should include a consideration of the stated aim in relation to the actual findings. Both the logic of the conclusions and any special problems with the methodology may be referred to here. Any wider implications of the study belong in this interpretative section.

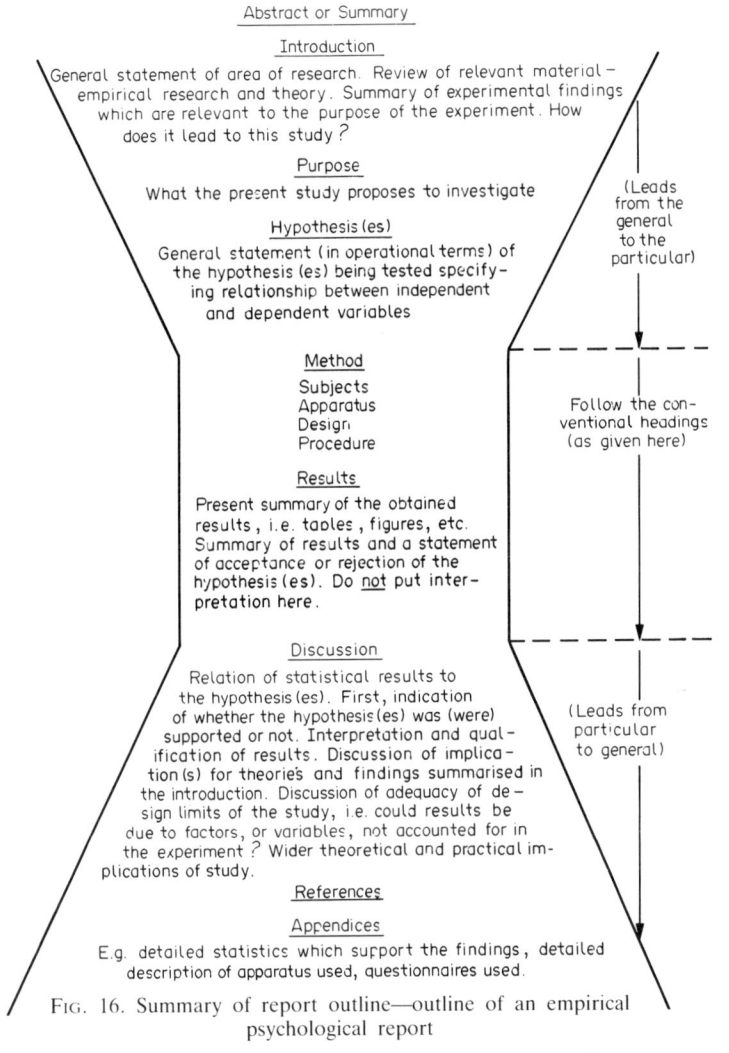

Abstract or Summary

Introduction
General statement of area of research. Review of relevant material — empirical research and theory. Summary of experimental findings which are relevant to the purpose of the experiment. How does it lead to this study?

Purpose
What the present study proposes to investigate

Hypothesis(es)
General statement (in operational terms) of the hypothesis(es) being tested specifying relationship between independent and dependent variables

(Leads from the general to the particular)

Method
Subjects
Apparatus
Design
Procedure

Follow the conventional headings (as given here)

Results
Present summary of the obtained results, i.e. tables, figures, etc. Summary of results and a statement of acceptance or rejection of the hypothesis(es). Do *not* put interpretation here.

Discussion
Relation of statistical results to the hypothesis(es). First, indication of whether the hypothesis(es) was (were) supported or not. Interpretation and qualification of results. Discussion of implication(s) for theories and findings summarised in the introduction. Discussion of adequacy of design limits of the study, i.e. could results be due to factors, or variables, not accounted for in the experiment? Wider theoretical and practical implications of study.

(Leads from particular to general)

References

Appendices
E.g. detailed statistics which support the findings, detailed description of apparatus used, questionnaires used.

FIG. 16. Summary of report outline—outline of an empirical psychological report

We pointed out earlier that the only road to perfection in report writing is to practise and to practise again. It is commonly acknowledged that present-day students are suffering from an inability to express themselves well in their written work—a weakness not confined to the English-speaking world but seemingly also noted in other idioms—and we recommend therefore that students pay special attention to the art of self-criticism. To help foster that art we have included as Appendix C a set of questions closely related to the recommendations for the form of an empirical report (see also Fig. 16). Students or beginners in the art of report writing may do well to use these questions on the final draft of their report and before presenting it to whom it may concern. We have also added, as Appendix B, an example of an empirical research report.

So far, we have dealt only with reports related to empirical psychological investigations but we stress that the technique of report writing and the criteria by which reports are judged are based on universal value. It will therefore not be necessary to repeat the general comments on report writing in our consideration of the specific characteristics of case reports and clinical reports.

It is perhaps stating the obvious to point out that clinical or case reports result from findings which are based on, or related to, quite specific considerations. In particular, case reports contain essentially results pertaining to an individual and are therefore often of an analytical kind.

Commonly, case reports are commissioned for some specific purpose (perhaps for referral to an institution or for a court of law). This feature often implies a tailored or focused account that addresses certain relevant issues. The form of a case report will therefore vary depending upon its purpose, to whom it is addressed and within what field it falls, e.g. clinical, forensic, social work, etc.

Notwithstanding these various orientations there are some common features to case reports, and we would like to suggest at least some of the more important ones. Firstly there are the logistic questions which occurred during the investigation and which should be spelt out early in the report:

(a) Who, in addition to the client, has been seen and interviewed?
(b) Where have they been seen and under what conditions?
(c) How often and for how long have they been seen or interviewed?

These points must be set down quite clearly in the report because these facts form the basis of the conclusion or recommendations.

It will be understood that a point of view derived from one source only may be all that is required but does entail the grave danger that it misses or misrepresents salient information.

Secondly, there is the structure of the report:

(a) How long should it be? It may be as brief as a one-page letter or as long as a minor thesis. Most commonly three to eight pages, say 1000 to 2500 words. This is not to say that appendices providing basic technical data should not be attached, because that relegation of detail to the end of the document allows one to construct a concise and flowing style which may be as scholarly or scientific as circumstances and the commissioning authority demand.

(b) In style, reports should be objective (as distinct from polemic), concise as well as precise, jargon-free and in clear prose.

The orientation of a case report may be one of three kinds; client-oriented, institution-oriented or mediational. A clinical report is usually of the first kind and a family case tends to be treated as of the third kind. There is, of course no fixed rule on this matter but it is an issue of which report writers should be very conscious.

The conclusions drawn in a case report must plainly follow from the given evidence and arguments. A useful rule of thumb is to bear in mind that any report may be produced in court and be subject to intensive scrutiny. Writers of case reports should imagine themselves defending their report under cross-examination. In drawing conclusions the realism of any recommendations should be considered. For example, if the case report is for a particular sort of treatment of great benefit for this kind of case, the treatment should be known to be available locally, properly administered, affordable, etc.

A third issue in case reports is that of being aware of pay-off issues wherein a client may be dissimulating to obtain a personal advantage of some kind. It is known that there are cases wherein a client or patient may wish to convey an impression of sanity or insanity in order to gain some advantage, such as seeking or evading deportation, to benefit under a will, or to enhance the prospects of a shorter or more appealing length or form of incarceration.

We have not included a sample of a case report because the format, for good reasons, cannot be standardized. Those involved in writing case reports will have served some form of internship and will, therefore, have received models and instruction. What is outlined here are some of the fundamental issues that should be considered when preparing a case report. For a comprehensive treatment of psychologists' case reports see Hollis and Donn (1979).

4. Publication

Those who, for whatever reason, aim at making the results of their researches more widely known will of course try to find a publisher, commercial or other. As this *Guide* is primarily directed at students and new entrants to the profession, we will restrict our remarks to the publication of relatively short contributions normally found in journals or produced by institutions in series closely related to their research programmes. We have pointed out repeatedly that it is our understanding of the structure of the profession that recent graduates and younger members find their feet, so to say, in the wake or under the tutelage of experienced (certainly relatively more experienced) psychologists, who in turn have gone through the same type of master–apprentice relationship and will offer guidance on all matters, including that of finding a suitable medium for one's first published paper. Even so, however, some benefit might accrue from an examination of Markle & Rinn's *Author's guide to journals in psychology, psychiatry and social work* (1977). Though now over 5 years old, this book contains useful hints on which journal might accept an article on a certain topic. It is not a great book—but it is the only one of its kind.

The very proposition of publishing raises a number of questions which should be well pondered before sending off half-baked ideas for exposure to a world of experts. To be judged by one's peers is proper; to be judged and found wanting is, of course, disastrous. Self-criticism is an art that can be acquired with practice and all the more easily if one has expert guidance. There can be no better help in this process than the statement by a former editor of the *Journal of consulting and clinical psychology* setting out the guidelines used by them for the evaluation of manuscripts submitted for publication. The salient critical points by which manuscripts are judged range from topic content—"Is the article appropriate to this journal?"—to style, introduction, method, representative design, statistics, factor analysis, figures, diagrams, and tables, to the breadth of the discussion and the verifiability of the conclusions. It will be found in Appendix D. If one bears in mind that this journal is one of the key publications of the APA, it will be understood that Maher's guidelines are more rather than less the "official" guidelines of the APA.

CHAPTER 11
The Profession

1. Psychological organizations

The intellectual development of any field of knowledge is fostered and accelerated by the exchange of ideas between those who are working in it or who are actively engaged in relevant research, whether this be in an academic institution or in some other environment.

Philosophers have, of course, since time immemorial, depended on the testing of their ideas through discussion with each other. One need scarcely remind readers that Plato cast all his teachings into the form of dialogues, but it may be useful also to remind ourselves that Plato already firmly recommended in his *Republic* that those who want to be cobblers or pilots or judges receive special education and training in the skills appropriate to their calling. In other words, he stressed the need for professionalism if the state was to flourish.

In our own terms, a profession is an occupation which demands highly specialized knowledge and skills acquired by the study at tertiary level of a body of theory and principles which have been determined as relevant by a group of appropriate experts, normally found among those who constitute the profession. Though this may appear to be tautologous, it reflects a historical development common to almost all professions now recognized as such.

The purpose of all professional organizations is to promote the discipline of the profession and not, in the first place, the well-being of the members of the organization. However differently the term "psychology" may be interpreted by individuals, most professional psychological organizations welcome, as members, all who are appropriately qualified and who genuinely profess psychology. Unfortunately, this ideal state has not, in the past, and probably does not now, represent absolute universality; there always have been associations within certain national and ethnic groups which lay more emphasis on the conformity of association members than on a free exchange of possibly opposing ideas.

Yet, for very sound reasons—linguistic, financial, administrative—most professional organizations are of a national character. These national groups have formed a small number of world-wide organizations with the specific purpose of bridging national barriers and to give reality to the universal uniformity of man.

There are some very good guides to the major international and national psychological organizations but not one of them covers the whole field exhaustively. It is therefore necessary to consult several of them if one wants to obtain a true conspectus and, in certain cases, to identify the kind of professional group best suited to one's requirements. It is worth noting here that the type of guide in question is normally found only in major research libraries in whose catalogues an approach via "Science–Associations" will reveal the presence of the directories here discussed.

A very general reference work on this topic, the *Encyclopaedia of associations,* published by the Gale Research Co., Detroit, Michigan is now in its 15th edition (1980) and covers national organizations of the USA and an updated edition appears almost every year. The first volume is arranged by subject, and lists an astonishingly long list of associations concerned with one aspect or another of psychology. Similar national listings can be found—albeit on a smaller scale—for many countries, and the Gale Research Co., in conjunction with CBD Research Ltd of Buckingham, Kent, England, has produced a *Directory of European associations* (3rd ed., 1981) which lists, under subjects, the principal national professional organizations (see Fig. 17). Other recent international directories are the *Guide to world science* and the *European research index,* two British publications likely to be found in some libraries but only of limited use because their subject indexing leaves a lot to be desired.

More specifically related to psychology is B. Wolman's *International directory of psychology* which appeared in 1979 and lists national societies and facts about the profession in short country-oriented surveys based on a questionnaire sent out in 1976. Wolman also provides details of membership for the two largest world organizations in this field: the International Union of Psychological Science (IUPS) and the Inter-American Society of Psychology or Sociedad Interamericana de Psicologia (SIP). The national psychological associations which constitute the IUPS are listed every 2 years in the official journal of the IUPS, the *International journal of psychology.*

Useful as the work by Wolman is in offering a state-of-the-art review at national levels, there is no certainty that it will be kept up to date and at any rate it does not provide a list of the hundreds of psychological associations that help make the community of persons interested in psychology into a profession proper. Lists of national organizations can be found in most libraries (cf. the note made earlier about how to find references to them in the library catalogues) and we have cited some of these in Appendix E at the end of this book.

Besides establishing the names of the hundreds of associations and societies concerned with professional aspects of psychology, these reference works also help us to identify, albeit only indirectly, the names of

CH Fédération Romande Immobilière (FRI)
= Westschweizerischer Hauseigenümerverband. 1925.
■ Rue du Midi 15, 1003 Lausanne. (021) 22 09 41.
M 5 cantonal org, with c 70,200 individual members.
● Conf - Inf - Stat - Res.
¶ Le Bulletin Immobilier - 24.

CH Schweizerischer Hauseigentümerverband.
Mühlebachstrasse 70, Postfach, 8032 Zürich.
(01) 69 22 70.
M c 95,000 i.
¶ Der Schweizerische Hauseigentümer.

D   Arbeitsgemeinschaft der Grundbesitzerverbände
> 2520 D

D   Zentralverband der Deutschen Haus-, Wohnungs- und
Grundeigentümer eV.
4000 Düsseldorf, Cecilienallee 45. (0211) 43 45 55;
43 45 85. tx ε 584 305.
M Regional & local associations of house- and landowners.

DK Grundejernes Landsorganisation (GLO)
= National Organisation of Houseowners. 1907.
■ Nørre Voldgade 2, 1358 København K. (02) 12 03 30.
M 75,000 i (members of local associations).
● Conf - Inf - Educ.
¶ Huset - Orientering for Grundejere - 12; DKr 56 yr.

I   Unione Piccoli Proprietari Immobiliari.
Corso S Martino 3, 10122 Torino. (011) 54 62 47.

L   Union des Propriétaires du Grand-Duché de Luxembourg asbl
(UP)
= Haus- und Grundeigentümerverband des Grossherzogtums
Luxemburg. 1937.

5935 PSYCHOLOGISTS
PSYCHOLOGUES
PSYCHOLOGEN

A   Berufsverband Österreichischer Psychologen. (BÖP) 1953.
1010 Wien, Liebiggasse 5.
M c 400 f.

B   Société Belge de Psychologie. (SBP) 1946.
See Introduction, 4(d).

CH Schweizerische Gesellschaft für Psychologie und ihre Anwendungen
(SGP)
= Société Suisse de Psychologie et de Psychologie Appliquée.
(SSP) 1941.
Postfach 197, 3000 Bern 7. (031) 22 93 31.
O   To promote research in psychology, university education in
psychology, & the further education of psychologists; to
protect the status of the profession.
M c 400 i.
● Conf - Educ.
¶ Revue Suisse de Psychologie Pure et Appliquée /
Schweizerische Zeitschrift für Psychologie und ihre
Anwendung - 4; FrS 48 yr. (Official organ;
published by Hans Huber & Co, Länggass-Strasse 76,
3000 Bern).

D   Berufsverband Deutscher Psychologen eV. (BDP) 1946.
■ Heilsbachstrasse 22, 5300 Bonn 1. (0228) 64 61 22.
M 4700 i.
● Conf - Inf - Stat - Educ.
¶ Report Psychologie - 6; DM 14,80 per issue.

DDR Gesellschaft für Psychologie der Deutschen Demokratischen
Republik. 1962.

FIG. 17. *Directory of European Associations*, 3rd ed., 1981; facsimile of p. 328 showing
beginning of list of European psychological associations

individual psychologists and of the specific conditions of membership in national professional organizations. It should be understood that, in general, individuals are members of national bodies, while international organizations consist of national groups on which they confer, through admission to membership, a well-defined status of professionalism. Complex as this may seem, it is a standard hierarchical structure common to almost all professional fields and scholarly endeavours.

The names, addresses and, in many instances, the specialism of individual psychologists can best be ascertained from membership lists of national associations, e.g. the American Psychological Association, the Australian Psychological Society, the British Psychological Society, the Canadian Psychological Association, to name but a few of the major ones.

The oldest of these associations is 90 years old. The APA was founded in 1892 and now has a membership of over 40,000 and its constitution, statutes and regulations have been imitated more or less closely by many other national societies. The BPsS is only just 40 years old, with about 7650 members, but it has been more directly linked with the professional societies in the British Commonwealth where daughter organizations have tended to model their independent status closely on the BPsS. Thus, the Australian Psychological Society which, in 1980, had already about 4000 members, evolved in 1966 from being the Australian Branch of the BPsS.

Though Canada's population is a third larger than that of Australia, the Canadian Psychological Association, which was established already before World War II, is considerably smaller in membership than the APsS; one obvious reason appears to be that the interchangeability of credentials with the much larger and more influential APA reduces the need for local professional identification.

The APA publishes, periodically, an updated list of its members and, given the large number of names involved, this is a major directory. Senior psychologists working outside the USA can be traced through the *International directory of psychologists, exclusive of the USA*. This important directory is sponsored by the IUPS and the 3rd edition has been prepared by the Zentralstelle für Psychologische Information und Dokumentation at the University of Trier, Germany, with the financial support of UNESCO and the US National Science Foundation. Besides citing the obvious personal data for every psychologist listed, the *International directory* also indicates his or her national affiliation and the major fields of interest. The arrangement of entries is by country but there is, unfortunately, no comprehensive name index. This is of some consequence because it is impossible to tell why so Italian a name as H. M. De Vetta should be listed under Zimbabwe. Particularly useful is the long list of national associations that completes this *Directory*. Again one can only regret the lack of an important detail: the full address.

One of the prime aims of professional societies, as has already been suggested, is the establishment and maintenance of professional standards. The objective is partly achieved by establishing and, of course, maintaining strict criteria for admission to membership. In practice this has led to different grades of membership with varying entry requirements; commonly, bona-fide students are admitted to student membership but some societies require applications to be supported by an approved teacher. Student membership normally allows the bearer to attend most meetings of the society and to receive some of the society's journals and other publications at a reduced (students) rate. For this and some other reasons, student membership of any one of the larger psychological societies depends on varying requirements. For instance, the APA requires all applicants to have completed a PhD before they are admitted to the professional register—strangely enough the PhD does not have to be in psychology; however, divisional membership is open only to those whose PhD is based on psychology, and the same holds for fellowships. By contrast, the BPsS's minimum requirement is a bachelor's honours degree in psychology—but anyone examining this in detail will soon find out that the BPsS insists, in fact, on a considerably larger psychology component in the educational preparation of applicants for professional membership than is commonly the case in North America.

In Australia the criteria for admission to the professional register of the APsS have been set at an academic qualification based on 4 years of study with psychology as a major plus 2 years (or equivalent part-time) of full-time supervised experience at postgraduate level. Other Commonwealth countries, e.g. Canada and New Zealand, stipulate a master's degree or a bachelor's degree at honours level.

One must, however, be careful when attempting to compare the membership grades between various countries. For instance, an associate member of the BPsS would be a full member of the APsS because of the different criteria of admission. At the same time, an "associate member" of the APsS has about the same status as a "graduate member" of the BPsS. Perhaps all of this should not be taken too literally. After all, most societies have vested in their council discretionary powers to admit some persons to an appropriate grade of membership according to their merit.

Matters are somewhat different with the high distinction of Fellow in the large and long-established psychological associations. While Honorary Fellows will, of course, always be very few in number—it is a distinction normally reserved to mark a quite outstanding career and distinguished contributions to the discipline—ordinary fellowships are attainable and are bestowed upon members who have considerable standing and experience in some branch of psychology. In the APA, it is a prerequisite for Fellows to have been members of the APA for 1 year, to have 5 years beyond the doctoral degree and to have made a significant contribution to psychology. Nominations come forward normally through the Divisions of the APA.

The position in the BPsS, the APsS, and the CPsA is similar though details of pre-election service differ as, for instance in the non-requirement of divisional membership of the BPsS and APsS. The APsS, for example, requires members to have held full membership for at least 7 years before being eligible to apply.

It is worth noting that many societies are divided into divisions—boards and sections sometimes on a geographic basis, sometimes on the basis of greater specialization. Clinical psychology or educational psychology are good examples of the type of sectional interest which has often led to sub-groups being formed within the large psychological associations. In most instances, admission to membership of such specialist sections is dependent on specialist qualifications or experience.

There are two objectives for which all professional associations strive: the establishment and maintenance of the theories and principles on which the profession rests; and the recognition and preservation of its code of professional conduct. The insistence on a continuing rational and theoretical basis of professional practice leads to a concern with teaching and research, with the standards of admission to the various grades of the profession, and ultimately with the institutions engaged in the education of recruits to the profession. This is a traditional though, of course, not necessarily a conservative pattern of the social fabric of most professions.

An excellent but now unfortunately dated guide to research establishments in many countries is the survey sponsored by the APA and the IUPS and published in 1966 under the title *International opportunities for advanced training and research in psychology*. The book lists, for about 90 countries, details of admission to higher degrees in universities and similar academic institutions, the status of psychological research and of the professional associations and conditions for visitors. This is by far the most useful compilation on this important topic and it is regrettable that a new edition has not been issued. The academic world is changing so rapidly that a revision of this guide should appear every 2–3 years. The establishment of a code of ethics (or Code of Professional Conduct as it is also known), and the efforts necessary to preserve it, are an essential objective of every profession and are fundamentally related to the standing of that profession in the wider community. A code of ethics relates to the respect a profession is paid by other professions, as well as by those who participate in other types of social groups. Such respect is partly expressed in terms of relative rates of professional remuneration, and the influence and authority members of the profession have in the community, and the extent to which the profession can defend itself against "poachers" and charlatans.

Both these objectives, the one related to professional standards and the other related to professional standing, have stimulated the production of journals of various kinds, have led to professional meetings at local, national and international levels and have been fostered by the establishment of government-audited registers of members.

On the aspect of journals a good deal more will be found in Chapter 3. Suffice it here to say that, commonly, the larger the professional society, the greater its financial resources—and consequently the more varied the ways in which it can foster communication between members. The obvious case in point is the APA, which has very large ranges of publications both in serial form and in the form of handbooks, guide books, manuals, etc.

If there is one lesson in all of this, it is surely that students should join their national psychological society as soon as possible. Membership rates for students are normally considerably lower than all other rates while nevertheless offering entitlements to journals and other publications. There are, furthermore, the tremendous informal advantages of meeting scholars and practitioners in the field, of participating in discussions both passively and actively, and of learning to observe.

2. Careers for Graduates in Psychology

Careers for graduates in psychology is a subject somewhat different from careers in psychology, and the reason for the distinction rests largely on the criteria applied by the professional societies for admission to their membership ranks. There are at least three options available to psychology graduates. The first of these is to use the qualification for a job for which a degree in psychology is equal to that of any other major. Examples of this are in business and general administration, the diplomatic corps, the armed forces, or as a precursor to studying for another profession, e.g. law. A good deal can be said for having studied psychology when one chooses an occupation which involves handling other people in some kind of supervisory activity, or which requires the assessment of actions in terms of human potential and performance.

The second option available is to use the degree for jobs in which psychology is directly relevant. Examples of this are in personnel administration, advertising and social work where quite obviously human behaviour is the root and reason for the professional activities which graduates are expected to perform.

The third option is to use the psychology degree as a basis for further research or training in some branch of psychology. Examples of this are the clinical, educational, management consultants, academic and forensic fields.

With regard to this third option one must acknowledge that some of the career paths are presently well served by experienced incumbents while others are not. An instance of a well-served speciality is that of the academic psychologist. The growth of tertiary education institutions is now substantially less than was the case about 15 years ago; further, that growth period was effected by recruiting relatively young staff who will not be retiring for some time yet. An instance of a less well-served speciality is that of clinical psychology. The demand for clinical skills is one that is likely to grow. A wider community acceptance, as well as a growing recognition of it by cognate professions, will help the expansion. This particular option has the added attraction of making its qualified and experienced members eligible for both institutional jobs and private practice.

In all countries the public service employs psychologists and it is interesting to note that such positions occur in a number of very different fields of psychology. Departments of transport (road, aviation, shipping) have need of trained psychologists, as do departments of education, mental health and public service employment services. The armed forces use psychologists; sometimes as commissioned officers within the forces and in other instances as civilians for a particular branch of the Department of Defence.

The general administrative or clerical stream of the Public Service provides an area of employment where qualification in psychology is an advantage but not a requirement. For instance, while there are special opportunities for graduates in psychology in the departments of employment and of industrial relations, applicants for positions will find that the opportunities for promotion from general administrative duties are facilitated also in other government departments for those who possess academic qualifications in one of the behavioural sciences.

Furthermore, the economic trends of the past few years have made many organizations increasingly aware of how "expensive" it can be to employ poorly selected and trained people. Management has become sensitive to the need for career and performance counselling, and to manpower planning and development within their organization. The increasing emphasis on staff development has meant that many professionals with behavioural science backgrounds are being utilized in "middle management" administrative positions. Many business firms and government departments, while not employing many psychologists directly, provide opportunities for psychology graduates to work as training officers or research officers at various levels.

In personnel work there is increasing scope for those with academic backgrounds to assist and advise management in the introduction of different organizational systems, e.g. industrial democracy and worker participation.

The "mixing" suggested here is of a career path, part of which is as a psychologist and part of which is as an administrator. In this instance one hopes that the "Peter Principle" would not apply, and that successful experience as a professional psychologist would result in an equally successful subsequent career in higher administration.

It is sometimes believed that jobs in psychology must be provided by governments as part of their social welfare or education programme and that private practice is a privilege of the medical profession because someone else picks up the tab for the fees. This is generally true, and so far has provided satisfactory employment for most graduates, but with recent cuts in government spending a feeling of gloom has settled on the professional community and those who plan to enter it. We suggest that, as in any other walk of life, graduates with initiative and flexibility have ample opportunities for employment where their psychological training is useful.

In the following paragraphs we outline some suggestions which may start a young graduate on a path towards earning a living as a psychologist but there will always be the need for initiative, as indeed the study of psychology and industrial relations clearly shows.

Most psychology departments turn out three types of graduates:

(1) Professionally trained psychologists with a diploma, masters or PhD degrees. In this group most are training for either clinical practice or research.
(2) Four-year pass or honours graduates (with at least half the courses in the discipline of psychology).
(3) Three-year pass graduates.

If psychologists with clinical skills cannot find government posts there are openings in private practice in which they may succeed even without the benefits of medical qualifications. These include weight control or smoking programmes, management of phobias, child management programmes for parents, and sexual counselling. Some of these could be self-management programmes with clinical support. Although fully qualified practitioners will have the necessary professional background, further specific training could be obtained through continuing education courses. Experience indicates that there is a large population in need of these services, who are willing to pay moderate fees for them without recourse to medical benefits. Since group and self-management programmes are not labour-intensive, moderate fees can add up to a sizeable income.

Psychologists with research degrees who are unable to find employment in universities or colleges should explore employment in industry on a variety of projects as consultants where research and numerical skills are required. Again, it depends on their flexibility and ingenuity to create a niche for themselves.

Four-year graduates are usually not regarded as having been adequately prepared to work without supervision. However, they may well explore the possibilities outlined for professionals and become attached to an organization which employs psychologists either on a part-time basis to carry out a specific investigation under the supervision of a more experienced researcher, or on a contract basis which would allow the employee some time for private practice.

It is worth bearing in mind that research costs money, and that unless the researcher derives funds from a private income he will have to seek support somewhere. There are a number of philanthropic trusts and private institutions who are at times willing to support a well-designed project, especially when this is of interest to non-profit organizations, or is designed to benefit the public in some particular manner.

The choice of a special field of psychology appropriate to one's own inclinations and ability is sometimes difficult, either because the implications of such a choice cannot always be foreseen, or because one has failed to identify one's ambition with the appropriate branch of the discipline. Undergraduate courses, and to a minor extent some early postgraduate courses, tend, quite properly, to give an overview of psychology rather than stress a particular area. However, by the time students embark upon a higher degree in psychology they should have a fairly definite idea of which area they want to specialize in.

It is obvious that experienced university teachers and practitioners should be consulted to formulate a career plan. If practitioners cannot be easily identified, the local branch of the regional or national society will at least provide a list of names of persons who may be consulted.

It will already have become evident that, in order to specialize in a field of psychology, students will need to complete a relevant specialist qualification and to gain supervised experience. Information on the education and experience required for registration as a specialist psychologist can be obtained from the government-controlled registration boards and from the institutions—academic or research—which offer relevant education and training.

Among such local expertise one would find experienced academics and experienced practitioners. If local experts are not readily identified then the local branch of the psychological society and/or the registration board are excellent resources. In this book, which deals substantially with library resources and methods of study and research, we would like to plead the notion that an interview with the relevant expert can pay handsome rewards. Work in the library will yield a number of names for particular fields of psychology and one could then correspond with those people seeking their advice and help.

The British Psychological Society offers very sound advice through its booklet *Careers in psychology*, which is updated from time to time. In addition the BPsS has issued a series of similar booklets on careers in special fields of psychology such as social psychology, occupational psychology, clinical psychology, educational psychology and on psychologists in the prison service. Obviously, specialist education and training cannot be obtained at every institution of tertiary education, whether it has a department of psychology or not. Courses in clinical psychology, though not taught everywhere, will be relatively easy to find, while a more exotic specialization such as Jungian psychology or humanistic therapy will be rare offerings in any university department of psychology. Those who are bent upon these rarer fields of psychology will have to be prepared to move about the world until they find the teachers and the courses congenial to them. Those who opt for this approach will unquestionably discover wider prospects of choice. Nor should this search for the right teacher be seen as a novel development; it has been a traditional procedure in Europe from the middle of the twentieth century. The economic conditions and the attempt at mass instruction in our time have tended to put a temporary stop to that excellent practice of yore.

This work would not be complete without a reference to a locator for North America. For these people the APA publishes *The consolidated roster for psychology: a location reference.* In this the APA cites the registration requirements for each state in the USA and for Canada for psychologists wishing to enter practice, showing what qualifications are necessary, experience required, exemptions likely to be granted, etc.

Another, and perhaps additional, tactic for those wishing to specialize is to undertake some voluntary work placement associated with a skilled professional. The dual benefits of such a placement are that one gets a realistic rather than glamorous view of what it is like to specialize in that field, and one meets people who know their way around and are in a strong position to give advice.

However, in the long run specialization in a field of psychology requires further study and the completion of both a relevant specialist qualification and supervised experience. Registration boards and institutions offering graduate specialist courses have a clear understanding of the practical training required and their advice must be heeded.

3. Further education and training in psychology

A little knowledge is a dangerous bit of equipment, and the same can surely be said of knowledge that has gone stale. The message of all we have said, until now, relates clearly to the many means available to the serious student and conscientious aspirant to professional status to find out more about specific fields in psychology. The practice of psychology, we have stressed, is a professional activity and it is dependent on continuing research. Such research may be undertaken by individuals or by teams, by persons in private practice or by members of an institution established to foster psychological research. Furthermore, such research may be clearly directed at a solution of specific problems or at theoretical solutions of universal questions. Finally, those who wish to engage in research may like to do so in order to upgrade their qualifications or in order to obtain practical experience in research methodology, or perhaps simply for the sake of intellectual curiosity. Those who are motivated by this last-named characteristic may well be getting the greatest deal of satisfaction—but that is another matter altogether.

It is obvious, then, that there are many variables in the fundamental motivation to engage in research. As readers may have expected, there are printed sources of information that may help to formulate a decision. But it must be remembered that the first step towards this goal has to be made by the individual concerned, even if the stimulus to do so lies in external circumstances. It is also assumed that the research here referred to begins, normally, after the successful completion of the tertiary education programme that led to an honours degree or the equivalent of a master's degree.

There are numerous guides to universities and colleges offering doctorates in psychology or related studies, and this is not the place to describe them. Every academic library and major public library will have the *World of learning* or the *Commonwealth universities year book,* or similar directories. More specifically oriented towards the needs of those aspiring to advanced study in psychology is the APA's list of about 500 institutions in the USA, entitled *Graduate study in psychology.* A guide to British institutions can be found in an in-house circular, the *Compendium of postgraduate studies* produced for a Committee of Heads of Psychology Departments in British universities by the Psychology Department of the University of Surrey.

Plans for the acquisition of higher academic qualifications are usually made in consultation with one's own first alma mater and, if one wants to move to another institution, with the head of the appropriate department in the university of one's choice. It should be clearly understood that admission to a programme of advanced studies is by no means automatic. The faculty and the candidate must approve of each other.

Students trying to decide whether they want to undertake advanced studies should, of course, have some idea in which field of psychology they would like to specialize; they should identify the head of department whose specialism is close to what they want to study and they would be well advised to accept a status of "famulus" or understudy if they want to gain the full benefit of association with a well-established scholar.

It is somewhat different with the attainment of the professional experience required to gain registration as a professional member of an association of psychologists. We have already referred in this chapter to the role and importance of professional associations. Here it will suffice to point out that details of requirements for registration may vary—seemingly slightly yet sufficiently to make it mandatory to seek advice from the respective registrar of the appropriate association whether a proposed or suggested practical experience programme meets the needs for registration. Such programmes may include one or more facets of experience as a psychologist working under supervision in a clinic, an occupational counselling bureau, a social services department, an educational institution or a manpower department of a factory. Some years ago, a conference on graduate education in social psychology was addressed by a number of distinguished scholars whose views were subsequently debated by a group of senior students. The results of this exchange of ideas was published in 1968 as *Higher education in social psychology*; in spite of the 14 years that have elapsed, the collection of essays is still worth reading.

Another, but no less important factor in further education is to find some financial support during the period of study, support which fairly frequently also has to provide for the scholar's wife and family. There exist a number of useful guides to organizations offering grants for study and research. Most of these guides have been compiled on a national basis and interested students should start their inquiries at the library reference desk. It would lead too far to list here such directories of grant-giving organizations. At the international level there is UNESCO's *Study abroad*, a frequently revised directory of organizations and institutions which support students from all parts of the world.

APPENDIX A
A Guide to Library Searches

THE preparation for, and writing of, essays, papers, reports and theses in psychology often throw up questions the answers to which can commonly be found in libraries. These questions tend to fall into four categories seeking data about

- a word;
- a fact or an event, biographical data;
- a reference to a journal article, a book or a document;
- an explanation or exposition of a concept or of a specific area in psychology.

Obviously, these categories reflect an increasing degree of complexity and each is representative of an almost infinite number of examples. We have made up four tables which illustrate the type of reference work that would be most suitable, in the first instance, to provide an answer within each category, but it cannot be emphasized enough that the sources of the "solution" are mere examples, that the titles suggested as possible sources of information are, in their turn, also only representative of categories of reference works.

To use the tables, read the questions presented on the left-hand side of the relevant table. If the question asked is applicable to your problem, follow it across the page to the relevant source. It should be noted that often, more than one question may be relevant to your problem.

The library user in search of bibliographic sources should proceed roughly as follows:

(1) Clearly define your inquiry.
(2) If authors or titles of relevant printed materials are known, identify their presence through the library's catalogues if in monograph form, or by locating the appropriate journal if published as a contribution to a periodical.
(3) If neither specific authors nor titles are known consult the subject catalogue of the library for entries under appropriate headings—bearing in mind the comments made on thesaurus terms in chapter 5 and identify the journals that deal with the subjects of interest. Note, however, that the subject headings for journals are of necessity very

broad, i.e. there will be lots of entries under the heading "Psychology —Periodicals" and some under more specialized headings such as "Psychology, Experimental—Periodicals" but there will be no entries, as has been said already, for the thousands of articles in those periodicals.
(4) It is time-wasting—up to a degree—to chase subject references by looking through every journal in the library; even if we consult the annual index to every journal this is not likely to produce a specific article on one's topic within a reasonable time. If one is looking for the current (i.e. periodicals-based) literature on a topic the only economic procedure is to consult the indexing and abstracting services held by the library or to make a search of the computerized data banks described in chapter IV.
(5) Once books and articles have been identified through the indexing and abstracting services, whether they have been examined manually or via a v.d.u., go back to step (2) above.
(6) It may occur that the library one is using does not hold the particular book or journal identified as being relevant to one's inquiry. In that case one should either try and identify another location (library) for it; a relatively simple procedure with the better-known journals is by consulting one of the union lists of serials mentioned in chapter IV, or consult a member of the library's reference staff whose task it is to help procure books and journals. Indeed, libraries will not normally lend materials to persons not registered as readers, and inquiries for material held in institutions other than the one to which the reader is affiliated must be made through the library where one is registered.

These are, broadly, the basic steps for a literature search. The library users should be aware that the financial restraints under which libraries operate, at the best of times, make it essential that as much as possible of the search is done by the user. Books, periodicals, or documents should be cited accurately when asking for them on interlibrary loan, including the source of information. Given the high cost of library staff time involved in the preparation of interlibrary loan requests, the cost of supplying them by the lending library and the eventual return to the latter, library users should not ask for materials which are not likely to be relevant to their topic.

The economics of the search steps here outlined will be obvious to all. Yet a rider should be placed on these recommendations: no serious student should fail to roam as often as opportunity permits through the stacks of an academic or research library. Some libraries require users to apply for a stack pass before they will allow free access to the research collection, but the importance of obtaining such a pass and of spending time browsing among all sections of the collection cannot be exaggerated. Psychology, as we have already observed at the beginning, is a discipline that is undergoing rapid development; shifts in emphasis and new lights in old tunnels necessitate frequent reorientation for psychologists. Classical works may present a dated view, and neglected aspects of research may suddenly attain new importance and significances. Psychologists must be well and widely read, and develop a broad frame of reference if they are to maintain a high level of scholarship.

1. Information about a word

Question	General type of reference work	Example of specific reference work
Do I understand what the words mean?	General dictionaries	*The Oxford English dictionary* (13 vols.) or *The shorter Oxford English dictionary* (2 vols.)
Is it a psychological word I don't know?	Psychological dictionary	Chaplin, J.P. *Dictionary of psychology*
Do I want more extensive information on that psychological word?	Psychological dictionary	Wolman, B.B. *International encyclopedia of psychiatry, psychoanalysis & neurology*
Do I want a word translated?	Bilingual or trilingual dictionary	See the relevant dual language dictionary *or* Duijker *et al*
Do I want a similar word or a synonym?	General thesaurus	*Roget's thesaurus*
Do I want a similar psychological word?	Psychological thesaurus	APA's *Thesaurus of psychological index terms*
Do I want to know what abbreviations, initials, acronyms, represent?	Book of acronyms, initials, etc.	Crowley, E.T. (Ed.) *Acronyms, initialisms and abbreviations dictionary*
Do I want to know the correct abbreviations or initials?	Reverse book of acronyms	Crowley, E.T. (Ed.) *Reverse acronyms, initialisms and abbreviations dictionary*

2. Information about people, events, etc.

Question	General type of reference work	Example of specific reference work
General knowledge question about someone or something	Encyclopaedia	*Encyclopaedia Britannica. Chambers's encyclopaedia* (The latest edition should normally be used, though the older editions are often significant for historical background.)
Who was that person?	Biographical dictionaries	*Dictionary of biography. Who's who* (Most of these reference works appear in a national context)
General knowledge question about someone or something well known in psychology	Psychological encyclopaedia or biographical registers, list of psychologists	Eysenck, H.J., Arnold, W. & Meili, R. *Encyclopaedia of psychology*
What are the entrance requirements to the local psychological association?	Handbooks or membership lists of national associations	
How many people in my city (county, state) are registered as insane?	Statistical yearbooks, Department of Health annual reports	Great Britain. Dept of Health and Social Security. Statistical research reports series. *In-patients statistics from the mental health inquiry.* Queensland. Dept of Health and Medical Services. *Annual report.*
Date and place of an international meeting on an aspect of psychology	House journal of national societies	British Psychological Association. *Bulletin* *World meetings: outside USA and Canada*
Correct date of a political or social event?	Contemporary social information	*Keesing's contemporary archives* *Facts on file.*

3. Literature retrieval

Question	Type of reference work	Comment and Examples
Do you want the latest extensive review of the theory of an area of psychology (or as it stood at a particular date?)	*Annual review of psychology*	Provides a review and present "state of the art" as well as comprehensive references on areas of psychology.
Do you want the latest work in an area of psychology or the latest work by someone?	*Psychological abstracts*	See the latest monthly edition under the relevant areas. For the latest work by someone, see the author index. If this fails, try the previous month.
Do you want information on an area or specific topic or within a specific period of time?	*Psychological abstracts*	"Cumulative Subject Index" of *Psychological abstracts* lists topic within the year specified (N.B. Index terms can be expanded with the *Thesaurus* mentioned above)
If *Psychological abstracts* was not enough what do I try next?	*Social science citation index* or *Index medicus*	Try reference works in cognate areas, e.g. biology, education, medicine.
What other institution has the journal in your city? Elsewhere in the country? Overseas?	The various guides to other library holdings, e.g. union lists of your own country or of other countries.	This is an area of expertise where reference librarians are best able to help; why not consult them.
Where is there a list of psychological journals?	*Psychological abstracts*	Covers many but not all.
If your library does not have a book, is it still in print? Who is the publisher? Who is the author of the book of which I have only the title and the author?	Lists of books currently in print (author or title index) or the *Cumulative book index*	*Books in print* (North American) (Also *British books in print, Australian books in print* and others.) Most are published annually. French and Spanish versions exist.
Do you want information on theses presented for higher degrees?		*Comprehensive dissertations index*, or *Dissertation abstracts international*
Do you want a list of higher degree theses within a country?	Use the appropriate national guide to accepted theses or dissertations, or use international reference guide.	*Guide to the availability of theses* by Borchardt & Thawley which lists theses bibliographies.

4. Extensive information on a specific area of psychology

Question	General or specific reference
Do I want extensive background information?	Subject catalogue of the library.
If no answer in library's catalogue by specific topic, then what?	*Thesaurus of psychological index terms* gives broader, related and narrower terms to look for in the subject catalogue.
Is the information about Human Behaviour, Psychology, Psychiatry, Mental Health?	An encyclopaedia of psychology or of the social sciences, e.g. *The encyclopaedia of human behaviour, psychology, psychiatry and mental health.*
Mental measurement: Issues	Anastasi, A. *Differential psychology.*
Test reviews, standardisation	Buros, O.D. (Ed.) *Eighth mental measurements year book.*
Personality tests	Buros, O.D. (Ed.) *Personality tests and reviews*
Tests in or out of print	Buros, O.D. (Ed.) *Tests in print.*
Problems of psychological testing	Cronbach, L.J. *Essentials of psychological testing educational measurement and evaluation.*
Framework or background in: Clinical psychology	Wolman, B.B. *et al.*, *Handbook of clinical psychology.*
Psychiatry	Arieti, S. (Ed.) *American handbook of psychiatry.*
Is the information about psychoanalysis?	Special reference source, e.g. *Encyclopaedia of psychoanalysis.*

APPENDIX B

Report Writing: a Model for Empirical Psychological Reports

TITLE
THE EFFECT OF READING TUITION ON ACADEMIC ACHIEVEMENT: VOLUNTEERING AND METHODS OF TUITION

Brief descriptive use of key words

SUMMARY

Volunteers were recruited from an introduction to Psychology course at an Australian university. Of the 197 students in the sample 108 volunteered for a reading improvement programme. From the group of volunteers 26 were chosen at random to undergo a course of reading improvement using a speed-reading projector. A further 27 were similarly chosen for a course on reading improvement but without the pedagogical use of mechanical aids. Both the groups receiving reading tuition improved over their starting rates. The non-projector group had greater speed but not greater comprehension. Neither the fact of volunteering, nor the non-receiving of tuition nor the form of tuition had an impact on examination performance. It is concluded that volunteering for, and the receiving of reading tuition do not bear upon performance at formal examinations. The presentation of relevant content in a reading improvement course does not enhance academic achievement.

Include with report if instructed to do so (about 150 to 200 words)

INTRODUCTION

In recent years there has been a heightened interest in reading rates. Among the features which have brought it to wider interest are those of its use by professional persons who need to keep up with extensive reading requirements, and the somewhat extravagant claims of some commercial reading improvement services.

What is the study about? Give the context.

There are a number of controversial issues associated with this area of research. The use of mechanical devices, the measurement of reading rate and adequacy of control groups are examples. Such issues are discussed in more detail by Berger (1968).

What issues emerge from debate in the literature?

In a recent article, Witty (1969) asserted that aspirations about reading rate should be more modest than are commonly advertised. With a starting rate of about 270 words per minute the average student might expect to improve by about 75 per cent to just over 470 words per minute. A related problem is that of comprehension of material. Berger cited a study in which the conclusion was drawn that comprehension depended less upon speed and more upon intelligence, the purpose of the reading, the difficulty level of the material and the opportunities for verification and perception of continuity. The results of an investigation of the Wood Reading Dynamics method by Liddle (1966) showed results which did not substantiate the claim that exceptional rates were obtained without a loss of comprehension.

Present findings and what others said on the issue. Take the views and illustrate each.

Carver (1972) maintained that most courses teach one to skim and that an increase in speed is not gained without sacrificing comprehension. The best way to improve reading, he says, is to read.

What issues emerge from debate in the literature?

Reading competence at the starting position has been shown to have little or no influence upon the magnitude of the change that can

Generalize the findings of repeated work to date.

be expected following tuition. Participants at both ends of the pre-test continuum appeared to gain equally well in reading achievement (Brim, 1968).

In several studies attention has been directed to the question as to whether machinery is necessary or desirable. McLaughlin (1969) has shown that speed readers appear to use their peripheral vision not only to examine the words on either side of each fixation but also to inspect the lines above and below. The use of a projector showing one line at a time prevents the development and exercise of this skill. Paperback scanning sessions in which training was given have been demonstrated to produce a significantly higher gain in reading rate than the use of either tachistoscope, controlled reader, or controlled pacing methods (Berger, 1967). Further confirmation is given by Witty who reports that studies repeatedly show that pacing devices do not produce results superior to those of nonpaced tuition.

Are there any general assumptions which could be challenged?

The issue of this study is important because (a) much time and effort is put into speed reading and, (b) if the proposal is demonstrated then it would be highly economical to teach substantive issues and a general skill simultaneously.

Say why you are addressing this issue. Why is this study important practically? theoretically?

At least three studies have considered the effect of reading competence on academic performance. Stebens (1968) has demonstrated that participation in a reading improvement programme improved academic performance. The gains were in reading comprehension, in vocabulary and in total reading performance. Reading rates continued to improve over a five semester period but gains in comprehension, although retained, did not improve. Confirmation of this general finding is given by Freer (1969). In that study the marks of students who had

Here the report becomes specific, discussing precise issues.

been given reading skill improvement training were significantly higher than for a control group.

Mouly (1952) used an experimental group of 155 students who took a remedial reading course for one semester. These were compared with a control group, using honour point ratios over a period of two years for those still in attendance and who had attended at least one full semester. Measures were calculated for both experimental and control groups and adjusted for initial differences in reading and psychological test scores. Only slight differences were found between the adjusted average honour-point ratio of the total for the experimental and control groups. Similarly, the groups were almost identical in drop-out rate semester by semester, and in the average number of credits accumulated over the period. However, when only that portion of the experimental group which had successfully completed the remedial reading programme was compared with the control group, significant differences in favour of the former were found. The conclusion was drawn that a remedial reading programme can result in an improvement in academic grades for those students who take the course seriously.

Report study(ies) that are closest to the present one. Leading to what conclusion?

The study being reported here is designed to draw together the following strands: methods of reading tuition, volunteering for reading courses, and the effect of these variables upon examination performance. Both the first and third points have received separate consideration in other studies. What is different in this study is that it brings in a new factor (volunteering) and compares *methods* of reading tuition in relation to academic performance.

What is original about this study and what variables are to be examined?

METHOD

The sample consisted of 197 university students enrolled for a course "Introduction to Psychology" during 1972. All students had passed a prerequisite course "Introduction to the Behavioural Sciences".

On initial contact with students it was stated that places were available in a reading improvement course and that much of the content would be relevant to the course they were studying. The reading improvement tuition was to occupy an hour a week for one semester. As a consideration, students participating would be excused one of the other specified hours of formal tuition.

Of the 197 students, 108 volunteered to participate in the reading improvement programme. For reasons of experimental design 55 of those volunteering were not included in the reading programme.

The reading improvement consisted of two forms: one form used an EDL Controlled Reader model V–45–P projector; the other form was conventional small group tuition without machinery.

Students undergoing tuition using the projector had specially prepared film-strips presented at an increasing pace both with and without left-to-right scanning. Both this group, and those who had conventional tuition on how to read, were told of scanning, eye movements, skimming, precis points, etc. Both groups used the same content materials.

To summarise this arrangement, there were four groups for comparison: one which had conventional reading tuition, one which had tuition based upon the EDL reading projector, one which volunteered for reading tuition but did not gain entry and a fourth

This is the "how one goes about it" section

Subjects

How subjects were instructed

Apparatus

This method has the advantage of . . . Are there logistic problems?

Method and design

group of non-volunteers. For all those who volunteered, randomisation was used to determine whether they were selected and to which form of tuition they were assigned.

How did the writer(s) go about the study?

There were two criterion measures, in addition to reading speed and comprehension; they were the students' mark on the examination ("Introduction to Psychology") and the mark on the examination for the prerequisite, and cognate course ("Introduction to the Behavioural Sciences").

What are the operational criteria?

RESULTS

An analysis of variance was carried out on examination performance of all four groups. No significant differences were found on the examination marks for the prerequisite course or the examination marks for the course under consideration.

This is a statement of what was found. No interpretation should be put here.

Of those receiving reading tuition, the projector group improved in speed over the semester by 28.3 per cent whereas the non-projector group improved by 33.0 per cent. This was a significantly greater improvement by the non-projector group over that of the projector group (F = 5.934; df = 1,51; P<.01. No difference was found on comprehension scores between the groups.

Main findings of significance.

To avoid giving the reading tuition groups practice in answering questions on course material, comprehension test passages given during the course were of general content. While the passages ranged over a variety of content areas, an attempt was made to keep them to comparable levels of difficulty. Sixty-seven per cent of the increase in reading speed for general material had occurred by the fourth week of tuition. However, at this stage comprehension had dropped significantly ("t" = 4.75; df = 179; P<.001.) During the remaining sessions, speed increased a further 23 per cent and

Make sure that no discussion creeps in. Keep tables to an absolute minimum. (They are often quite unnecessary). Use graphs, figs. where they are indispensable for clarity.

comprehension returned to the generally satisfactory pre-test level.

The question also arises as to the possibility that some confounding might have taken place as a result of different initial competence. To examine this, an analysis of covariance was carried out using the mark of the prerequisite course as a covariate with reading speed improvement. No significant differences were found between the two reading tuition groups in their final examination marks (F = 1.326; df = 1,49; (n.s.)

DISCUSSIONS AND CONCLUSIONS

It was the purpose of this paper to examine some linked propositions. These propositions were the role of volunteering for reading tuition courses, the efficacy of different forms of tuition, the extent of reading improvement and the effect of reading improvement on examination performance.

Lead into the discussion.

The results showed most clearly that volunteering for reading tuition courses bears no significant relationship to examination performance. Also, that despite the current interest in pedagogical machinery no advantages apparently attach to its use. The group which received the reading tuition without the aid of the projector fared better on speed improvement than the group which did use the projector. The groups were not distinguishable from each other by their ability to comprehend the passages read.

What do the results mean?

Does the study achieve its stated aim?

It is noted that both groups receiving tuition improved their reading speed by an average of 30.9 per cent, but the group receiving tuition with the EDL projector improved 4.7 per cent less than the group taking ordinary classroom reading tuition.

What is the general conclusion?

The study implies that money spent on machinery to improve reading competence is not well spent. Personal contact in teaching

What are the implications?

would seem to bring better results in reading performance.

In terms of cost effectiveness one needs to consider the percentages of improvement which result from different regimes with varying costs.

Might the findings give rise to advice?

From the results of this study it does appear that the extravagant claims made for speed reading improvement programmes are not substantiated (Woody Allen's "I read *War and Peace* in two hours!—it was about Russia?" is an apt comment).

Speed of reading is one important variable, understanding is another and reading and browsing for pleasure is a third. We should be clear about what is our aim before teaching speed reading.

Give consideration to alternative explanations.

REFERENCES

Berger, A. Effectiveness of four methods of increasing reading rate, comprehension, and flexibility. *Dissertation abstracts*, 1967, 27 (12A), 4160.

Berger, A. Controversial issues pertaining to reading rate. *Research in education*, 1968, 3,89.

Brim, B. J. Impact of a reading improvement program. *Journal of educational research*, 1968, 62, 177–182.

Carver, R. P. *Sense and nonsense in speed reading*. Maryland, Revrac Publications, 1972.

Freer, I. J. A study of the effects of a college reading program upon grade point average in Odessa College. *Journal of reading*, 1969, 13, 9–14.

Liddle, W. An initial investigation of the Wood Reading Dynamics method. *Dissertation abstracts*, 1966, 27 (3–9), 605.

McLaughlin, G. H. Reading at "impossible" speeds. *Journal of reading*, 1969, 12 (6), 449–454, 502–510.

Mouly, G. J. A study of the effects of a remedial reading program on academic grades at college level. *Journal of educational psychology*, 1952, 43, 459–466.

Stebins, L. D. A study of the relationship between reading skills and academic achievement in specific subject matter areas, *Dissertation abstracts*. 1968, 28 (12–19), 4881.

Witty, P. A. Rate of reading—a crucial issue. *Journal of reading*, 1969, 13, 102–106, 154–163.

Cite only those works referred to in the text.

Are they cited properly? Do they show evidence of having been properly searched?

APPENDIX C
Self-testing for Authors of Empirical Reports

Title   Have you used key words and terms?

Introduction
   What is the study about? Is the context clearly stated?
   What have other researchers and commentators said on the issues?
   Take the various conceptual viewpoints and illustrate each before drawing a conclusion.
   What unresolved issues emerge from the debate in the literature?
   Do they lead to what your study is about?
   Why are you addressing this issue now and what importance does it have either practically or theoretically?
   What are your underpinnings, rationale, frame of reference etc.?
   How is your study different from others and what do you hope that it will resolve?
   What is the exact aim of the study and what are the precise hypotheses?

Method
   What is (are) the independent variable(s)? What is (are) the dependent variable(s)?
   Are the concepts operationally definable?
   How did you go about conducting the study? Did you pay attention to the subjects and their recruitment? What operations were performed upon them or upon their yielded data?
   Is the presentation clear enough so that another researcher could repeat the study from the information contained in the report?
   Are there any logistic problems? How were they overcome?

Results
   Does this section contain only the findings and no interpretation?
   Are the data expressed in the most economical and meaningful form?
   Are the analyses performed appropriately making sure that the techniques have satisfied assumptions (e.g. skew, kurtosis etc.)?
   Are the conclusions sufficiently clear with respect to significance?

Discussion
  What do the results mean? Are the hypotheses accepted?
  Does the study achieve its stated aim?
  Are alternative explanations possible for what was found?
  Have possible criticisms been rebutted?
  With the new found knowledge could a better study be prescribed?
  What implications are there for these findings?

References
  Are they cited properly?
  Do they show evidence of having been properly searched?
  Are there any glaring omissions in the citations?

APPENDIX D

A Reader's, Writer's, and Reviewer's Guide to Assessing Research Reports in Clinical Psychology

Brendan A. Maher

Harvard University

The Editors of the *Journal of Consulting and Clinical Psychology* who served between 1974 and 1978 have seen some 3,500 manuscripts in the area of consulting and clinical psychology. Working with this number of manuscripts has made it possible to formulate a set of general guidelines that may be helpful in the assessment of research reports. Originally developed by and for journal reviewers, the guidelines are necessarily skeletal and summary and omit many methodological concerns. They do, however, address the methodological concerns that have proved to be significant in a substantial number of cases. In response to a number of requests, the guidelines are being made available here.

Topic Content

1. Is the article appropriate to this journal? Does it fall within the boundaries mandated in the masthead description?

Style

1. Does the manuscript conform to APA style in its major aspects?

Introduction

1. Is the introduction as brief as possible given the topic of the article?
2. Are all of the citations correct and necessary, or is there padding? Are important citations missing? Has the author been careful to cite prior reports contrary to the current hypothesis?

3. Is there an explicit hypothesis?
4. Has the *origin* of the hypothesis been made explicit?
5. Was the hypothesis *correctly* derived from the theory that has been cited? Are other, contrary hypotheses compatible with the same theory?
6. Is there an explicit rationale for the selection of measures, and was it derived logically from the hypothesis?

Method

1. Is the method so described that replication is possible without further information?
2. Subjects: Were they sampled randomly from the population to which the results will be generalized?
3. Under what circumstances was informed consent obtained?
4. Are there probable biases in sampling (e.g., volunteers, high refusal rates, institution population atypical for the country at large, etc.)?
5. What was the "set" given to subjects? Was there deception? Was there control for experimenter influence and expectancy effects?
6. How were subjects debriefed?
7. Were subjects (patients) led to believe that they were receiving "treatment"?
8. Were there special variables affecting the subjects, such as medication, fatigue, and threat that were not part of the experimental manipulation? In clinical samples, was "organicity" measured and/or eliminated?
9. Controls: Were there appropriate control groups? What was being controlled?
10. When more than one measure was used, was the order counterbalanced? If so, were order effects actually analyzed statistically?
11. Was there a control task(s) to confirm specificity of results?
12. Measures: For both dependent and independent variable measures—was validity and reliability established and reported? When a measure is tailor-made for a study, this is very important. When validities and reliabilities are already available in the literature, it is less important.
13. Is there adequate description of tasks, materials, apparatus, and so forth?
14. Is there discriminant validity of the measures?
15. Are distributions of scores on measures typical of scores that have been reported for similar samples in previous literature?
16. Are measures free from biases such as
    a. Social desirability?
    b. Yeasaying and naysaying?
    c. Correlations with general responsivity?
    d. Verbal ability, intelligence?

17. If measures are scored by observers using categories or codes, what is the interrater reliability?
18. Was administration and scoring of the measures done blind?
19. If short versions, foreign-language translations, and so forth, of common measures are used, has the validity and reliability of these been established?
20. In correlational designs, do the two measures have theoretical and/or methodological independence?

Representative Design

1. When the stimulus is a human (e.g., in clinical judgments of clients of differing race, sex, etc.), is there a *sample* of stimuli (e.g., more than one client of each race or each sex)?
2. When only one stimulus or a few human stimuli were used, was an adequate explanation of the failure to sample given?

Statistics

1. Were the statistics used with appropriate assumptions fulfilled by the data (e.g., normalcy of distributions for parametric techniques)? Where necessary, have scores been transformed appropriately?
2. Were tests of significance properly used and reported? For example, did the author use the p value of a correlation to justify conclusions when the actual size of the correlation suggests little common variance between two measures?
3. Have statistical significance levels been accompanied by an analysis of practical significance levels?
4. Has the author considered the effects of a limited range of scores, and so forth, in using correlations?
5. Is the basic statistical strategy that of a "fishing expedition"; that is, if many comparisons are made, were the obtained significance levels predicted in advance? Consider the number of significance levels as a function of the total number of comparisons made.

Factor Analytic Statistics

1. Have the correlation and factor matrices been made available to the reviewers and to the readers through the National Auxiliary Publications Service or other methods?
2. Is it stated what was used for communalities and is the choice appropriate? Ones in the diagonals are especially undesirable when items are correlated as the variables.
3. Is the method of termination of factor extraction stated, and is it appropriate in this case?

4. Is the method of factor rotation stated, and is it appropriate in this case?
5. If items are used as variables, what are the proportions of yes and no responses for each variable?
6. Is the sample size given, and is it adequate?
7. Are there evidences of distortion in the final solution, such as singlet factors, excessively high communalities, obliqueness when an orthogonal solution is used, linearly dependent variables, or too many complex variables?
8. Are artificial factors evident because of inclusion of variables in the analysis that are alternate forms of each other?

Figures and Tables

1. Are the figures and tables (a) necessary and (b) self-explanatory? Large tables of nonsignificant differences, for example, should be eliminated if the few obtained significances can be reported in a sentence or two in the text. Could several tables be combined into a smaller number?
2. Are the axes of figures identified clearly?
3. Do graphs correspond logically to the textual argument of the article? (e.g., if the text states that a certain technique leads to an *increment* of mental health and the accompanying graph shows a *decline* in symptoms, the point is not as clear to the reader as it would be if the text or the graph were amended to achieve visual and verbal congruence.)

Discussion and Conclusion

1. Is the discussion properly confined to the findings or is it digressive, including new post hoc speculations?
2. Has the author explicitly considered and discussed viable alternative explanations of the findings?
3. Have nonsignificant trends in the data been promoted to "findings"?
4. Are the limits of the generalizations possible from the data made clear? Has the author identified his/her own methodological difficulties in the study?
5. Has the author "accepted" the null hypothesis?
6. Has the author considered the possible methodological bases for discrepancies between the results reported and other findings in the literature?

Many detailed responses to a first draft were reviewed. Particular acknowledgment is due to Thomas Achenbach, George Chartier, Andrew Comrey, Jesse Harris, Mary B. Harris, Alan Kazdin, Richard Lanyon,

Eric Mash, Martha Mednick, Peter Nathan, K. Daniel O'Leary, N. D. Reppucci, Robert Rosenthal, Richard Suinn, and Norman Watt.

Requests for reprints should be sent to Brendan A. Maher, Department of Psychology and Social Relations, Harvard University, Cambridge, Massachusetts 02138.

This material may be reproduced in whole or in part without permission, provided that acknowledgment is made to Brendan A. Maher and the American Psychological Association.

APPENDIX E
Psychological Societies

THIS book is intended primarily, though not exclusively, for English-speaking countries. The prospects of professional interchange are greatly enhanced by the use of professional psychological societies. We append here the addresses of the more prominent psychological groups within the English-speaking world.

The Australian Psychological Society (APsS)
191 Royal Parade
Parkville 3052 Victoria   AUSTRALIA

The Canadian Psychological Association (CPsA)
1390 W Sherbrooke St.
Montreal H3G 1K2   CANADA

The New Zealand Psychological Society (NZPsS)
Box 12367
Wellington   NEW ZEALAND

The South African Psychological (SAPsS)
Box 4292
Johannesburg 2000   SOUTH AFRICA

The British Psychological Society (BPsS)
48 Princess Rd. East
Leicester LE1 7DR   UNITED KINGDOM

The American Psychological Association (APA)
1200 N.W. 17th St.
Washington D.C. 20036   UNITED STATES OF AMERICA

Those wishing to find the address of any other psychological society or association may consult the *World guide to scientific associations and learned societies* the 3rd edition of which was issued in 1981 by Verlag Dokumentation, München.

Bibliography

The list of books set out below provides the basic bibliographic data necessary for the identification of titles cited in the text with the exception of general reference works. The latter can be identified through Dr. G. Chandler's work *How to find out*. The form of citation here given conforms with the style recommended by the APA *Publication manual*. No attempt has been made to offer multiple access to works written, compiled or edited by several persons. For ease of reference journals have been placed at the end of this list. We have provided no page references for the latter because they represent a sampling only of major serial publications in the field and only a few of them are discussed in the text.

All works referred to should be available in the major libraries serving academic institutions that offer courses in psychology and in the large national or regional research libraries.

The list, we stress once more and even at this point, is not intended as a bibliography of psychology or a list of recommended readings in this discipline. It is conceived as an aid for students of psychology who have access to a major library.

Monographs, Bibliographies, Indexes, and Abstracting Services

Alexander, F. G. & Selesnick, S. T. *The history of psychiatry: an evaluation of psychiatric thought and practice from prehistoric times to the present*. New York: Harper & Row, 1966..85, 87

Altschule, M. D. *The development of traditional psychopathology: a sourcebook*. Washington: Hemisphere Pub. Corp., 1976...85

American Behavioral Scientist. *The ABS guide to recent publications in the social and behavioral sciences*. New York: Author, 1965. (Continues as *Recent publications in the social and behavioral sciences*.) 49

American doctoral dissertations. 1955/56– . Ann Arbor: University Microfilm 40

American Psychological Association. *The consolidated roster for psychology in the United States and Canada; a locator-reference;* John A. Lago, Ed. Washington: Author, 1973..47

American Psychological Association. *Graduate study in psychology*. 1968/69– . Washington: Educational Affairs Office, American Psychological Association 148

American Psychological Association. *International opportunities for advanced training and research in psychology*. Washington: Author, 1966..............................142

American Psychological Association. *Publication manual of the American Psychological Association* (5th ed.). Washington: Author, 1974.......................... 109–11, 128

American Psychological Association. *Standards for educational and psychological tests*. Washington: Author, 1974 79

Anastasi, A. *Psychological testing* (4th ed.). New York: Macmillan, 1976........................80

Anderson, J. *et al. Theses and assignment writing*. Sydney: Wiley, 1970.......................129

Bibliography

Ansbacher, H. L. (Ed.). *Psychological index: abstract references of 1–35, 1894–1928.* Columbus: American Psychological Association, 1941 44

Arasteh, A. R. & Arasteh, J. D. *Creativity in human development: an interpretative and annotated bibliography.* Cambridge, Mass.: Schenken Pub. Co., 1976 78

Arasteh, A. R. *Creativity in the life-cycle.* Leiden: Brill, 1968 77–8

Ardila, R. "Desarollo de la psicolojia Latina Americana". *Revista Latina Americana de psicolojia,* 1969, *1*(1), 65–71 13

Ardila, R. "La psicolojia en America Latina". *Revista de psicolojia general y aplicada,* 1971, *26*(110–111), 359–369 13

Ardila, R. *La psicolojia en Colombia: desarollo historico.* Mexico: Trillas, 1973 13

Atherton, A. L. *International organizations: a guide to information sources.* Detroit: Gale Research Co., 1976 38

Australia. Dept. of Immigration and Ethnic Affairs. *Please listen to what I'm not saying: a report on the survey of settlement experiences of Indochinese refugees, 1978–80.* Canberra: Australian Government Publishing Service, 1982 33

Australian Council for Educational Research. *ACER annotated catalogue of educational tests and materials.* Hawthorn, Vic.: Author, 1981 80

Australian education index. 1958– . Hawthorn, Vic.: Australian Council for Educational Research 50, 83

Baldwin J. M. *Dictionary of Philosophy and Psychology, including many of the principal conceptions of ethics, logic, aesthetics, philosophy of religion, mental pathology, anthropology, biology, neurology, physiology, economics, political and social philosophy, philology, physical science and education, and giving a terminology in English, French, German and Italian . . . with . . . extensive bibliographies.* New York: Macmillan, 1901–5. Vols. 3 & 4. Rand B. *Bibliography of philosophy, psychology and cognate subjects.* 1905; New ed. 1928 .... 3–4, 26

Bartz, W. R. *et al.* Effects of reducing student anxiety in a statistics course. *Australian psychologist,* 1981, *16*, 347–353 119

Bibliographie der psychologischen Literatur der sozialistischen Länder. Berlin: Volk & Wissen, 1957/58–1966 14

Bibliography of world literature on mental retardation, January 1940–March 1963. By Rick Heber . . . and others. Washington: US Dept. of Health, Education and Welfare, 1963. Supplement, March 1963–December 1964. By Rick Heber & Patrick J. Flanigan. Bethesda, Md.: US Dept. of Health, Education and Welfare, 1965 87

Biological abstracts: a comprehensive abstracting and indexing journal of the world's literature in theoretical and applied biology, exclusive of clinical medicine. 1926– . Philadelphia: Biological Abstracts 49, 64

Biology as a social weapon: the Ann Arbor Science for the People Editorial Collective. Minneapolis: Burgess Pub. Co., 1977 22

Bishop, O. B. *Canadian official publications.* Oxford: Pergamon Press, 1981 34

Blalock, H. M. *Causal inferences in nonexperimental research.* Chapel Hill: University of North Carolina Press, 1964 125

Bolton, N. *Philosophical problems in psychology.* London: Methuen, 1980 21

Boneau, C. A. "The effects of violations of assumptions underlying the 't' test". *Psychological bulletin,* 1960, *57*, 49–64 121

Borchardt, D. H. (Ed.). *Australian official publications.* Melbourne: Longman Cheshire, 1979 34

Borchardt, D. H. & Thawley, J. *Guide to the availability of theses.* Munich: K. G. Saur, 1981 41

Boring, E. G. *A history of experimental psychology* (2nd ed.). New York: Appleton-Century-Crofts, 1957 16

Boston studies in the philosophy of science. 1– , 1962– . Boston: Reidel 19

British education index. 1954– . London: Library Association 50, 83

British Psychological Society. *Careers in psychology.* Leicester: Author, 1977 146

British Psychological Society. Standing Committee on Publications. *Suggestions to contributors.* Leicester: Author, 1979 128

British union-catalogue of periodicals: a record of the periodicals of the world, from the seventeenth century to the present day, in British libraries. London: Butterworth Scientific Publications, 1955–58 51

Bibliography 177

Supplement to 1960. London: Butterworths, 1962.
New periodical titles. London: Butterworths, 1964– .
Brožek, J. M. & Slobin, D. I. (Eds). *Psychology in the USSR: an historical perspective.* White Plains NY: International Arts and Sciences Press, 1972..................................13
Bulletin signalétique C (19–24): sciences humaines. 1961– . Paris: Centre de Documentation du CNRS 29
Buros, O. K. (Ed.). *Personality tests and reviews, including an index to the mental measurements yearbooks.* Highland Park, NJ: Gryphon Press, 1970 79
Buros, O. K. (Ed.). *Tests in print: a comprehensive bibliography of tests for use in education, psychology, and industry.* Highland Park, NJ: Gryphon Press, 1961 78–79
Buros, O. K. *Tests in print II: an index to tests, test reviews, and the literature on specific tests.* Highland Park, NJ: Gryphon Press, 1974 78–79
Butler, F. *Biofeedback: a survey of the literature.* New York: IFI/Plenum, 1978..................74
Butler, F. & Stoyva, J. (Eds). *Biofeedback and self-regulation: a bibliography.* Denver, Biofeedback Research Society, 1973 74
Campbell, D. T. "Factors relating to the validity of experiments in social settings". *Psychological bulletin,* 1957, **54,** 297–312 124
Campbell, D. T. & Stanley, J. C. *Experimental and quasi-experimental designs for research.* Chicago: McNally, 1963.. 123
Carter, R. M. *Communication in organizations: an annotated bibliography and sourcebook.* Detroit: Gale Research Co., 1972...84
Cattell, R. B. *Handbook of multivariate experimental psychology.* Chicago: Rand McNally, 1966 124
Chandler, A. R. & Barnhart, E. N. *A bibliography of psychological and experimental aesthetics, 1864–1937.* Berkeley: University of California Press, 1938.........................77
Chandler, G. *How to find out: a guide to sources of information for all, arranged by the Dewey Decimal Classification* (4th ed.). Oxford: Pergamon Press, 1974 .... 27, 175
Chapman, D. J. & Jones, D. M. *Models of man.* Leicester: British Psychological Society, 1980...21
Chemical abstracts. 1907– . Columbus, Ohio: American Chemical Society....................48
Chicorel index to mental health book reviews. 1976– . New York: Chicorel Library Pub. Corp...85–6
Child development abstracts and bibliography. 1927– . Washington: National Research Council 82
Chin, R. & Chin, A. S. *Psychological research in Communist China, 1949–1966.* Cambridge, Mass.: MIT Press, 1969 14
Chun, K., Cobb, S. & French, J. R. P. *Measures for psychological assessment: a guide to 3000 original sources and their applications.* Ann Arbor: Survey Research Center, Institute for Social Research, 1975...79
Cleary, A. *Instrumentation for psychology.* New York: Wiley, 1977 125
Coelho, G. V. & Irving, R. (Eds.). *Coping and adaptation: an annotated bibliography and study guide.* Rockville, Md.: National Institute of Mental Health, 1981 87
Commonwealth retrospective national bibliographies: an annotated directory. Compiled by the IFLA International Office for UBC. London: Commonwealth Secretariat, 1981 ...24
Comprehensive dissertation index, 1861–1972. Ann Arbor, Mich.: Xerox University Microfilms, 1973 40
Corsini, R. J. & Putzey, L. J. *Bibliography of group psychotherapy, 1906–1956.* Beacon, NY: Beacon House, 1957..87
Crabtree, J. M. & Moyer, K. E. *Bibliography of aggressive behavior: a reader's guide to the research literature.* New York: A. R. Liss, 1977...77
Crews, F. *The Pooh perplex: a student casebook.* London: Barker, 1964.........................21
Crime and delinquency abstracts and current projects: an international bibliography. 1–8; 1963–1972. Bethesda, Md.: US National Clearing House for Mental Health Information, National Institute of Mental Health..89
Criminal justice abstracts. 1970– . Hackensack, NJ: National Council on Crime and Delinquency 89
Criminology and penology abstracts. 1960– . Amstelveen, Kugler Publications 89
Cronbach, L. J. *Essentials of psychological testing* (3rd ed.). New York: Harper & Row, 1970 79–80

Bibliography

Cumulated index medicus. 1960– . Chicago: American Medical Association 49, 86
Cumulative book index. 1898/99– . New York: H. W. Wilson Co 24–5
Current contents: behavioral, social & management sciences. 1– ; 1969– . Philadelphia, Institute for Scientific Information 45
Current index to journals in education. 1969– . New York: CCM Information Sciences 50
Dennis, W. *Readings in the history of psychology.* New York: Appleton-Century-Crofts, 1948 10
Dimitrov, Th. D. *Documents of international organisations: bibliographic handbook covering the United Nations and other intergovernmental organisations.* Chicago: American Library Association, 1973 38
Dissertation abstracts international. 1– ; 1938– . Ann Arbor, Mich.: University Microfilms. *Retrospective index, I–XXIX.* Ann Arbor, Mich.: Xerox University Microfilms, 1970 40
Dorsch, F. *Psychologisches Wörterbuch.* Bern: H. Huber, 1976 7
Driver, E. D. *The sociology and anthropology of mental illness: a reference guide* (Rev. and enl. ed.). Amherst: University of Massachusetts Press, 1972 87
Duijker, H. C. J. & Rijswijk, M. J. van (Eds). *Trilingual psychological dictionary. Dictionnaire de psychologie en trois langues. Dreisprachiges psychologisches Wörterbuch.* Bern: H. Huber, 1975 7
Dunnette, M. D. (Ed.). *Handbook of industrial and organizational psychology.* Chicago: Rand McNally College Publishing Co., 1976 90
Education index. 1929– . New York: H. W. Wilson Co 50, 83
Edwards, A. L. *Statistical analysis for students in psychology and education.* New York: Rinehart, 1946 120
Edwards, A. L. *Statistical methods* (3rd ed.). New York: Holt, Rinehart & Winston, 1973 120
Ellis, W. D. *Gestalt psychology and meaning.* Berkeley: Sather Gate Book Shop, 1930 76
Ellis, W. D. *A source book of Gestalt psychology.* New York: Humanities Press, 1967 76
Encyclopedia of psychology. Eds: H. J. Eysenck, W. Arnold and R. Meili. London: Search Press, 1972 5
Engineering index. 1906– . New York: Engineering Index 48
English, H. B. & English, A. C. *A comprehensive dictionary of psychological and psychoanalytical terms: a guide to usage.* New York: Longmans Green, 1958 6
English, H. B. *A student's dictionary of psychological terms* (4th ed.). New York: Harper, 1934 6
Ennis, B. *Guide to the literature in psychiatry.* Los Angeles: Partridge Press, 1971 86
Farberow, N. L. *Bibliography on suicide and suicide prevention, 1897–1957, 1958–1970.* Chevy Chase, Md.: National Institute of Mental Health, 1972 88
Fearing, F. *Reflex action: a study in the history of physiological psychology.* Cambridge, Mass.: MIT Press, 1970 16
Fisher, R. A. & Yates, F. *Statistical tables for biological, agricultural and medical research* (6th ed., rev. and enl.). New York: Hafner Pub. Co., 1963 120
Flugel, J. C. *A hundred years of psychology, 1833–1933.* New York: Basic Books, 1964 9
Flugel, J. C. *A hundred years of psychology. Part V: 1933–1963.* Rev. and supplemented by D. J. West. New York: International Universities Press, 1970 9
Fodor, N. & Gaynor, F. (Eds). *Freud: dictionary of psychoanalysis.* New York: Philosophical Library, 1950 74
Foreign language tests and reviews: a monograph consisting of the foreign language sections of the seven Mental measurement yearbooks (1938–72) and Tests in print II (1974); Ed. by O. K. Buros. Highland Park, NJ: Gryphon Press, 1975 79
Fryer, D. H. & Henry, E. R. *Handbook of applied psychology.* New York: Rinehart, 1950 90
Galton, Sir F. *Memories of my life.* London: Methuen, 1908 18
Ginsburg, G. P. (Ed.). *Emerging strategies in social psychological research.* New York: Wiley, 1979 125

Glick, I. D. & Haley, J. *Family therapy and research: an annotated bibliography of articles and books published 1950–1970*. New York: Grune & Stratton, 1971 86

Goldenson, R. M. *Encyclopedia of human behavior: psychology, psychiatry and mental health*. Garden City, NY: Doubleday, 1970 5

Goldstein, K. *The organism: a holistic approach to biology derived from pathological data in man*. Boston: Beacon Press, 1963 17

Goodstein, L. D. & Reinecker, V. M. "Factors affecting self disclosure: a review of the literature". Vol. 7 of series: *Progress in experimental personality research*, New York, Academic Press, 1974 81

Graham, E. C. & Mullen, M. M. (Comps.). *Rehabilitation literature, 1950–1955: a bibliographic review of the medical care, education, employment, welfare and psychology of handicapped children and adults*. New York: Blakiston, 1956 88

Gray, J. A. (Ed. and trans.). *Pavlov's typology: recent theoretical and experimental developments from the laboratory of B. M. Pavlov*. New York: Macmillan, 1964 13

Greenberg, B. *How to find out in psychiatry: a guide to sources of mental health information*. New York: Pergamon Press, 1978 85

Grinstein, A. *The index of psychoanalytic writings*. New York: International Universities Press, 1956 75

Grinstein, A. *Sigmund Freud's writings: a comprehensive bibliography*. New York: International Universities Press, 1977 75

Guilford, J. P. & Fruchter, B. *Fundamental statistics in psychology and education* (5th ed.). New York: McGraw-Hill, 1973 120

Handbook of child psychology, (Ed. by P. H. Mussen), 4th ed., New York: Wiley, 1983. 4 Vols 82

Handbuch der Psychologie. Eds K. Gottschaldt *et al*. Göttingen: Verlag für Psychologie, 1959– 4

Hankin, J. & Oktay, J. S. *Mental disorder and primary medical care: an analytical review of the literature*. Washington: US Dept. of Health, Education and Welfare, Public Health Service, Alcohol, Drug Abuse and Mental Health Administration, 1979..87

Hare, A. P. *Handbook of small group research* (2nd ed.). New York: Free Press, 1976 84

The Harvard list of books in psychology. Compiled and annotated by the psychologists in Harvard University (4th ed.). Cambridge, Mass.: Harvard University Press, 1971 27–8

Hearnshaw, L. S. *A short history of British psychology, 1840–1940*. London: Methuen, 1964..12

Heidenreich, C. A. *A dictionary of personality: behavior and adjustment terms*. Dubuque, Iowa: W. C. Brown Book Co., 1968 76

Henle, M. (Ed.). *Documents of Gestalt psychology*. Berkeley: University of California Press, 1961 76

Herrnstein, R. J. & Boring, E. G. *A source book in the history of psychology*. Cambridge, Mass.: Harvard University Press, 1965 10

Hesse, M. B. *Models and analogies in science*. Notre Dame, Ind.: University of Notre Dame Press, 1966 19–20

Heuss, E. *Bibliographie der philosophischen, psychologischen und pädagogischen Literatur in der deutschsprachigen Schweiz, 1900–1940*. Basel: Verlag für Recht und Gesellschaft, 1944 15

Higher education in social psychology. Ed. by S. Lundstedt. Cleveland: Press of Case Western Reserve University, 1968 149

Hilgard, E. R. (Ed.). *American psychology in historical perspective, 1892–1977: addresses of the presidents of the American Psychological Association, 1892–1977*. Washington: American Psychological Association, 1978 12

Hinsie, L. E. & Campbell, R. J. *Psychiatric dictionary* (4th ed.). New York: Oxford University Press, 1970 85

A history of psychology in autobiography. New York: Appleton-Century-Crofts, 1930– 11

Hollis, J. W. & Donn, P. A. *Psychological report writing: theory and practice*. Muncie, Ind.: Accelerated Development, 1979 134

Bibliography

Huff, D. *How to lie with statistics*. New York: Norton, 1964. 120
Hunter, R. A. & Macalpine, I. (Eds). *Three hundred years of psychiatry, 1535–1860: a history presented in selected English texts*. London: Oxford University Press, 1963 85
Index medicus. 1879–1926; 1960– . Washington: American Medical Association ... 49, 64, 87
Index to theses accepted for higher degrees in the universities of Great Britain and Ireland. 1– , 1950/51– . London: Aslib 40
Indian psychological abstracts. 1972– . Bombay: Somaiya Publications 50
Insight books. 1961– . London: Van Nostrand...20
International directory of psychologists, exclusive of the USA (3rd ed.). Amsterdam: North Holland, 1980 140
International journal of abstracts: statistical theory and method. 1959– . Edinburgh: Oliver & Boyd.. 121
Internationale Bibliographie der Zeitschriften-literatur aus allen Gebieten des Wissens. International bibliography of periodical literature covering all fields of knowledge. Bibliographie internationale de le littérature périodique dans tous les domaines de la connaissance. 1965– . Osnabruck: F. Dietrich 29
James, W. *Principles of psychology*. New York: Dover, 1950. (First published 1918: there are numerous reprints.).. 18–19
Johnson, H. H. & Solso, R. L. *An introduction to experimental design in psychology: a case approach* (2nd ed.). New York: Harper & Row, 1978 123
Jones, E. *The life and work of Sigmund Freud*. New York: Basic Books, 1961 17
Kantor, J. R. *The scientific evolution of psychology*. Chicago: Principia Press, 1963–69..13
Kazdin, A. E. *Research design in clinical psychology*. New York: Harper & Row, 1980 126
Kelley, T. L. *The Kelley statistical tables* (Rev. ed.). Cambridge, Mass.: Harvard University Press, 1948 120
Kendall, M. G. & Stuart, A. *The advanced theory of statistics* (3rd ed.). London: Griffin, 1969 120
Kessen, W. *The child*. New York: Wiley, 1965 81
Kiell, N. *Psychiatry and psychology in the visual arts and aesthetics: a bibliography*. Madison: University of Wisconsin Press, 1965 77
Kiell, N. *Psychoanalysis, psychology and literature: a bibliography*. Madison: University of Wisconsin Press, 1963 75
Klein, D. B. *A history of scientific psychology: its origins and philosophical backgrounds*. New York: Basic Books, 1970 9
Kling, J. W. & Riggs, L. A. *Woodworth and Schlosberg's experimental psychology* (3rd ed.). New York: Holt, Rinehart & Winston, 1971 16
Koch, S. (Ed.). *Psychology: a study of a science*. New York: McGraw-Hill, 1959........... 5, 20
Kochen, M. *Principles of information retrieval*. Los Angeles: Melville Publishing Co, 1974 117
Köhler, W. *Gestalt psychology*. New York: H. Liveright, 1929...............................17, 76
Koestler, A. *The act of creation*. London: Hutchinson, 1964..19
Kuhn, T. S. *The structure of scientific revolutions* (2nd ed., rev.). Chicago: University of Chicago Press, 1970. (International encyclopedia of unified science, vol. 2 no. 2).........19
Lafon, R. *Vocabulaire de psychopédagogie et de psychiatrie de l'enfant* (4th ed.). Paris: Presses universitaires de France, 1979 82
Lagacé, R. O. *The nature and use of HRAF files: a research and teaching guide*. New Haven: Human Relations Area Files, 1974..41
Lake, D. G., Miles, M. B. & Earle, R. B. *Measuring human behaviour: tools for the assessment of social function*. New York: Teachers College Press, 1973 79
Lang, A. *Rorschach-Bibliography; Bibliographie Rorschach; Rorschach bibliography, 1921–1964*. Bern: H. Huber, 1966 81
Langer, S. K. *Philosophy in a new key: a study in the symbolism of reason, rite and art*. Cambridge, Mass.: Harvard University Press, 1951 19
Laplanche, J. & Pontalis, J. B. *The language of psychoanalysis*. London: Hogarth Press, 1973..75
Lawlis, G. F. & Chatfield, D. *Multivariate approaches for the behavioral sciences: a brief text*. Lubbock, Texas: Texas Technical Press, 1974 124

Bibliography

Leland, H. & Deutsch, M. W. *Abnormal behavior: a guide to information sources.* Detroit: Gale Research Co., 1980 85
Lindzey, G. & Aronson, E. *The handbook of social psychology* (2nd ed.). Reading, Mass.: Addison-Wesley, 1968–69 84
Lindzey, G. et al. *Theories of personality: primary sources of research* (2nd ed.). New York: Wiley, 1973 21
Lowry, R. *The evolution of psychological theory, 1650 to the present.* Chicago: Aldine Atherton, 1971 ...... 9, 21
Lubin, B. & Lubin, A. W. *Group therapy: a bibliography of the literature from 1956 through 1964.* East Lansing: Michigan State University Press, 1966 87
Lyerly, S. B. *Handbook of psychiatric rating scales* (2nd ed.). Rockville, Md.: National Institute of Mental Health, 1973 80
Lynn, R. *Personality and national character.* Oxford: Pergamon Press, 1971 126
McLeish, J. *Soviet psychology: history, theory, content.* London: Methuen, 1975 ...... 13, 34
Maison des Sciences de L'Homme, Paris. Service d'échange d'information scientifiques. *List mondiale des périodiques spécialisés, psychologie. World list of specialized periodicals, psychology.* Paris: Mouton, 1967 29
Markle, A. & Rinn, R. C. (Eds). *Author's guide to journals in psychology, psychiatry and social work.* New York: Haworth Press, 1977 ...... 31, 135
Marshall, J. G. & Trahair, R. C. S. *Industrial psychology in Australia to 1950.* Bundoora, Vic.: La Trobe University Library, 1981 90
Marx, M. H. & Hillix, W. A. *Systems and theories in psychology* (2nd ed.). New York: McGraw-Hill, 1973 20
Marx, M. H. & Goodson, F. E. (Eds). *Theories in contemporary psychology* (2nd ed.). New York: Macmillan, 1976 21
Masters abstracts: abstracts of selected masters theses on microfilm. 1– , 1962– . Ann Arbor, Mich.: University Microfilms 40
Matlin, M. W. *Human experimental psychology.* Monterey, Calif.: Brooks-Cole, 1979 122
Meissner, W. W. *Annotated bibliography in religion and psychology.* New York: Academy of Religion and Mental Health, 1961 90
Menninger, K. A. *A guide to psychiatric books in English* (3rd ed.). New York: Grune & Stratton, 1972 86
Mental health book review index. 1956– . New York: Council on Research in Bibliography. (Continued by *Chicorel index to mental health book reviews.*) 85
Mental measurements yearbook. 1938– . Highland Park, NJ: Gryphon Press 79
Miller, A. J. & Acri, M. J. *Death: a bibliographical guide.* Metuchen, NJ.: Scarecrow Press, 1977 88–89
Miller, C. & Swift, K. *Words and women.* Garden City, NY: Anchor Press, 1976 129
Minnesota studies in the philosophy of science. 1– , 1956– . Minneapolis, University of Minnesota Press 19
Modgil, S. & Modgil, C. *Piagetian research: compilation and commentary.* Windsor, Ont.: NFER, 1976 ...... 77, 83
Morehead, J. *Introduction to United States public documents* (2nd ed.). Littleton, Col.: Libraries Unlimited, 1978 34
Morgan, C. T. *Physiological psychology* (3rd ed.). New York: McGraw-Hill, 1965 16
Morrison, D. E. & Hornback, K. E. *Collective behavior: a bibliography.* New York: Garland Publishing Co., 1976 84–5
Morrow, W. R. *Behavior therapy bibliography, 1950–1969: annotated and indexed.* Columbia: University of Missouri Press, 1971 86
Mosak, H. H. & Mosak, B. *A bibliography of Adlerian psychology.* Washington: Hemisphere Publishing Co., 1975 75
Moss, C. *Bibliographical guide to self-disclosure literature, 1956–1976.* Troy, NY: Whitston, 1977 81
Muensterberg, H. *Psychology and industrial efficiency.* Boston: Houghton-Mifflin, 1913 90
Murchison, C. A. *A handbook of child psychology* (2nd ed. rev.). Worcester, Mass.: Clark University Press, 1933 82

Murdock, G. P. et al. *Outline of cultural materials* (4th rev. ed.). New Haven: Human Relations Area Files Inc., 1967 41
Murphy, G. & Kovach, J. K. *Historical introduction to modern psychology* (3rd ed.) New York: Harcourt Brace Jovanovich, 1972 9
Murphy, G. & Murphy, L. B. (Eds). *Western psychology; from the Greeks to William James*. New York: Basic Books, 1969 13
National Library of New Zealand *Union list of serials in New Zealand libraries* (3rd ed.). Wellington: Author, 1969– 51
New serial titles: a union list of serials commencing publication after December 31, 1949. 1953– . Washington: Library of Congress 51
New serial titles, 1950–1970: subject guide. New York: Bowker, 1975 51
Nie, N. H. *SPSS: statistical package for the social sciences* (2nd ed.). New York: McGraw-Hill, 1975 122
Nixon, M. C. & Taft, R. (Eds) *Psychology in Australia; achievements and prospects.* Sydney: Pergamon Press, 1977 13
Nunnally, J. C. *Educational measurement and evaluation;* with the collaboration of Nancy Almond Afor (2nd ed.). New York: McGraw-Hill, 1972 80
Nunnally, J. C. *Psychometric theory.* New York: McGraw-Hill, 1967 21
O'Connor, N. (Ed.). *Recent Soviet psychology.* Oxford: Pergamon Press, 1961 13
O'Neill, W. M. *The beginnings of modern psychology* (2nd rev. ed.). Sydney: Sydney University Press, 1982 10
Osgood, C. E. *Method and theory in experimental psychology.* New York: Oxford University Press, 1953 16
Payne, T. R. *S. L. Rubenstejn and the philosophical foundations of Soviet psychology.* Dordrecht: Reidel, 1969 74
Pemberton, J. E. *British official publications* (2nd ed.). Oxford: Pergamon Press, 1973 34
Periodicals in South African libraries; Tydskrifte Suid-Afrikaanse biblioteke (2nd ed.). 1971– . Pretoria: South African Council for Scientific and Industrial Research and Human Sciences Research Council 51
Piéron, H. *Vocabulaire de la psychologie* (6th ed.). Paris: Presses Universitaires de France, 1979 7
Popper, Sir K. *The logic of scientific discovery* (Rev. ed.). London: Hutchinson, 1968 19
Prentice, A. E. *Suicide: a selective bibliography of over 2,200 items.* Metuchen, NJ: Scarecrow Press, 1974 88
Primakovskiĭ, A. P. *Ukazatel' statei retsenziĭ i zametok napechatannykh v zhurnale "Voprosy filosofiĭ i psikhologiĭ" za 1889–1918 gg.* Moscow: Akademiĭa nauk SSSR, 1939 14
Psychological abstracts. 1927– . Lancaster, Pa.: American Psychological Association 44–7, 53, 61, 70–1, 86–7
Psychological documents. 1– , 1983– . Washington: American Psychological Association. (From 1971 to 1982 as *JSAS catalogue of selected documents in psychology.*) 42
Psychological index . . . an annual bibliography of the literature of psychology and cognate subjects. Nos 1–42, 1894–1935. Princeton: Psychological Review Co 44–6
Psychological reader's guide. 1973– . Lausanne: Elsevier Sequoia SA 44–5
Psychology survey. 1– , 1978– . London: Allen & Unwin 20
Psychopharmacology abstracts. 1961– . Washington: National Institute of Mental Health 87–8
Rahmani, L. *Soviet psychology: philosophical, theoretical and experimental issues.* New York: International University Press, 1973 .... 13, 74
Recent publications in the social and behavioral sciences. 1966– . New York: American Behavioral Scientist 49
Referativnyi Zhurnal. 1953– . Moscow: Akademiĭa Nauk SSSR. (Appears in over 60 subject areas.) 29
Research in education. 1966– . Washington: Educational Resources Information Centre 83
Research studies in education: a subject and author index of doctoral dissertations, reports and field studies for an eleven year period. 1941/51– . Bloomington: Phi Delta Kappa 41

Bibliography

Resources in education. 1966– . Washington: US Dept. of Health, Education and Welfare, National Institute of Education 50, 83

Rickman, J. *Index psychoanalyticus 1893–1926, ein Register der Autoren und deren Werke uber die Psychoanalyse; being an author's index of papers on psycho-analysis; un catalogue des auteurs sur la psychoanalyse.* London: Hogarth Press and the Institute of Psychoanalysis, 1928 75

Riviere, M. *Rehabilitation of the handicapped: a bibliography, 1940–1946.* New York: National Council on Rehabilitation, 1949 88

Roback, A. A. *Behaviorism and psychology.* Cambridge: University Bookstores, 1923 76

Roback, A. A. *History of psychology and psychiatry.* New York: Philosophical Library, 1961 .... 10, 12

Robinson, P. W. & Foster, D. F. *Experimental psychology: a small-N approach.* New York: Harper & Row, 1979 125

Roos, C. & Barry, J. *Bibliography of military psychiatry 1952–1958.* Washington: US Library of Medicine, 1959 91

Rosenthal, R. *Experimenter effects in behavioral research.* New York: Appleton-Century-Crofts, 1966 125

Rosenthal, R. & Rosnow, R. L. *The volunteer subject.* New York: Wiley, 1975 125

Rossmassler, S. A. & Watson, D. G. *Data handling for science and technology: an overview and a source book.* Amsterdam: North Holland, 1980 117

Rothenberg, A. & Greenberg, B. *The index of scientific writings on creativity: creative men and women.* Hamden, Conn.: Archon Books, 1974 78

Rycroft, C. *A critical dictionary of psychoanalysis.* London: Nelson, 1968 74

Savage, C. W. (Ed.). *Perception and recognition: issues in the foundations of psychology.* Minneapolis: University of Minnesota Press, 1978 19

Schmaltz, L. W. *Scientific psychology and social concern.* New York: Harper & Row, 1971 126

Schmeckebier, L. F. & Eastin, R. B. *Government publications and their use* (2nd rev. ed.). Washington: Brookings Institution, 1969 34

Scientific serials in Australian libraries. 1967– . Melbourne: Commonwealth Scientific and Industrial Research Organization 51

Serials in Australian libraries, social sciences and humanities. 1964–74. Canberra: National Library of Australia 51

Supplement. 1974– . Canberra: National Library of Australia.

Shaffer, L. F. *Preparing doctoral dissertations in psychology: a guide for students* (5th ed.). New York: Teachers College Press, 1967 129

Sheehy, E. *Guide to reference books* (9th ed.). Chicago: American Library Association, 1976 .... 24, 40, 52

Supplement. Chicago: American Library Association, 1980.

Shock, N. W. *A classified bibliography of gerontology and geriatrics.* Stanford: Stanford University Press, 1951 84

Shonfield, A. & Shaw, S. (Eds). *Social indicators and social policy.* London: Heinemann Educational, 1972 124

Sidowski, J. B. *Experimental methods and instrumentation in psychology.* New York: McGraw-Hill, 1966 125

Siegel, S. *Nonparametric statistics for the behavioral sciences.* New York: McGraw-Hill, 1956 121

Simon, B. (Ed.) *Psychology in the Soviet Union.* London: Routledge & Paul, 1957 13

Simpson, M. A. *Dying, death and grief: a critically annotated bibliography and source book of thanatology and terminal care.* New York: Plenum Press, 1979 88

Singer, B. *Distribution-free methods for non-parametric problems: a classified and selected bibliography.* Leicester: British Psychological Society, 1979 121

Skinner, B. F. *About behaviorism.* New York: Vintage Books, 1974 76

Snodgrass, J. G. *The numbers game: statistics in psychology.* Baltimore: Williams & Wilkins, 1977 123

Social sciences citation index. 1973– . Philadelphia: Institute for Scientific Information 48–9, 64

Spiegelberg, H. *The phenomenological movement: a historical introduction* (2nd ed.). The Hague: Nijhoff, 1965 90

Spiegelberg, H. *Phenomenology in psychology and psychiatry: a historical introduction.* Evanston, Ill.: Northwestern University Press, 1972 90
Sternberg, R. J. *Writing the psychology paper.* Woodbury, NJ: Barron's Educational Series, 1977 129
Stevens, S. S. *Handbook of experimental psychology.* New York: Wiley, 1951 120
Stevenson, L. F. *Seven theories of human nature.* Oxford: Clarendon Press, 1974 20
Stibic, V. *Personal documentation for professionals: means and methods.* Amsterdam: North Holland, 1980 116
Stodgill, R. M. *Leadership: abstracts and bibliography.* Columbus: Ohio State University, 1977 85
Strunk, W. & White, E. B. *The elements of style* (2nd ed.). New York: Macmillan, 1972 129
Study abroad: international handbook: fellowships, scholarships, educational exchange. 1– ; 1948– . Paris: UNESCO 149
Swingle, P. G. *Social psychology in natural settings: a reader in field experimentation.* Chicago: Aldine Pub. Co., 1973 124
Synoptic tables concerning the current national bibliographies. Leipzig: Deutsche Bücherei, 1975 24
Taulbee, E. S., Wright, H. W. & Stenmark, D. E. *The Minnesota Multiphasic Personality Inventory (MMPI): a comprehensive annotated bibliography* (1960–1965). Troy, NY: Whitston, 1977 80–1
Teevan, R. C. & Birney, R. C. (Eds). *Theories of motivation in personality and social psychology: enduring problems in psychology: selected writings.* London: Van Nostrand, 1964 20
Textor, R. B. (Comp.). *A cross-cultural summary.* New Haven: HRAF Press, 1967 41
Thesaurus of psychological index terms (2nd ed.). Washington, American Psychological Association, 1977 .... 8, 47, 56–63
Theses in the social sciences: an international analytical catalogue of unpublished doctorate theses, 1940–1950. Paris: UNESCO, 1952 40
Thinès, G. *Phenomenology and the science of behaviour: an historical and epistemological approach.* London: Allen & Unwin, 1977 90
Tompkins, M. & Shirley, N. (Comps.). *A checklist of serials in psychology and allied fields.* Troy, NY: Whitston, 1969 28–9
Trahair, R. C. S. & Marshall, J. G. *Australian psychoanalytic and related writings, 1884–1940: an annotated bibliography.* Bundoora, Vic.: La Trobe University Library, 1979 75
Troland, L. T. *The principles of psychophysiology: a survey of modern scientific psychology.* New York: Greenwood Press, 1969 74
Ulrich's international periodicals directory. 1932– . New York: Bowker 29
Underwood, B. J. *Experimental psychology* (2nd ed.). New York: Appleton-Century-Crofts, 1966 123
Union list of higher degree theses in Australian university libraries: cumulative edition to 1965. Hobart: University of Tasmania Library, 1967 40
Supplements, 1966/68– . Hobart: University of Tasmania Library, 1971–
Union list of serials in libraries of the United States and Canada (3rd ed.). New York: H. W. Wilson, 1965 51
Union list of serials in New Zealand libraries 3rd ed. Wellington, 1969/1970 6 vols. Supplement, 1970–1975 51
United Nations. *Everyone's United Nations* (9th ed.). New York: Author, 1979 38
UNDOC: *Current index: United Nations Documents index,* 1979– New York, United Nations. (Earlier titles varied) 39
United Nations Educational, Scientific and Cultural Organization. *Unesco List of documents and publications.* 1973– . Paris: Computerized Documentation Service 39
US Children's Bureau. *Research relating to emotionally disturbed children.* Washington: Children's Bureau Clearinghouse for Research in Child Life, 1968 83
Varela, J. A. *Psychological solutions to social problems: an introduction to social technology.* New York: Academic Press, 1971 125
Viney, W., Wertheimer, M. & Wertheimer, M. L. *History of psychology: a guide to information sources.* Detroit: Gale Research Co., 1979 28

Bibliography

Voos, H. *Organizational communication: a bibliography.* New Brunswick, NJ, Rutgers University Press, 1967 84
Voutsinas, D. *Documentation sur la psychologie française.* Paris: Groupe d'études de psychologie de l'Université de Paris, 1957 14
Watson, J. B. *Psychology from the standpoint of a behaviorist* (3rd ed. rev.). Philadelphia: Lippincott, 1929 17
Watson, R. I. (Ed.). *Eminent contributors to psychology.* New York: Springer, 1974–76 10
Watson, R. I. *The great psychologists from Aristotle to Freud* (3rd ed.) Philadelphia: Lippincott, 1971 10
Watson, R. I. *The history of psychology and the behavioral sciences: a bibliographic guide.* New York: Springer, 1978 ....9, 76
Webb, E. J. et al. *Unobtrusive measures: nonreactive research in the social sciences.* Chicago: Rand-McNally, 1966 124
Wellek, A. (Ed.). *Gesamtverzeichnis der deutschsprachigen psychologischen Literatur der Jahre 1942 bis 1960.* Göttingen: Verlag für Psychologie, 1965 14
Westfall, G. *French official publications.* Oxford: Pergamon Press, 1980 34
Westland, G. *Current crises of psychology.* London: Heinemann Educational, 1978 21
White, R. A. & Dale, L. A. (Comps.). *Parapsychology: sources of information.* Metuchen, NJ: Scarecrow Press, 1973 91
Winchell, C. A. *The hyperkinetic child: a bibliography of medical, educational and behavioral studies.* Westport, Conn.: Greenwood Press, 1975 83–4
Winton, H. N. M. *Publications of the United Nations systems: a reference guide.* New York: Bowker, 1972 38
Wolman, B. B. (comp. & ed.). *Dictionary of behavioral science.* New York: Van Nostrand Reinhold Co., 1973 6
Wolman, B. B. (Ed.). *Handbook of developmental psychology.* Englewood Cliffs, NJ: Prentice-Hall, 1982 82
Wolman, B. B. *International directory of psychology: a guide to people, places and policies.* New York: Plenum Press, 1979 138
Wolman, B. B. (Ed.). *International encyclopedia of psychiatry, psychology, psychoanalysis, and neurology.* New York: Produced for Aesculapius Publishers by Van Nostrand Reinhold Co., 1977 5
Woodworth, R. S. *Contemporary schools of psychology.* In collaboration with Mary R. Sheehan (3rd ed.). New York: Ronald Press Co., 1964 15
Wright, L. *Bibliography on human intelligence: National Clearinghouse for Mental Health Information: an extensive bibliography.* Chevy Chase, Md.: US National Clearinghouse for Mental Health Information, 1969 80
Young, M. N. *Bibliography of memory.* Philadelphia: Chilton Co., 1961 77
Zaretsky, I. I. & Shambaugh, C. *Spirit possession and spirit mediumship in Africa and Afro-America: an annotated bibliography.* New York: Garland Publishing Co., 1978 91
Zimpfer, D. G. *Group work in the helping professions: a bibliography.* Washington: Association for Specialists in Group Work, 1976 87

Journals

Advances in experimental social psychology. 1964– . New York: Academic Press.
Advances in psychological assessment. 1968– . San Francisco: Jossey-Bass Pub.
American psychologist. 1– , 1946– . Washington: American Psychological Association.
L'Année psychologique. 1894– . Paris: Presses universitaires de France.
Annual review of psychology. 1950– . Stanford: Annual Reviews.
Canadian psychological review; Psychologie Canadienne. 1– , 1950– . Montreal: Canadian Psychological Association. (To 1974 as *Canadian psychologist.*)
Contemporary psychology: a journal of reviews. 1956– . Baltimore: American Psychological Association.
Excerpta medica. Section 8: Neurology and neurosurgery. 1948– . Amsterdam: Excerpta Medica Foundation.
Excerpta medica: Section 32: Psychiatry. 1948– . Amsterdam: Excerpta Medica Foundation.
The German journal of psychology. 1977– . Toronto: C. J. Hogrefe.

Information bulletin of Australian criminology. 1974– . Canberra: Australian Institute of Criminology.
International journal of psychology 1– , 1970– . Westport, Conn.: Greenwood Periodicals.
Journal of abnormal psychology. 1906– . Lancaster, Pa.: American Psychological Association.
Journal of consulting and clinical psychology. 1– , 1937– . Washington: American Psychological Association. (To 1967 as *Journal of consulting psychology.*)
Journal of creative behavior. 1967– . Buffalo: Creative Education Foundation.
Journal of experimental psychology. 1–103, 1916-1974. Washington, American Psychological Association.
Journal of experimental psychology: animal behavior processes. 104– , 1975– . Washington: American Psychological Association. (Supersedes in part *Journal of experimental psychology.*)
Journal of experimental psychology: general. 104– , 1975– . Washington: American Psychological Association. (Supersedes in part *Journal of experimental psychology.*)
Journal of experimental psychology: human learning and memory. 104– , 1975– . Washington: American Psychological Association. (Supersedes in part *Journal of experimental psychology.*)
Journal of experimental psychology: human perception and performance. 104– . 1975– . Washington: American Psychological Association. (Supersedes in part *Journal of experimental psychology.*)
Journal of the history of the behavioral sciences. 1965– . Brandon, Vt.: Psychology Press.
Science. 1880– . Washington: American Association for the Advancement of Science.
Voprosy filosofiĭ i psikhologiĭ. 1–28, 1889–1917. Moscow: Akademiya Nauk.
Zeitschrift für experimentelle und angewandte Psychologie. 1953– . Göttingen: Verlag fur Psychologie.
Zeitschrift für Psychologie. 1907– . Leipzig: J. A. Barth.
Zentralblatt fur die gesamte Neurologie und Psychiatrie. 1910– . New York: Springer-Verlag.

Subject Index

APA *see* American Psychological Association
Abnormal psychology 3, 85
Abstracting and indexing services 43–50
Adler, A. 18, 75
Affective psychology 77
Aging *see* Gerontology
American Association for the Advancement of Science 10
American Philosophical Association 10
American Psychiatric Association 6
American Psychological Association 6, 12, 140–3
Anthropology and psychology 91
Applied psychology 90–1
  see also Industrial psychology; Military psychology; Organizational psychology
Aristotle 10, 17, 85
Australian Psychological Society 140
Australian psychology 13
Austrian psychology 15

Baldwin, James Mark 11
Behaviourism 3, 17, 76
Bibliographic citations *see* Citations, bibliographic
Bibliographies 26–7, 28
Bibliographies, national 23–5
Biography *see* Psychology–biography
Bliss, Henry 1–2
Book reviews 27–8
Boring, Edwin G. 11
British Psychological Society 140
British psychology 12
Buhler, Karl 11
Buros, O. K. 78

Canadian Psychological Association 140
Careers in psychology 143–7
Case work reporting *see* Report writing—case work reporting
Child, I. L. 18
Child psychology 3, 64, 66, 81–4
Chinese psychology 14
  see also Oriental psychology
Citations, bibliographic 109–111

Clinical psychology 3, 85
Code of ethics 142
Cognition 77
Comparative psychology 17
Computers *see* Data storage and retrieval systems—computer based
Council of European Social Sciences 42
Creativity 77–8
Criminology 89
Current contents 45

DSM *see* Diagnostic and Statistical Manual
Data Archives 42
Data storage and retrieval systems computer based 53–71
Death 88–9
Developmental psychology 81–4
Dewey Decimal Classification 96–101, 106
Diagnostic and Statistical Manual 6
Dictionaries *see* Psychology—dictionaries
Dissertations *see* Theses

Education, postgraduate 148–9
Educational psychology 3, 48, 49–50, 64, 83
Encyclopaedias *see* Psychology—encyclopaedias
Ethics, code of *see* Code of ethics
European Consortium for Social and Political Research 42
Existential psychology 18, 20
Experimental design 122–6
Experimental psychology 16
Eysenck, H. J. 11

Forensic psychology 85, 89
French psychology 14
Freud, S. 10, 17, 20, 74

Galton, Sir F. 18
Genetics 6
German psychology 14–15
Gerontology 84
Gestalt psychology 3, 17, 76
Government publications 32–9

Subject Index

HRAF *see* Human Relations Area Files
Hearnshaw, L. S. 12
Helmholtz, Hermann 74
Hippocrates 85
History of Science Society 10
Human Relations Area Files 41
Humanistic psychology 18

ICPSR *see* Intergroup Consortium for Political and Social Research
Indexing and abstracting services 43–50
Industrial psychology 3, 48, 90
Intergroup Consortium for Political and Social Research 42
International Federation of Data Organizations 42
International Social Council 42
Islamic psychology 13

James, William 9, 11, 18–19
Journals *see* Periodicals
Jung, C. G. 18

Kuhn, T. 19

Latin American psychology 13
Legal deposit libraries 25
Library catalogues 25–6, 107
Library of Congress Classification 102–6
Library use 151–6
Literature searches *see* Library use
Loeb, J. 17
Lombroso, C. 12
Lorenz, K. 17, 20

MMPI test *see* Minnesota Multiphasic Personality Inventory
Mathematical formulae 7
Mental deficiency 85
Mental disorders *see* Mental illness
Mental health 3, 5, 85–9
Mental illness 6
Mental measurement *see* Tests
Merleau-Ponty, M. 18
Military psychology 90–1
Minnesota Multiphasic Personality Inventory 80–1
Monographs 23–8
Morgan, C. L. 17
Murchison, Carl 11

National bibliographies *see* Bibliographies, national

Neurology 5, 6, 16, 85
Neuropsychology 4, 16
North American psychology 12

Organizational psychology 90
Oriental psychology 20
   see also Chinese psychology
Osgood, C. E. 11
Osler, Sir William 94

PsycINFO 64–5
Parapsychology 91
Pathological psychology 85
Pavlov, I. P. 13
Periodicals 28–31
   union lists 50–2
Personality 21, 80–1
Pharmacology 6, 7, 17
Phenomenology 90
Philosophy 3–4
Phrenology 12
Physiological psychology 15–16, 49, 64, 74
Piaget, J. 82, 83
Polish psychology 14
Professional associations *see* Psychological societies
Psychiatry 5, 6, 85–9
   history 10
Psychoanalysis 3, 5, 6, 12, 17–18, 74–5
Psychological societies 137–43, 173
Psychological tests *see* Tests
Psychologists 7
   professional ethics 6
Psychology
   biography 9–12
   dictionaries 6–7
      trilingual 7
   encyclopaedias 4–5
   history 9–15
   theories 18–22
   thesauri 7–8, 56–61
   see also geographical aspects, e.g. Austrian psychology
Psychology, pathological *see* Abnormal psychology
Psychometrics 21
   see also Tests
Psychopathology *see* Pathological psychology
Psychotherapy 85
Punched card systems 112–17

Religion and psychology 89–90
Report writing 127–35, 157–66
   case work reporting 133–4

Subject Index

Research 93–108
  see also Experimental design; Punched card systems; Report writing; Statistics
Research report 41–2, 167–71
Roback, A. A. 12
Rorschach test 80–1
Russian psychology 13–14, 20

SDI see Selective dissemination of information
Science 19–20
Selective dissemination of information 54
Skinner, B. F. 20
Social psychology 84–5
Statistics 119–22
Suicide 88
Swiss psychology 15

Tests 3, 7, 78–81
Thesauri see Psychology—thesauri
Thesaurus of psychological index terms 56–61
Theses 39–41
Titchener E. B. 16

UNESCO 42
Unesco see UNESCO
Union lists of periodicals see Periodicals—union lists
United Nations 38–9

Watson J. B. 17
Watson R. I. 9, 10, 76
Woodworth, R. 16
Wundt, Wilhelm 9, 16, 78

FUNDERBURG LIBRARY
MANCHESTER COLLEGE

WITHDRAWN
from
Funderburg Library